THE BUYING
BRAIN

THE BUYING
BRAIN

Secrets for Selling to the Subconscious Mind

Dr. A.K. PRADEEP

WILEY

John Wiley & Sons, Inc.

Published by John Wiley & Sons, Inc., Hoboken, New Jersey.
Published simultaneously in Canada.

For general information on our other products and services or for technical support, please contact our Customer Care Department within the United States at (800) 762-2974, outside the United States at (317) 572-3993 or fax (317) 572-4002.

Wiley also publishes its books in a variety of electronic formats. Some content that appears in print may not be available in electronic books. For more information about Wiley products, visit our web site at www.wiley.com.

Library of Congress Cataloging-in-Publication Data:

Pradeep, A. K., 1963–
    The buying brain : secrets for selling to the subconscious mind / Dr. A.K. Pradeep.
        p. cm.
    Includes index.
    ISBN 978-0-470-60177-8 (cloth)
    ISBN 978-0-470-64684-7 (ebk)
    ISBN 978-0-470-64678-6 (ebk)
    ISBN 978-0-470-64661-8 (ebk)
    1. Neuromarketing.   2. Consumer behavior.   3. Shopping–Psychological aspects.
4. Marketing–Psychological aspects.   I. Title.
    HF5415.12615.P73 2010
    658.8'342–dc22

                                                                    2010003830

Printed in the United States of America.

10 9 8 7 6 5 4 3 2 1

For my dear children, Alexis, Shane, and Devin,
whose intelligence and laughter light up my life.

CONTENTS

Part 2
ENGAGING THE BUYING BRAIN

FOREWORD

As a professional marketing strategist, my entire career has been about getting into the heads of buyers. I've used tools that are familiar to generations of marketers, conducting primary research about my buyers by interviewing them, and drawing on secondary sources such as analysts' opinions and studies. Then, armed with that information, I've directed my teams of both staffers and agencies to create advertisements, websites, or trade show booths and tested these efforts via a focus group or A/B testing.

Damn, I thought I was really doing it right—until I read *The Buying Brain*, that is.

In these pages, I learned that I've been focused for all these years on just a tiny part of my buyers' brains! Like most marketers, I've been obsessing over the tip of the iceberg—that part of the consumer that we can see, touch, and hear.

I've asked questions designed to probe consumers' *conscious* minds. But the answers to questions like "Do you like this ad?" and "When I mention this brand, what animal do you think of?" and "Would you prefer red or green for that button?" seem downright quaint when compared to the potential fruits of probing the enormous activity in buyers' *subconscious* brains.

In this remarkable book, Dr. A. K. Pradeep shows us that as many as 95 percent of buyer decisions are made by the subconscious mind. Yes, you read that correctly!

Use of the word *secret* in many marketing book titles is an exaggeration at best and a fabrication at worst. But that accusation is absolutely untrue of *The Buying Brain: Secrets of Selling to the Subconscious Mind*, because this book unlocked mysteries for me (a reasonably knowledgeable marketing author and practitioner) in every chapter. I learned that there are differences between male and female brains that have profound importance to marketers. I learned that your brain changes with age, and knowing the nature of this transition can make your marketing to various age groups come alive. I even learned how to market effectively to new mothers (yup, her brain changes, too).

Because Pradeep is the guiding force behind the world's top neuromarketing lab, many of the world's largest and most sophisticated companies are using his ideas. These companies are applying the latest advances in neuroscience to create brands, products, websites, package designs, marketing campaigns, store environments, and more.

Now these powerful neuromarketing ideas are available to you in this engaging and easy-to-digest book.

Marketers have known for years that if you understand the human brain, you will design better offerings, create better marketing, and sell more products. Now, finally, marketers possess a more complete understanding of the entire human brain.

—David Meerman Scott
Business Week best-selling author of
The New Rules of Marketing & PR
www.WebInkNow.com
twitter.com/dmscott

Acknowledgments

Many people were involved not only in creating this book, but in creating the new field of neuromarketing. They are:

All the clients of NeuroFocus, who gave us the opportunity to explore previously unchartered domains of knowledge.

The employees of NeuroFocus across the globe, whose amazing brilliance and insanely hard work made the extraction of these insights possible. Special thanks to Julie Penfold and Tom Robbins, whose literary magic wands transformed these insights into the right words and stories to bring them to life on these pages.

Dr. Robert Knight for unlocking the mysteries of the human brain and clearing a pathway to bring neuroscience to the world of business.

Ram and Dev for creating the technical infrastructure that made these insights possible. Caroline Winnett, Russ Dunham, Andrew Pohlmann, Deepak Varma, Joakim Kalvenes, Steve Miller, and Steve Genco for our fruitful debates on the frameworks and ideas behind this book. Michal Levinson and Karthik Kasinathan for their exceptional mastery of data collection and analysis. Jack Lester for minding the store while I worked on this book. Ronen Gadot and Felipe Jaramillo for helping to bring NeuroFocus around the globe. Oksana Teicholz for her beautiful cover design. NeuroFocus marketing for getting this book out of my computer and onto these pages. Ajit Nazre, Ray Lane, and John Doerr for strengthening my resolve to make NeuroFocus a brilliant success. Al Gula and Jim Johnson, who helped me early on when the field of neuromarketing did not yet exist.

The NeuroFocus Advisory Board, for their outstanding contributions to the very foundations of everything we do.

Dave Calhoun, Thom Mastrelli, John Burbank, Itzhak Fisher, Cindy Shin, Dave Harkness, Susan Whiting, Dave Thomas, and Frank Stagliano for being great partners.

Jaya Kumar, Ann Mukherjee, Pam Forbus, Michelle Adams, Christine Kalvenes, Jack Marquardt, Steve Springfield, Craig Wynett, Ricardo Hungria,

Efrain Rosario, Betsie Kasner, Stan Sthanunathan, David Poltrack, Mel Berning, Frank Cooper, Alan Wurtzel, Horst Stipp, Peter Leimbach, Jon Mandel, Chris Moloney, Yong Park, Dermot Boden, Kwanwoo Nam, Gregory Lee, Byung Do Yoon, Patricia Roxas, Robert Atencio, Ramon Portilla, Rick Smith, the Advertising Research Foundation, and Jack Wakshlag for their ideas and inspiration.

THE BUYING
BRAIN

PART 1

INTRODUCING THE BUYING BRAIN

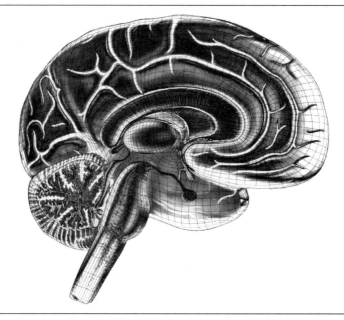

Source: Photo by BigStock.com

Understanding the human mind in biological terms has emerged as the central challenge of science in the twenty-first century.
—Dr. Eric Kandel, Neuroscientist and winner of the Nobel Prize for Physiology or Medicine; NeuroFocus Advisory Board Member.

CHAPTER 1

$1 TRILLION TO PERSUADE THE BRAIN

Millions of people in our global economy have jobs that depend on communicating with and persuading human brains. A trillion dollars is spent on this effort every year.

Yet few of us understand how all those human brains really work—what is attractive to them, how they decide what they like and don't like, or how they decide to buy or not buy the infinite variety of products and services presented for their consideration every day.

This book is about **how and why brains buy**. It dips into a wellspring of new knowledge that has been pouring out of the neurosciences over the last few decades, especially the last five years, and describes actionable insights for businesspeople and marketers that can be derived from that knowledge and applied directly to the global industry of persuasion.

These are remarkable times. It is a rare event when a science, its enabling technology, and a set of real, practical problems come together all at once to revolutionize and expand our capabilities in the world. It happened with chemistry in the eighteenth century, physics in the nineteenth century, microbiology in the twentieth century, and now neuroscience in the twenty-first century. As Charlie Rose said in a recent series of interviews devoted to the neurosciences, "we have learned more about the brain in the last five years than in all human history combined."

I am lucky to be surrounded by the best neuroscience team in the world to help me understand these developments and I am going to share them with you in this book.

What have we learned?

The basic lesson is that human brains process much of their sensory input subconsciously. This is, of course, counterintuitive because we can't think about how we think when we're not aware of the thinking we're thinking about! But the basic fact is undeniable and is validated by literally thousands of scientific studies. Most of the work our brains are doing day and night occurs below the threshold of our personal conscious awareness. Imagine all the work your brain was doing (that you weren't aware of) just decoding the second sentence in this paragraph!

Scientists have tried to express the ratio of subconscious to conscious brain activity in many ways. I like the formulation I first came across in Timothy Wilson's book, *Strangers to Ourselves: Discovering the Adaptive Unconscious.*

Our senses are taking in about 11 million bits of information every second. Most of that comes through our eyes, but all the other senses are contributing as well—hearing, touch, smell, taste, and spatial sensations. Our conscious brains—that part of thinking in which we are aware of thinking—can only process, at best, 40 bits of information per second. All the rest is processed subconsciously. That's a ratio, if I'm doing my math correctly, of 99.999 percent subconscious to conscious processing. No wonder our brains often appear to be a mystery to us.

The challenge for marketers and product developers is obvious. "How do I get into that 40 bits of consciously considered information?" That's what this book is about.

It is written for marketers and businesspeople. There are enough books about the brain that make me go "wow!" They are written by neuroscientists, social scientists, and psychologists. They create a sense of wonder for the brain and what it does.

In this book I tackle the question that my Fortune 500 clients ask me, "Brain science is nice, but, *so what*? Tell me how I use this knowledge. How do I change my brand strategy using neuromarketing? How do I change product design and pricing using neuromarketing? How do I analyze packages to make sure they will pop on the shelf? Are there things I should be doing in the store in the aisles to make our consumers desire our products? How can I make sure I get the returns on our investment in advertising?"

"And by the way," (clients tell me) "neuromarketing cannot be a set of 'cool, cute ideas,' but must be a systematic process and framework that can live and flourish in the workplace and workflow of my corporation."

This book explains those frameworks, workflows, and processes that enable a Chief Executive Officer (CEO), Chief Marketing Officer (CMO), Vice President of Brands, Vice President of Insights, and a Market Researcher to implement brain-based marketing in a corporation. These frameworks are born from analyzing thousands of brands, products, designs, pricing mechanisms, packages, in-store Point-of-Sale (POS) elements, Web storefronts, TV advertising, print advertising, Internet advertising, and more in our NeuroLabs across the world.

The frameworks and actionable concepts presented in this book will also be invaluable to those in the supply chain: brand marketing consultants, product designers, pricing clinicians, package design firms, in-store designers, Web design firms, and advertising agencies.

The interplay of conscious and subconscious processes in the human brain presents a fundamental challenge for people in the business of developing products and getting other people to buy and try them. Marketers and product developers have suspected this for years.

If people do not have access to all the sources of their decisions and behaviors, then **they can't tell us why they do what they do**. So if we only listen to their articulated reports of what they like and don't like, we may well be led astray. An 80 percent failure rate of new products in the marketplace, with all the economic costs that implies, gives us some pretty strong evidence that this is the case!

The problem for marketers and product developers is how to find out what people really want and need. That's where brain scientists come in.

I love helping companies do marketing and product development. I love being able to apply these new neuro-based tools to making products and messages more effective. The business I lead has worked with many companies—large and small, domestic and global—and I can tell you this: Companies come to us with humility and tremendous respect for their current and potential customers. They all want to know the same things:

- Do consumers notice us?
- Do consumers like us?
- Do consumers remember us?

In a free marketplace of competing ideas, the consumer is, and will remain, the boss. Giant corporations still rise and fall at the whim of the consumer, based on their ability to meet that consumer's wants and needs better than their competition.

So here are the basic principles that drive everything you are going to read in this book.

- Neuromarketing provides a real competitive advantage in a crowded and cluttered marketplace.

- While the languages of people and the ways they express themselves change from country to country and culture to culture, the language of the brain is universal, thus opening the door for global norms.
- Neuro-design of products and services opens the door to design products and services that appeal to the inner truths and aesthetic sensibilities within all of us.
- Every aspect of brands, products, packages, in-store, and advertising is changed by neuromarketing today, and that trend is explosive.
- My goal is to get you to put the book down and apply what you learned in your work tomorrow.

CHAPTER 2

NEUROMARKETING TECHNOLOGY

At the end of this chapter, you'll know and be able to use the following:

- Why it's critical to use a dense array of EEG sensors to cover the whole brain
- Why neurological testing can rely on sample sizes far smaller than surveys and even some focus groups, and get results that are more scientifically accurate
- The differences between EEG, fMRI, and biometrics

So much attention is being paid to the advances that neuromarketing is making in today's marketplace that its origins have gone largely unnoticed. I want to shine a little light on the reasons why this marriage of science and marketing was consummated, and the driving forces behind it.

It usually surprises audiences I address to learn that electroencephalography (EEG), the basic technology underlying most brainwave-based neuromarketing and the form of neurological testing that we use at NeuroFocus, is not really new. In fact, it is the staple methodology used in neuroscience laboratories around the world.

Hans Berger made the first practical application of EEG measurement in the 1920s. He was the first scientist to design sensors to pick up electrical signals naturally emanating from the brain, and his discovery is directly responsible for our ability today to capture brainwave activity as accurately and reliably as we do. He understood from the start that his invention could and should be used to measure the brain's full range of activity, not just an extremely small portion of it. When you consider how limited the state of neuroscience knowledge was some eight decades ago compared to today, Dr. Berger's comprehension and foresight is all the more impressive.

But in some key respects, his invention was the classic example of a great idea ahead of its time. EEG sensors could acquire the previously elusive tiny microvolts of electricity that are produced by brain activity, but the technology to integrate and fully analyze them was lacking. It would remain so until the advent of transistors, microprocessors, and the subsequent blossoming of digital technology many years later. Combined, these elements enabled us to untangle the complex interplay of brain electrical dynamics. It really took matching microchips with those microvolts before we could take full advantage of Berger's Flapper Age discovery.

It was quite a span of time from the Depression to the Digital Dawn, but EEG methodology coupled with fast, large memory-capacity computers enabled scientists at last to explore and, most importantly, understand the inner workings of the brain for the first time. However, even today, with all the processing power we have at our fingertips, we are still plumbing the depths of this amazing organ and making new discoveries on a daily basis.

CORTICAL GEOGRAPHY

The second element in the birth of neuromarketing is what we have learned about the brain's basic structure and the way it functions. Hopefully you won't tire of this fact, because I mention it in these pages several times, but it is central to grasp the concept that **the brain is really an incredibly complex and interwoven series of neural networks.** The chapters on the brain and the senses delve into this phenomenon in great detail, but it's worth noting here because it is at the core of EEG measurement of brainwave activity.

There are seemingly endless statistics about the brain, but a few call out for mention here:

 The brain—that supercomputer inside your skull—is capable of roughly 200 million billion calculations per second.

This massive interconnectivity is what enables the human brain to perform all the amazing things we do, from walking upright and chewing gum at the same time, to scoring operas, performing brain surgery, and everything in between. As much as we have learned by isolating and identifying the brain's many specific regions and structures, if we hope to understand the real majesty and meaning of our minds, we have to adopt a "systems approach."

Hans Berger's breakthrough paved the way towards gaining that neurological knowledge.

 A man-made supercomputer has about 60,000 miles of wiring inside. The brain's equivalent amount of interconnectivity would amount to more than 200,000 miles of "wiring"!

One more statistic illustrates how important full-brain measurement is for neuroscience, medicine, and neuromarketing:

 Sixteen EEG sensors are the minimum number required by a clinical standard for determining brain death in humans.

This is why NeuroFocus applies high density arrays of EEG sensors to cover the full brain. Only this full brain coverage provides marketers with the entire scope of brainwave activity that occurs across multiple brain regions. Measurement across the entire brain is critical for understanding how the brain is responding to stimuli.

As groundbreaking as this combination of neuroscience with digital technology has been, it would not have given birth to neuromarketing without a third causative effect at work. And that is the state of market research methodologies and challenges at the dawn of the neuromarketing age.

MARKET RESEARCH CHALLENGES AND OPPORTUNITIES

The fact is, as sophisticated, and in many ways useful, as market research has become in modern economies, there have always been fundamental shortcomings associated with the various methodologies that are employed. These flaws have vexed both clients and researchers for decades, and no one has been able to devise comprehensive solutions without a deeper understanding of the brains being studied.

There are two basic reasons for this: first, traditional methods are inherently unable to duplicate what the brain does, how it operates, and how it forms perceptions of things like products, services, stores, ads, and everything else connected with modern marketing.

Behind the second reason is a fascinating neurological finding:

 When asked to recount how it reacted to something, in the course of responding *the brain actually alters the original data it recorded.*

This is the basic problem with surveys and focus groups—so-called "articulated" or "self-reported" responses. These research methods can work reasonably well when used to capture **facts** recounted by participants. But not so much when it comes to probing how consumers truly felt about or remembered something. It is extraordinarily difficult for people to describe in precise words the emotions that they experienced when exposed to a stimulus. We are asking our conscious mind to reconstruct what our subconscious mind recorded, and translate that into specific language that accurately reflects how we felt or what we remembered at an earlier point in time.

Traditional market research must try to work around this structural shortcoming, plus a couple of others. Focus groups can be influenced by one or more strong-voiced, opinionated participants. Surveys must cover large numbers of respondents in order to compensate for the inherent "noise" or error in any individual's responses. These limitations are built-in for such "articulated response" methodologies.

So the third element in the birth of neuromarketing has been the fundamental **need in the market research world for more accurate, reliable, and actionable knowledge** in order to make more informed business decisions. This need is made all the more urgent by ever more competitive companies and economies.

Combine this need with the exponential growth in scientific knowledge of the brain, the advancement in computer technology, and the challenges of existing research approaches, and the advent of neuromarketing appears nothing less than inevitable.

Sample Size

One frequently asked question (FAQ) we encounter periodically has to do with sample size. Happily, here again neuroscience supplies the answer.

Traditional research methodologies require substantial sample sizes to approximate statistical validity. Fairly large numbers of people must be sampled in surveys to overcome variables such as language, education, culture, and other factors that can and do influence consumers' articulated responses.

In sharp contrast, neurological testing achieves more scientifically sound, rigorously reliable, and actionable results—and requires far smaller sample sizes to do so. Brainwave activity measurement dives below the surface of the consumer's conscious mind, to the deep subconscious level where the brain's initial registration of and reaction to stimuli occurs. While the human brain differs in some respects—for example, between men and women, or young children and seniors—**the fact is that our brains are far more alike than they are different.**

Because our brains are so remarkably alike, a thorough and scientifically sound neuromarketing research project **requires about 10 percent of the test subjects** required by conventional surveys.

No matter how large the sample size may be, conventional research results are also vulnerable to a basic neurological fact: what our brains actually perceive and recall is different from what we say we perceived and recalled when we're asked. The process of accessing that stored information and translating it into a physical response actually causes the brain to alter its original response. NeuroFocus measures at the stage of the cognitive timeline before that alteration occurs.

Alphabet Soup, with a Side of Biometrics

As with any new field, the terminology, technology, and methodology associated with what is now commonly referred to as neuromarketing can be daunting and confusing to nonscientists. While some might maintain that there's a marketing advantage to this aura of complexity, I disagree and firmly side with the late retail magnate Sy Syms, who said in his ads, "an educated consumer is our best customer."

So herewith is **a brief overview** of the two main technological pillars upon which the neuromarketing category is built. And a third methodology that really has nothing to do with neurological measurement per se, but is often thrown into the mix (especially by its practitioners, who dearly love to embrace all that is great about the brain, without actually measuring it at all!).

EEG

As you now know, this acronym stands for electroencephalography. It is a "passive" technology, using sensors (essentially, tiny and highly sensitive microphones) to capture the minute electrical signals that brainwave activity produces. It is completely noninvasive and comfortable. Neuroscience laboratories worldwide have used EEG technology for decades.

For full-brain coverage, which again is the sole scientific standard that any reputable EEG-based neurological testing company relies on, EEG sensors are embedded in a lightweight cap (closely resembling a typical swim cap) and deployed in high-density arrays. They measure the extremely low-voltage signals emitted by neurological activity at up to 2,000 times a second at each sensor's location.

At NeuroFocus, we apply high density arrays of EEG sensors to achieve full-brain monitoring. We do so for several reasons. **Many areas of the brain are responsible for several functions,** and because of this, we rely on full-brain coverage to know exactly which regions are operating simultaneously and in concert in response to a specific stimulus. If you only measure a very small number of areas, you are going to miss this essential element of interconnectivity—and your results will be woefully inadequate by any recognized neurological standards.

Sensor placement is key as well. EEG sensors are so sensitive that they pick up a certain amount of artifacts—"noise," in signal processing parlance—along with brainwave activity. A classic example is eye blinks. Muscle movements like blinks can generate up to 100 times the electrical voltage that brainwave activity creates—so you can see that it is critical in the analysis phase to screen for and eliminate that noise, to ensure that what is being analyzed is only the pure brain activity data, uncorrupted by muscle activity or other extraneous signals. If you only place EEG sensors in certain limited areas—such as on the temples or forehead alone—you are going to pick up an inordinately large ratio of artifacts, or "noise," from muscle activity in that area, compared with the brainwave activity recorded.

Relying exclusively on full-brain testing assures not only that brainwave activity across all the relevant and interconnected regions of the brain is being captured, but also that sufficient overlapping data streams are being acquired to allow for artifact removal, and still have more than enough brainwave data to conduct accurate analysis.

To put this into perspective, the importance of full-brain testing is reflected in the fact that NeuroFocus *discards* as artifact as much data as some other EEG-based neuromarketing companies collect in their **full set of data.**

We combine this full-brain EEG testing methodology with sophisticated eye-tracking equipment that records exactly where a person is looking while experiencing a stimulus. This combination allows us to correlate, with precision, exactly how that person's brain is responding to a certain stimulus in terms of our three primary NeuroMetrics of Attention, Emotional Engagement, and Memory Retention, with exactly where that person's eyes are focused at the same millisecond.

fMRI

This stands for functional Magnetic Resonance Imaging. If you've ever had a physical injury for which you've had an MRI scan, you're familiar with the technology. It's been in productive use in the medical community for years, and in the fMRI format, is a valid and useful form of neurological research.

A test subject is scanned by lying down in a long, narrow, tube, surrounded by extremely powerful magnets. Activation of these magnets produces electrical fields, which computer imaging converts to reveal inner body structures, or in fMRI applications, brain functionality.

In short, fMRI measures the increase in oxygen levels in the flow of blood within the brain. Hence, it can accurately indicate when activity in a certain area of the brain is increased. When neurological activity increases, the brain calls for added oxygen-bearing blood to fuel that activity—and fMRI scans pick that increase up.

The shortcoming of fMRI technology for marketing research purposes is that **it can take up to 5 seconds** for that added blood supply to reach that specific area of the brain. So, for example, if you're testing a consumer's neurological reaction to a TV commercial, their brain might respond instantaneously to a red car appearing in the spot—but the added blood that the brain called for in response to that heightened activity might take as long as 5 seconds before it reaches the activated area.

Therefore, relying on fMRI, it becomes problematic to attempt to link with temporal precision the exact stimulus—that red car appearing—with the indication of the brain's response to it, because of the elapsed time between the two events.

In comparison, EEG testing captures the brain's response in milliseconds.

Additional shortcomings for fMRI today include its cost—the equipment, specialized testing facilities, and trained staff **cost many millions**—and the demands on the person being tested: Only one subject can be tested at a time, and each subject must remain prone and completely motionless throughout the testing procedure, or the entire session will be invalid. If there is head movement of as little as three millimeters, it can render test results useless. So fMRI, while scientifically sound and medically valuable as a diagnostic tool, currently has specific structural drawbacks that limit its effectiveness as a marketing research methodology.

Having said this, I do see significant potential of fMRI as the technology improves. Reflecting this belief, NeuroFocus recently obtained the core patent underlying the use of fMRI for neuroimaging purposes in marketing research.

Biometrics

This is an overall term that represents measurements of physiological responses in the body—not directly in the brain—to external stimuli we experience with our senses. Examples of biometric measures include heart and respiration rates, eye movements, blinking, galvanic skin response (GSR), facial muscle movement, and body movements.

Some biometric measurements are limited for marketing research purposes in that they are "lagging indicators," not direct measures, of primary brain activity. That is, the brain may issue an order to the body well before the physiological effect actually occurs. In an ideal world, we want to know when the order is issued, not just when it is carried out.

Similar to the temporal problem with fMRI measurements, **this lag time is a definitive shortcoming.** Various human physical systems not only respond at different rates in comparison to each other; physiological responses in general can be dissimilar between different individuals; and even within one individual the complex of response rates may vary depending upon a whole host of factors (fatigue, medical conditions, environmental influences, and so forth).

Although much effort has been put into adjusting and calibrating all these timing differences, to date it has not been scientifically feasible to "time link" all the body's responses to stimuli with the brain's original reactions in any consistent, reliable way. There are simply too many variations in the timing to do so.

To sum up: Biometrics do not delineate between specialized brain responses. They provide a secondary, time-lagged, and confounded measure of arousal. They cannot stand alone as reliable indicators of emotion or cognition.

This is not to say that biometric measurements cannot be useful. They can definitely serve as secondary, peripheral confirmations of what the brain has already registered and responded to. But make no mistake: they are **not** primary indicators of neurological activity—only direct electrical measures of brain activity can provide that data. **And EEG is exactly that:** The direct measure of electrical activity in the brain, registered at the true speed of thought.

To illustrate the dichotomy between basic physiological reactions and active "thought," consider that a comatose patient can still exhibit physical reactions to certain stimuli, like a loud hand clap. In other words, biometric response does not necessarily correspond with cognitive response, at either conscious or subconscious levels. The brain's basic systems may still trigger a measurable response from the body's physical systems—but that doesn't alter the fact that the patient is still in a coma.

The brain is where the initial, and most complex and meaningful, responses to stimuli are formed. More specifically, the subconscious level of the brain is where elements that are essential to marketing success such as initial product interest, purchase intent, and brand loyalty are formed, and where they reside.

The preceding explains why the most accurate and reliable measurements are made at the subconscious level of the brain, relying on full-brain EEG-based testing, and using biometrics for what they are: secondary confirmations of what the brain has already responded to several seconds earlier.

These fundamental facts are vital to understand accurately the field of neuromarketing, and to separate marketing claims from neurological/scientific truths.

CHAPTER 3

YOUR CUSTOMER'S BRAIN IS 100,000 YEARS OLD

At the end of this chapter, you'll know and be able to use the following:
- Key ways to engage the primal part of the human brain
- Core mechanisms the brain uses to determine whether to pay attention to your message
- The three ways in which the brain can be frustrated, and how to avoid them in your marketing
- The four triggers the brain loves and how to use them in marketing

CAVEMAN IN A WIRED WORLD

The neuroscience of the human brain builds from the understanding that it is a freshly evolved miracle. Travel back with me 100,000 years or so, when newer, larger prefrontal cortexes in early man first previewed the modern brain we all share today.

Life is nasty, brutish, and short. Competition for food is fierce. Predators are fast and omnipresent. To survive, the relatively slow and weak humans develop a secret weapon: fine hand movements allow them to refine tools and weapons to become extremely efficient at both hunting and defending against others who hunt. At around the same time, the human trachea descends into the throat to make vocalizations more distinct and communications suddenly very effective. Communication is honed and increases in importance with the evolving social system and the need for cooperation. The ability to determine friend from foe is crucial in this nascent society, as is the ability to predict what someone will do (lie or tell truth, cooperate or attack).

This is all good news for the hominids, bad news for their prey. Our rise up in the food chain begins as our brains become larger to accommodate these

17

critical new skills of working in cooperative groups, planning, hunting, and remembering.

But, in a classic catch-22, there is a price to pay. As brain size increases, so must the skull that carries it. And here's the rub: If the skull continues to grow in pace with the rapidly evolving brain, the pelvis of the females will need to be so wide that they will no longer be able to run. Plus, that gorgeous new brain requires significantly more oxygen, glucose, and blood than previous versions, making it more expensive to operate over time.

 In fact, our brain is the most metabolically expensive organ to operate—representing only 3 percent of the body's weight, yet requiring up to 20 percent of its energy.

Advertisers take note: The "ease of processing" of your message is therefore very important to the brain. A complicated ad that requires cognitive resources **will likely be ignored** by the brain. So as you balance the complexity of an ad with ease of processing, lean toward ease. Package designers note that simplified "Zen" like packaging (Apple being a prime example) appeals to the brain—as it consumes fewer cognitive resources. In-store designers and Web and storefront designers, keep in mind that simplified organization and ease of cognitive processing trumps clutter and complex hierarchies. While it is true that "simple puzzles" intrigue and attract the brain, if the puzzle requires more than a few seconds to resolve, the brain **gives up**, and often rejects the message, with prejudice against your brand (aka negative priming).

So evolution offers a twofold compromise: First, the large brain begins folding in on itself, creating grooves and valleys to fit within the skull (see Figure 3.1).

Second, infants are born while their heads are still small enough to pass through the mother's pelvis, but long before they are ready to face the world. Helpless and dependent, **human babies require their mothers to stay put,** at least for some time. They require fathers to provide for the mothers. They require group cooperation and an increasingly complicated social structure to support them. Because of the need to operate in a complex social group, the brain continues to evolve and grow in size, developing empathy, deception, altruism, and the building of coalitions.

This big, complex brain separates us from every other animal on Earth and gives us extraordinary capacities like linear thinking, complex language

Figure 3.1
To compensate for limited space inside the skull,
the brain develops folds and ridges.

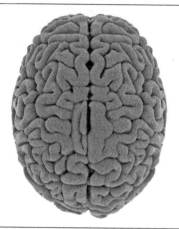

Source: Photo used with permission from istockphoto.com

development, the ability to understand symbols and metaphors, to develop and comprehend the complex strategies of mathematics, and to communicate with purpose and grace.

> Large, complex brains exist in other species such as some whales, dolphins, great apes, chimpanzees, and orangutans. These mammals are typically highly social also, have long lives with long gestational and developmental periods, living in complex groups that hunt together and form life-long bonds. They also require planning and memory to hunt, adapt, and mate successfully.

As humans work and live in small groups, natural selection favors greater intelligence. We grow smarter still until the brain, **around 100,000 years ago,** reaches its current size and configuration. It becomes exquisitely attuned to its social and environmental needs. Always alert for predators, forever searching for food, warmth, shelter, and suitable mates to pass on genes, the human brain—the same model we share today—developed hard-wired abilities and responses honed to the survival of the species. Encounters were filtered and filed primarily via six human emotions: sadness, fear, anger, disgust, happiness, and surprise, and possibly a seventh, contempt. The prefrontal cortex (the most advanced part of the brain), began conducting its symphony (including long range planning, storing and planting food, and hunting and finding animals in season), learning socially-appropriate behavior and task switching. Soon it launches humans into a new world beyond daily survival into a dance of possibilities—featuring representations of objects further removed in time and space and manipulated with logic and emotion. This big new brain absorbs and exudes culture, bringing itself to full modernity. Figurative art, music, self-ornamentation, trade, burial, and consciousness of an afterlife become imbedded in—the society, which begins to thrive rather than just survive.

> The human brain is emotional at its very core. While women process messaging with more emotion than men, both genders **must be engaged emotionally** for a message to be remembered and acted upon. Advertisers must uncover the key emotional triggers their product inspires and pinpoint them in their messaging. Package designers must carefully imbue their designs with palatable, even visceral, emotive imagery and shapes. Merchandisers must make the experience of shopping an emotionally engaging, self-satisfying one **if they seek repeat visits.**

Traditions develop and concepts, ideas, patterns, folklore, and customs are passed down through generations. Eventually, small, tightly bound groups begin to migrate, to explore, to adapt. One hundred thousand years later, they—we—have conquered the Earth, and are beginning to explore the planets and galaxies that surround it.

Day One

And it all started with the debut of our large, multilayered brains, first in evidence 100 millennia ago. On a typical day on that dry savannah, you awake with the sun, hungry and perhaps cold. Your goal-oriented brain propels you to seek food. Grabbing your spear, you go out, and away from your shelter. Your anxiety level is high; your senses are on alert, ears monitoring every crunch of dry grass; eyes scanning the horizon; nose filtering the scents of animals, water, and plants; your mouth is dry, and every muscle is tense and at the ready. Your breathing is fast and your heart rate is elevated.

Goal-driven behavior is the frontal lobe's command to the body to seek and find what it needs most. This type of pressing, urgent search mode prompts the brain to scan for novel or precisely-attuned messages or images that satisfy its consuming goal. When dealing with products or messages that have **an indispensable** place in consumer's lives, provide clutter-free, clear, accurate directions for finding and obtaining the goal. In advertising, packaging, and in-store merchandising, use active verbs and dominant imagery to tell the brain "What you need is here."

Some two hours into your journey, your eyes, ears, and nose alert you: Something is moving in the tall grass. Is it friend or foe? You freeze, hold your breath, and wait. Soon, a tail switches and a leopard rises to meet your gaze. In blazing speed, your brain calculates your next move. The leopard is faster than you are. Should you flee? Your spear is deadly and you have not eaten in days. Do you fight? **In milliseconds, the answer is determined.**

The leopard, too, is hungry, starving from the drought. In her eyes, you see stark determination as the big cat growls softly, showing you her teeth. Her whiskers tremble as she moves into high alert mode. She made her life-and-death decision the moment she rose to meet you from her hidden spot in the tall grass. You are two predators, each deadly, each hungry. Only one of you will survive this confrontation.

Your heart pounds as you advance, your body sweats, your muscles tremble as you confront today's life and death scenario. The fighting is brief but ruthless. Wounded and bleeding, you manage to drive the spear home. As the leopard collapses, your body is flooded with endorphins, a feel-good hormone that produces feelings of euphoria. Your mouth waters at the prospect of food. You drag the heavy cat back over the miles you've come, fighting back scavengers all along the way. When you limp back to your shelter, the members of your tribe greet you with joy, prepare your prize for eating, and mend your wounds. **The reward circuits in your brain light up** as the feeling of pride and accomplishment settles deep into your psyche, driving you to go out and hunt another day.

When the brain comes across a "rewarding behavior" (one that it wants to be repeated or continued), it releases a potent dose of dopamine as a powerful reward to motivate trial and repetition, Over time, repeated behaviors that spark the reward circuits lay down neurological pathways to prompt the performance of those behaviors with greater ease and frequency. The pleasure/reward circuit—at its extreme—is responsible for everything from addicts to Olympians. So what? Motivate consumers to try or to continue using your brand or product by activating their pleasure/reward circuits by focusing on powerful images of the emotional "payoff" elements of your product: the luscious depiction of the chocolate, or the smooth leather seats of the high-performance automobile.

Physically, emotionally, and mentally exhausted, you fall into a deep, restorative sleep. And a new day dawns.

Same Brain, Different Day

This morning, you wake to the sound of an alarm buzzing. You are warm and comfortable. **Instead of focusing on finding food** to ensure your survival, you examine your refrigerator to see which option has the *fewest* calories. Rarely—if ever – is the search for sustenance your prime motivator for the day's activities. But your ancient brain still **feels compelled to hunt, to achieve,** and so it elevates today's missions into life-and-death scenarios as it has evolved to handle.

Checking your e-mail, you see that a contract that should have been signed lingers in Legal. Exactly as you did when faced with hunger in the savannah, your anxiety rises, you become tense and hyperalert. Your brain urges you to seek relief.

You grab your cell phone and laptop and begin your commute. Sitting in traffic, your brain feels hunted. Horns blast and your amygdala fires (the part of your brain that responds immediately to stress), your blood pressure rises, and your breath becomes shallow and fast. Messages assault and seduce you without relief. The radio plays. The stock market is down. Your sense of security is shaken again. Irritation grows as other cars attempt to squeeze into your space. You masterfully outmaneuver and do not allow others to outpace you.

Arriving at work, **you gather your electronic spears,** and walk from the parking deck. Along the way, a group of young men appears, sweating and shaking, demanding money and all of your electronics. Your defensive instincts swing into action. You yell and try to move around the men. Confronted, they are now angry rather than just desperate. Now they want your life, not just your laptop. Your heart pounds and your muscles tremble. Just at that moment, a security guard rounds the corner, and the men flee.

You collapse in relief. But hours, days, and weeks later, your brain replays the event. You dream about it in symbols every night. Your fear is heightened and your safety is threatened. And unlike your earlier self, you do not run or fight or walk off the anxiety. Instead, you enter your office and sit. You interact with your colleagues all day, in well-spoken struggles for influence and power.

As your cortisol level rises, this "stress hormone" improves your alertness and performance.

You are "on your game," aligning yourself with those who support your goals, scanning for motives of those who might undermine it, eyes on the prize all day long, 100 percent of the time.

When you emerge, night has fallen and blinking signs surround you. Your brain fights to make sense of the many messages hurtling toward it (see Figure 3.2).

Figure 3.2
Times Square. Your brain constantly struggles to make sense of a flood of messages and images.

Source: Photo by Bart Penfold

Many are cast aside, irrelevant. Some of the more relevant or novel messages reverberate in your hippocampus to be stored more permanently in your cortex and throughout your brain.

> When the brain is exposed to too many messages, or interrupted in its drive to complete a task, it purposefully drives distracting messages or images into the background so that it can focus on the task at hand. The brain can ill afford to attend to each note of the cacophonous barrage it encounters. Frustrated, the brain ignores **all of the messaging,** which has run together to form an irritating diversion. Whenever possible, position your message or product in scenarios without clutter. If clutter is unavoidable in your crowded category, make sure your message, image, package, or product is clean and clear, and uses white space and simple, direct messaging to offer a breath of fresh air to the frustrated brain viewing it.

Arriving home, you turn to one of your three screens (perhaps all of them), and monitor messaging for the rest of the night (read more about multimedia screens in Chapter 14). You fall into a restless sleep, which is essential for your memory to consolidate important information that may help you adapt tomorrow.

CAVEWOMAN IN A CAR POOL

As you see here in Chapter 3 and in Chapter 5, the brains of men and women are very different. They evolved to serve best the needs of each gender as early human society developed. So, in the service of equality, let us look at how a typical female brain experiences two typical days—100,000 years apart.

Day One

You wake weary with a hungry newborn in your arms. You feed and clean your baby, and then set about finding some food for yourself. You are dangerously thin and very thirsty, the child's needs stripping you of your stores of fat.

With the child always in tow, you venture out into the area around your dwelling. The other women, adolescent girls, and children of your tribe soon join you. Together, you return to a chaparral where you've found tubers and berries before. When the children sleep, one or two women guard and comfort them, while the others continue to gather grains, roots, and occasionally, small rodents or snakes. The women's band stays close, always on the alert for predators, prepared to stand between danger and the children. Yet they do not attack larger, dangerous animals. As their large prefrontal cortex knows, such "all or nothing" attacks could leave their infants unguarded, vulnerable, or dead. While they don't comprehend it, this caution permits them to fulfill their primary evolutionary goal: to procreate successfully.

The band of women and children spend the day gathering food, communicating, and in general supporting each other (but if a person can sneak or lie —use deception—to gain an advantage that may be beneficial to her survival and genetic fitness, she will). The women tend the sick and use their superior empathic skills to know what they need. **Quickly, they learn to "read" each other** and the babies of the tribe, who can only communicate with facial expression and eye contact. Without words, successful mothers can tell quickly, within a range of different abilities, if her baby's cry means hunger, anger, fear, boredom, sleepiness, or irritation. As she nurses the child throughout the day, oxytocin flows through her system, keeping her calm, even slightly sedated, and most certainly deeply, thoroughly devoted.

> Women, particularly mothers, are supremely skilled at empathic skills, watching others and knowing what they're feeling and, often, what they need. The female brain is hard-wired to seek out community and uses this enhanced empathic ability to foster it. When presenting a message, package, product, or store environment to a largely female audience, engage her empathic mind. She engages immediately with faces, particularly when they're making direct eye contact with her; she reacts positively to women in groups, enjoying a shared activity; and she cannot look away from a baby making eye contact with her.

As the shadows lengthen, the men of the tribe return. One has made a large kill that will provide vital protein and calories for his family. The women celebrate and reward this hunter and they become cautious and timid around the frustrated hunters, careful not to anger these larger, now irritated and aggressive males. At the same time, the women carefully notice which of the men would be a better mate, the more successful hunters, and purposefully associate with them to father their children.

As the small group shares its food of the day and hears the stories of the hunts that provided it, you settle next to your mate, sleeping baby always in your arms.

Same Brain, Different Day

You wake to your alarm and quickly shower and dress. It's still dark outside, giving you your best chance of completing the day's first round of duties.

You pack the children's lunches and their backpacks. You check each of their schedules, sign a permission slip for a field trip, and write a note to remind the nanny that your son has a dentist's appointment and your daughter has a soccer match. You check the refrigerator and make a list of what's missing—and what's available for after-school snacks. You pay your bills before it's time to wake your sleeping children and speed them on their way. Your brain has evolved to multitask, just as your ancestors did while gathering food, caring for children, and guarding their friends. You are a master of efficiency.

The female brain is designed to multitask. With many more connections between her right and left hemispheres than a typical male brain, the female brain juggles tasks, emotions, logical input, and to-do lists with ease. So what? Marketers speaking to the female brain should be aware that she is attending to many "mission-critical" tasks as your message makes its way into her consideration. She will pay attention to information that helps make her job easier, and to material that celebrates her individuality and her mastery over the many critically important "little things" she gets done. See Figure 3.3.

Figure 3.3
The corpus callosum, which connects the two hemispheres, is more developed in the female brain.

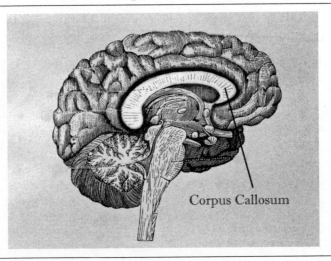

Corpus Callosum

Source: Used with permission from istockphoto.com

Each child requires multiple wake-ups and constant reminders to brush, wash, and dress. A wardrobe drama ensues with your daughter, with tears and frustration leading the way from house to car. Your superior empathic skills read her distress and dissolve the problem quickly. You grab your laptop and cell phone and jump behind the wheel, making it almost all the way to school before you remember that it's your turn to drive car pool today. You turn around, now late and frustrated, to drive by three more houses and endure the disapproving stares of the moms who load their now-tardy kids into your car.

You unload the children at school and head for the freeway. Aggressive drivers edge into your lane, horns blast, and brake lights flash quickly. Your brain senses it's in a life-and-death situation. Your heart pounds, your anxiety peaks, cortisol floods your system. **Your brain has prepared you** to deal with imminent danger and a probable attack. And it does so twice a day, every day—in every commute.

You go to the office, hurrying in, breathless and late for your first meeting. As you present to your colleagues, part of your brain is drawn back to your children. Did you remember to pack fruit? Is the runny nose an allergy or the flu?

You hunker down to your work, flying through requests and proposals, your multitasking brain accessing both hemispheres effortlessly. You skip lunch because you're a little behind. At 2:30 P.M. the nanny calls. She is sick. Your children will be waiting alone at school in 30 minutes. Your brain is now flashing alarm signals to your entire system. The children must be protected. You pack your bags and leave early, again, to the disparaging expressions of your boss and teammates.

Again, your brain warns you: Ostracism from the group is a dangerous consequence.

You pile your electronics back into your car and repeat, quickly, the trek home. Constantly monitoring the time, you're panicked, breathing shallow and fast. At every signal, you urge "Come on! Come on!"

You arrive at school 15 minutes after pick-up. Your children are sullen and angry. You drop your son off at the dentist's, drive your daughter to soccer practice, leave to get your son, return to pick up your daughter. You didn't see a moment of practice; you didn't sit with your son at the dentist. Yet your brain craves the stimulation and comfort of their presence.

You return home at 5:45 P.M. to an empty refrigerator. You've been up for 12 hours and have not spent 15 minutes with either of your children. You hurry them to their homework, phone for pizza delivery, and open your laptop to continue the work of the afternoon. After a 10-minute dinner break, you and your children move to separate rooms to complete your separate tasks. As a born connector, you feel uneasy, as you haven't connected at all today with your children, your husband, or the friends upon whose empathy you depend.

At 9:00 P.M., you check homework and put the children to bed. You start a load of laundry and make calls for another parent to cover you (again) at pick-up. Your husband returns somewhere in the middle, and before returning to your separate work, you fill each other in (briefly). He makes a quick trip to the grocery store while you unload the dishwasher.

Exhausted, you fall into bed at midnight, and dream of symbolic threats and attacks as your brain struggles to make sense of your day.

> Compared to her ancient predecessor, the modern female brain has much more on her plate. Her ability to maintain close, daily contact with a network of friends and family is severely hampered in today's commuter society, full of two-earner households and "bedroom communities." So what? Let your brand, product, or store become a networking hub for your prospects and customers. Provide your female customers with Twitter or Facebook updates and links, in-store cooking lessons, chat rooms, and other resources to help her feel more connected to her world—and your brand or product.

THE PRIMAL BRAIN IN THE MODERN WORLD

As these vignettes make clear, **it's not always easy for a 100,000-year-old brain** to make its way in the modern world. Exquisitely evolved to react to threats, danger, aggression, and to determine the true from false to avoid being deceived, our brains often find themselves in "emergency mode" simply due to the pace and overstimulation of modern life.

In fact, one school of thought wonders why our brains created environments for which they are ill-suited. Why, for example, would a highly-evolved, successful hominid create a world with the stressors ours embodies?

The answer, I'd argue, is that we are both ambitious and creative. We are not content with what is, and seek ever-better solutions. One could certainly argue that we've paid a high price for our creations, but we've also gained high rewards. Diseases have been eradicated, magnificent art has been created, the human genome has been decoded, and we can communicate with anyone, anywhere in the world, in seconds.

So the question becomes, how do we **engage with the primal brain**—embedded deep within us—in this modern world? How do we soothe and seduce it? How do we send it messages that are important enough to be noticed and remembered? How do we stand out from the amazing barrage of sensory stimuli to be the one product or brand that makes sense and is embraced by the brain? How do we make life easier and more fun for this miracle of nature that's perpetually on guard? More importantly, how do we start treating our customers as the smart, evolved people they are? With respect and dignity, compassion and caring, delivered in a way that invites and engages, but doesn't overstimulate or alarm.

Until very recently, we've not had a way to learn "how the brain feels" about the messages, products, packages, and shopping environments we create. But with game-changing improvements in EEG consumer testing and interpretation coinciding with huge leaps in computer algorithmic and analyses capabilities and, of course, the burst of knowledge and experience both have allowed us, we can now **know** with certainty, what the brain likes and what it rejects.

The brain is frustrated by:

- Tasks that take too long to resolve,
- Clutter, and
- Messages that distract or don't apply.

THE NEUTRAL BRAIN

At their emotional core, the brains of modern humans are remarkably alike. They respond similarly to key stimuli and react along the same lines to messages. The most primal, emotional sections of our brains react at a pure, precognitive level, in milliseconds. They are honest and unambiguous, unaffected by language, education, or culture. The universality of the human brain allows us to make highly accurate projections and draw extremely specific conclusions and recommendations based on the results we obtain from capturing and analyzing brainwave activity.

The brain can't ignore:

Novelty is the single most effective factor in effectively capturing its precious attention. Novelty recognition is a hard-wired survival tool all primates share. Whether looking for prey or berries or suitable mates, our brains are trained to look for something brilliant and new, something that stands out from the landscape, something that looks delicious. A novel message, product, package, and/or layout is the key to penetrating their busy and selective subconscious minds. Breaking through the clutter in this way helps products stand out at the shelf and elevates a great logo from a sea of competing symbols and letters. To be embraced, a consumer touch point must first be noticed. (In Chapter 12 you can find more about novelty, how to achieve it, and what it means to the buying brain.)

Eye contact is particularly important to a social species such as ours. Activating challenge or empathy, depending on its depiction, displaying eyes is a certain way to gain the brain's attention.

Pleasure/reward images are irresistible to our brains. The trick is to find out exactly what those are, and exactly the best ways to present them to each consumer group. EEG testing in particular is moving this goal from pipe dream to reality every day.

Throughout this book, you'll find dozens of additional, actionable tactics—based on years of brain analysis—to allow you to learn the secrets of every consumer's brain, category by category.

But first, it is important to understand the workings of the brain itself.

BACK FROM THE BRINK

As little as 70,000 years ago, there were as few as 2,000 mating pairs of humans. Driven to the brink of extinction by severe East African droughts during the years referred to as our evolutionary "bottleneck," those endangered humans spanned out over hundreds of miles, innovating and adapting to survive. Eventually, their numbers recovered enough for the small isolated tribes to reunite and form larger, supportive and, sometimes, warring groups, punctuated by dynamism, stasis, and equilibrium. Today, there are 6.6 billion humans on every corner of the Earth (plus a dozen or so in space).

Here's a summary of what we learned in this chapter:
- Engage the primal brain by honoring the brain's precious resources—its limited processing ability, and its restricted, focused attention. The brain is determined to protect these resources. Make your interaction quick, clear, and interesting.
- Be interesting. The brain loves puzzles and humor.
- Use emotion to reach out to consumers, especially women.
- Clear your message of clutter. Use white space and clear, simple imagery and copy, particularly if your product lives in a crowded, loud category.

- If your brand or product is likely to be part of some "goal-seeking behavior" use active, direct verbs to guide the brain swiftly and directly to its goal.
- If your brand or product is likely to activate pleasure/reward circuits, indulge the brain in messaging, images, displays, and environments that celebrate the sensuality and deep pleasure likely to be derived from use.
- Celebrate the multitasking wizardry of your female consumers in images and copy.
- Provide networking opportunities through your brand, product, or environment for female consumers.

CHAPTER 4

THE BRAIN 101

At the end of this chapter, you'll know and be able to use the following:
- How the brain works and the process of engaging the brain.
- The structuring principles of the brain.
- How this will help you understand your customers' wants and needs.

To apply neuroscience—the study of the brain—to the consumer marketplace, we must begin with a better understanding of the brain itself. Easily the most complicated organ, and one of the most complex systems in the universe, the human brain warrants lengthy tomes dedicated to its mysteries. For our purposes, however, allow me to provide you with an introductory tour of the brain and how it works in your daily life, in your relationships, in your business, and in the **why of what and how you and your customers buy.**

In this decade after "the decade of the brain," we have learned a great deal about how the brain works. Yet a great deal begs to be discovered: How does the brain produce the delightful individuality of human beings, their personalities, their talents? Where does the concept of "I" begin? Where does idea of "You" come in?

These lofty questions are zipping through your brain—alongside your shopping list and your knowledge of how to tie your shoes. Every behavior, every intention, every dream begins in the brain.

BRAIN CELLS

So let's begin at the beginning of our journey of understanding: the brain's cells. The human brain is a network of a hundred billion individual cells, called neurons. Complex and intertwined, those neurons, each electrically charged, could be compared to an endless, sparkling display of stars across a clear, cold night sky. But the metaphor is incomplete. Imagine instead that every one of

33

those stars is pulsing with electricity, communicating with other star systems through a complex interplay of electrical signals and brain chemicals. Now imagine that each star migrated to its particular place in the universe, pulled by its target system. Imagine further that every newly energized, purposeful star system sets in motion every aspect of your humanity, from breathing and balance, to creativity and insight, to charity and love. It sets us apart from all other species by allowing us to walk on the moon, to compose symphonies and sonnets, to fall in love, and to ponder the universe.

Neurons are the basic working units of the brain and the central nervous system, designed to transmit information to other nerve, muscle, or gland cells.

Neurons consist of a **cell body, dendrites,** and an **axon** (see Figure 4.1). The cell body contains the nucleus and cytoplasm of the cell. The electrically-excitable axon extends from the cell body to the target and often gives rise to many smaller branches called dendrites. These dendrites extend from the neuron cell body and receive messages from other neurons. **Synapses** are the contact points where one neuron communicates with another. So if you look at it from another vantage point, a neuron or a neural system is a one-way traffic light, receiving electrical impulses from another neuron, transporting them along the axon, and dispersing them at the target, where neurochemicals and electricity prompt or prohibit movement of that target. As neurons transmit

Figure 4.1
The working unit of the brain, a neuron.

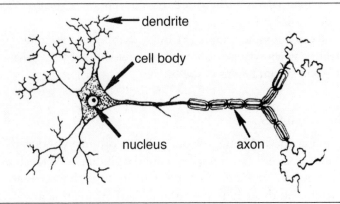

Source: NeuroFocus, Inc.

electrical impulses along their axons (which range in length from a tenth of an inch to three feet or more!), this electrical current produces tiny voltage changes across the neuron's cell membrane. These small but highly predictive, sometimes chaotic and noisy, and at other times regular electrical changes allow us to measure with precision how the brain reacts to any stimuli, from medical conditions to marketing messages. But more about that later. We have a bit more to learn about the brain in light of recent scientific breakthroughs.

So, back to the neuron. When a nerve impulse is initiated, a dramatic reversal in the electrical potential occurs at one point on the cell's membrane, when the neuron switches from an internal negative charge to a positive charge. This change, called an **action potential**, then passes along the membrane of the axon at speeds of up to 100 miles per hour. At this dramatic speed, a neuron can fire impulses up to about 1,000 times a second.

When they reach the end of an axon, these voltage changes trigger the release of **neurotransmitters**, the brain's chemical messengers. Neurotransmitters are released by nerve terminals and bind to receptors on the surface of the target cell. These receptors then act as on-and-off switches for the next cell. There may be tens of thousands of such connections on a neuron modifying the target cell, which has to compute inputs from many cells that contact it—tens of thousands of connections, a thousand times a second in a binary and algorithmic computational dance. Amazing!

How Neurons Gather into Functional Areas of the Brain

Neurons connect with each other and with distant muscle and gland cells. These connections form trillions of specific patterns that re-form, grow, and migrate over the course of our lives.

This spectacular neuron specification and migration begins in the human embryo, where the right types of neurons must form in significant numbers to complete their preordained tasks and then must migrate to the appropriate places to form functional units that make up the brain. After they've reached their destination, which could be inches or feet from where they started, the neurons extend axons and dendrites to connect to each other.

Remarkably, the axons are then guided, even pulled, by the targets they will activate.

For example, a newly-born neuron that has migrated to the motor area of the brain will extend its axon to the bottom of the spinal cord where it will target another motor cell that will then control the muscle that moves your big toe. If nurtured properly by its target, that pathway then thrives and functions in a neurochemical partnership.

Birth of Neurons

About four weeks after conception, the ridges on the flat plane of the embryo fold, and fuse to form the hollow neural tube. This primitive structure grows and evolves in truly spectacular fashion, with the fetal brain at times producing a quarter of a million new neurons **every day**. In addition to neurons, the mature nervous system contains glial cells, which clean up leftover chemical transmitters, guide migrating neurons, and serve as the infamous blood/brain barrier, which prevents toxins in the blood from killing brain tissue.

Neurons collect together to form each of the various brain structures, acquire specific ways of transmitting nerve messages, and learn unique ways to process and control interactions with the environment, from motor tasks (like throwing a ball) to complex memory tasks (like guiding a submarine).

After its spectacular period of growth in the fetus, the neural network is pared back to create a more efficient system. Neurons are removed when they lose their battle with other neurons to receive life-sustaining chemical signals produced by the target tissues. So the same cells that draw them forward, in many cases, then deprive them of life. This pruning process explains why **children actually have more brain cells than adults.**

Those extra brain cells also form too many connections at first. In humans and other primates, children have twice the number of connections between neurons that adults have. For example, the neural connections between the two eyes and the brain initially overlap, but then migrate to separate territories devoted to one eye or the other. The connections that are active and generating electrical currents survive, whereas those neurons with little or no activity fade away. Thus, the circuits of the adult brain are formed, at least in part, by sculpting away incorrect or unused connections to leave only the correct ones, in the most elemental example of "use it or lose it."

What's left is a precisely elaborated adult network of 100 billion neurons capable of body movement, perception, emotion, and thought.

Once the neurons reach their final location in the brain, they must make the proper connections for a particular function to occur, such as vision or hearing. They do this through their axons. These thin appendages can stretch out a thousand times longer than the cell body from which they arise, from one side of the brain to the other. The journey of most axons ends when they meet thicker appendages, called dendrites, of other neurons. Enlargements of the axon's tip, called growth cones, actively explore the environment as they seek out their precise destination.

Once axons reach their targets, they form synapses, which permit electric signals in the axon to jump to the next cell, where they can either provoke or prevent the generation of a new signal.

Each neuron receives thousands of synapses, and the astounding information-processing power of the brain works by turning on or off the huge number of electric signals that pass through the synapses.

The human brain is what makes us human.

Every Neuron Has a Target

As they grow and begin to migrate throughout the body, each neuron makes connections at a precise point with a specific target. Each neuron somehow knows to bypass all other points and other targets, and arrives at a destination that is predetermined to fit that neuron and that neuron alone.

Once in place in its network, the neuron generates an action potential (an electrical current) along the axon in response to stimuli. The current may be tiny (from a few microvolts), fast (up to 100 meters a second), or powerful and permanent. Once the cell body has summed all the inputs that excite or inhibit an electrical current, the neuron fires off its action potential. Once fired, it **goes**! The action potential carries the same voltage all the way to its target destination. These action potentials give us great insight into the impact a given stimulus, perhaps a television commercial, or a brand logo, has made on the brain.

Parts of the Brain

The growth, migration, and pruning of neurons leaves them in remarkably purposeful sections of the brain, each dedicated to finely-tuned and interdependent functions that run a body and make a mind.

For this section of Brain 101, let's start at the top with the cerebral cortex. This part of the brain is divided into four large regions: the occipital lobe, the

Figure 4.2
Major parts of the brain.

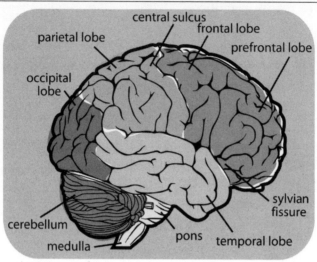

Source: Courtesy by Acxiom Corporation, Wellsphere.com

temporal lobe, the parietal lobe, and the frontal lobe (see Figure 4.2). Functions, such as vision, hearing, and speech, are distributed in these regions. Some regions perform more than one function. And assigning a specific function with a specific region is a less than perfect science as we are all subtly different and that is reflected in our brains' organization. For instance, in an amputee, just after losing a limb, the brain's neurons still represent that body part, even though the limb isn't there. Later that representation fades away as other adjacent limb functions migrate over or begin to activate into that valuable tissue.

The cerebral cortex performs **the highest intellectual functions**— thinking, planning, and problem solving. The **hippocampus** is involved in memory. The thalamus serves as a relay station for almost all the information coming into the brain. Neurons in the hypothalamus—the master of the master gland—serve as relay stations for internal regulatory systems—body temperature, eating, mating—by monitoring information coming in from the nervous system and issuing orders to the body through those nerves and the pituitary or "master" gland.

On the upper surface of the midbrain are two pairs of small hills that are called colliculi, collections of cells that relay sensory information from sense organs to the brain. The hindbrain consists of the pons and medulla oblongata, which help control respiration and heart rhythms, and the cerebellum, which helps control movement as well as cognitive processes that require precise timing.

Where do memories live? It's an interesting question. Many studies of human and animal memory have led scientists to conclude that no single brain center stores memory. It most likely is stored in distributed collections of brain processing systems—the same systems that are involved in the perception, processing, and analysis of the material being learned. In short, many parts of the brain contribute to permanent memory storage. For example, the hippocampus, parahippocampal region, and areas of the cerebral cortex (including the prefrontal cortex) compose a system that supports declarative, or cognitive, memory, such as remembering phone numbers. Different forms of behavioral memory, such as knowing how to throw a ball, are supported by the amygdala, striatum, and cerebellum.

LANGUAGE

One of the most important human abilities is language, a complex system involving many components, including sensory motor functions and memory systems. Although the neural basis of language is not fully understood, scientists have learned a great deal about this function of the brain from studies of patients who have lost speech and language abilities owing to stroke, traumatic brain injury, and also from brain imaging studies of normal people. It has long been known that damage to different regions within the left hemisphere (in most right-handed people) produce different kinds of language disorders, or aphasias.

Researchers once believed that all aspects of language ability were governed only by the left hemisphere. Recognition of speech sounds and words, however, involves both left and right temporal lobes. In contrast, speech production is a strongly left-dominant function. However, the emotional content in speech, which comes via voice inflection, is a mostly right hemispheric (emotional hemisphere) function.

Sections of the Brain Work Together Like a
Highly Coordinated Team

The brain handles many mental functions through multiple regions. For example, the brain pathways used to read words are different from those we use to hear or speak them. Still another pathway gives us the meaning of the word. The more pathways that are involved, the more complicated the action becomes. Prosody—or the tone of voice we use when we speak that lets others know whether we're happy, sad, or excited—originates in the right hemisphere of the brain. But the logical content of language, for example, that "the truck is red," originates in the left hemisphere.

In fact, **all** mental functions can be divided into subfunctions that work interdependently to give us a representation of consciousness and self. Perception, language, thought, movement, and memory all link to multiple regions of the brain. That's why the entire brain must be measured to catch these electrical impulses as the separate regions "talk to" and react with each other.

Each Section Interacts with the Next

The final discovery in our tour of the brain is that each part of the brain interacts with its neighbors, creating topographical maps that science can use to find disorders and lesions. A final interesting but imperative fact: The functional systems on one side of the brain control the opposite side of the body. So the sensory/motor activations on the left side of the body are mediated by the cerebral hemisphere on the right side of the body.

In this chapter, we celebrated the spectacular beauty of the brain, a masterpiece of connected neurons, functional centers, and hemispheres. The one clear takeaway from all the facts, the electricity, symphony, and dance**: The brain makes behavior.** Every millisecond of every day, the brain creates your world and the world of your consumers. It alone decides what's important enough to pay attention to, to remember, and to act on. Only through your enhanced knowledge of the brain, and the enhanced messaging you create and deliver to it, can you reliably expect your brand, product, package, message, or experience to be granted an audience with this literal master of the universe.

CHAPTER 5

THE FIVE SENSES AND THE BUYING BRAIN

At the end of this chapter, you'll know and be able to use the following:
- How each of the five senses "works"
- How to construct messages, products, experiences, and ideas that reach the brain through the five senses
- How the five senses interact with each other to construct our reality, day by day
- Relevant, new information about each of the five senses

What a gorgeous, vivid, delicious, melodic, aromatic, sensual world we live in! The human brain is beautifully evolved to make the most of the sensory input available on the Blue Planet. It's true that other animals have better senses. Your eyes can't compare with a peregrine falcon's "eagle eye" for sense of sight, nor is your nose a match for your dog's exquisitely finely tuned sense of smell. Dolphins hear more than you ever will, and so do the felines and rodents in your house or neighborhood.

So why sing the praises of the five senses of the human brain? First, our sensory intake is remarkable because we have access to all of our senses. Many animals with expert sensory perception in one area developed that extreme sensitivity to counterbalance the absence of other senses. A mole, for example, has six times the touch receptors that we have, but he can't see. The falcon doesn't "touch" with anything other than his beak and claw, and our cats have no idea of the range of tastes we're able to discern.

So if the first cause for sense celebration is that we are generalists, the second is that we're voluptuaries. We revel in our senses, create art and music to celebrate them, and stand in awe of the beauty they bring. That, of course, is a self-perpetuating cycle: The more we revel, the more neural pathways we put down to enjoy, and the more and more delight we're able to create and appreciate, so the more we revel, and so on.

Defining Consciousness

All of our knowledge and insight is gathered through our senses, and our emotions and feelings are expressed using them.

Our senses make sense of everything we encounter.

In the following sections are a top-down view of the five senses of humans, how they work, and what they mean to the buying brain.

VISION

The reason for our attention to the things we *see* is deep-seated and, of course, evolutionary. **About one-fourth of the human brain is involved in visual processing,** much more real estate than is devoted to any other sense.

About 70 percent of the body's sense receptors are in our eyes. To a large degree, we understand our world mainly by looking at it. The easiest and most successful way to capture the Buying Brain's attention is through great visuals. We have evolved to put our visual senses at the top of our sensory hierarchies, and therefore, visual components tend to trump all others. When vision and sound are presented together, for example, the brain places greater credibility and impact on the visual portion. For example, that's why the spoken portion of an animated spot with audio/visual synchrony out of sync will be discarded.

Interestingly, vision does not happen in the eyes, but in the brain.

The eyes gather light and enhance focus. But the brain makes sense of the colors, shapes, facial expressions, and landscapes it sees. That's why we remember scenes in vivid detail months and years after they happen . . . why we "see" imaginary daydreams with ultra realism . . . why the dreams we have at night are vivid, full of detail, and often more "real" than reality itself.

The memory peak for visual impressions is in the age range of roughly 15 to 30 years. Researchers ask people in their seventies what memories they associate with a selection of words or pictures, and they report most memories from when they were in that age range. One reason for this is that the years from 15 to 30 are very dynamic for most people—they move away from home, for instance, they get married for the first time, and develop their own identity preferences when it comes to such things as music and literature.

In addition, remember that color doesn't occur in the world, but in the brain. Our brains "assign" the colors we see as the spectrum of light available to us bounces off objects around us. Not everyone sees the same colors; some of us are color-blind and others are color-gifted. Cézanne once wrote, "The same subject seen from a different angle gives a subject for study of the highest interest and so varied that I think I could be occupied for months without changing my place, simply bending more to the right or left."

Bipedal Luxury

Our visual acuity became our core sensory attribute the minute we moved from four legs to two. Suddenly, we were further from the ground and the smells left by our prey, predators, and tribe. But, just as suddenly, we were able to scan the savannah around us, to track animals as they moved, and to visually project where they would be by the time we got to them. This same scanning, aiming, and projecting is evident every day, sometimes spectacularly. For example, on the football fields and hockey rinks, when a quarterback throws a missile right into the waiting hands of an open receiver who appears, magically, just where the ball is thrown, or a player zooms a puck before the stick of a teammate who appears in the nick of time.

> Our brain's ability to scan an area, to locate an object in three dimensions, and to predict where that object *will be* over the course of seconds or minutes is hard-wired. So what? Keep this scanning and locating expertise in mind when laying out store designs and planograms. Be sure, for example, that **nothing** obscures your customer's view of the object(s) s/he is scanning for. Overly tall shelves that obscure the landscapes behind them, signage with dense text and no visuals, and canyon-like narrow aisles all detract from this hard-won ability and frustrate the Buying Brain.

All primates, including humans, have well-developed vision using two eyes, called **binocular vision.** Visual signals pass from each eye along the million or so fibers of the optic nerve to the optic chiasm, where some nerve fibers cross over, so both sides of the brain receive signals from both eyes. Consequently, the left halves of both retinas project to the left visual cortex and the right halves project to the right visual cortex. This means that things on the observer's left go to the right hemisphere and things on the observer's right go to the left hemisphere.

PREDATOR ME

Look at yourself in the mirror. Gaze at your spouse eye-to-eye over your morning coffee, have a staring contest with your children. In each case, you're looking into the eyes of a dangerous predator. Using eyes set directly on the fronts of their heads, **the eyes of humans are perfectly positioned** to find and track prey. Front-focusing eyes also provide much better depth perception, a crucial element for keeping up with another animal's movements. Human eyes have discrete mechanisms that gather light, focus on novel images, pinpoint them in space, follow them as they attempt to evade.

Prey (deer, squirrels), on the other hand, have eyes on the sides of their heads for excellent peripheral vision. Side-facing eyes gain advantages in field of view, but lose advantages in depth perception. This configuration is great at letting them know when something is sneaking up on them. Not so great in helping them anticipate and "catch" something ahead of them, but then again, that is not their goal.

MIRROR, MIRROR

As an extremely visual species, it should come as no surprise that a person's appearance, fair or unfair, has an effect on those s/he encounters. For instance:

Men prefer women whose pupils are dilated, as happens naturally during sexual arousal. Women during the Renaissance took small quantities of the deadly belladonna plant to make their pupils dilate. They also painted their skin white with arsenic to be more attractive to potential mates, giving a new meaning to making sacrifices in the name of beauty.

Attractive criminals receive shorter sentences.

Prettier babies are treated better than their peers are by care providers in nurseries.

Given the same resumes, people who are more attractive get the job.

Attractive children get higher grades overall, possibly because all of the positive feedback they've been given provides confidence.

Vision in the Marketplace

The visual elements of your message or environment will have the most impact on your consumers.

- To avoid being lost in the clutter, emphasize clean, clear lines delivered at eye-level.
- Use the **"cathedral effect."** When entering a cathedral, our eyes are drawn upward within the structure. For signage, outdoor and print ads, place the object of interest at the top of the ad.
- Use puzzles that are easily solved to draw in and delight the brain.

SMELL

Our olfactory bulbs are, in fact, part of our limbic system, the deepest, most primitive part of our brains. They are separated by only two synapses from the amygdala, the seat of memory and emotion, and six synapses from the hippocampus, the brain organ responsible for storing memories. Carefully consider and create the scent that will be forever linked to your offering. Never discount the power of smell. Remember the smell of Play-doh? How about Listerine mouthwash? Now imagine them switched. End of story.

Think of it: Every other sensory system must follow a long and winding path to the brain, full of transfers and hand-offs. But **smells are mainlined** directly into our centers for emotion and memory.

Emotive and powerful, however, our olfactory senses are perhaps the least of all the weapons in our sensory arsenal. While 60 percent of our brain is devoted to sight, a scant 1 percent is devoted to smell. As the least necessary of our senses, Helen Keller called our sense of smell the "Fallen Angel."

How Smell Works

When we inhale with every breath, we send particulates up through our nostrils, past the cilia that wave them along, and directly into the olfactory bulbs, which deliver them without further ado, into our brains. If we're experiencing a familiar or highly evocative scent, the full memory of our first contact ignites both in our amygdala and hippocampus. For a friend, for example, stepping into a barn immediately transports her back to her days as a child, playing in her grandmother's barn, with the warm, earthy scents of hay and horses, the buzz of the bugs, and the promise of lemonade all part of the picture. Another of my friends can eat a certain macaroon and find herself, for a few moments, back on the streets of Paris, the hot, sweet smells of pastry mixing with the metallic, slightly copperish smell of falling rain on cobblestone streets.

In evolutionary terms, it's little surprise that **prey smells great to the hunter** (steak, anyone?) and predator smells foul to the prey (if you ever get close enough to a large predatory cat, such as a lion, or even a large scavenger, like a hyena, you will be alarmed and possibly disgusted by their musk, their breath, or both). Our sense of smell was critical to our species' survival. In its earliest uses, we relied on smell not only to find food, but also to find a healthy, genetically different mate and to identify our children in the dark. In the early days of medicine, smells allowed for the diagnosis of some diseases: Diabetes smelled like sugar, for instance, and measles like feathers. Trained dogs are our new partners in disease detection, able to sniff out melanoma, epileptic seizures, low blood sugar, and heart attacks. There is great interest in the medical field in developing new ways for dogs to sniff out disease in its earliest stages. By far, the best smellers are four-legged mammals. We have 5 million olfactory cells, while sheepdogs have 220 million.

The Secret to Scent Memories

The special memory system for senses, for things that you remember, is episodic memory. We have many other memory systems: procedural, semantic, short-term, long-term, and so forth.

But, episodic memory is the function that may best be described as a mental time machine that stores memories about **"what, where, and when."** This system is younger and more complex than our other memory systems, and is most developed in human beings.

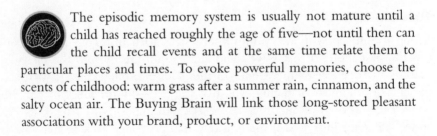 The episodic memory system is usually not mature until a child has reached roughly the age of five—not until then can the child recall events and at the same time relate them to particular places and times. To evoke powerful memories, choose the scents of childhood: warm grass after a summer rain, cinnamon, and the salty ocean air. The Buying Brain will link those long-stored pleasant associations with your brand, product, or environment.

While humans generate the most lasting visual or audio memories between the ages of 15 and 30 (that's why the songbook of your adolescence remains so poignant), the more powerful memories that have to do with smell are a pony ride straight back to childhood. Studies have consistently found that humans' **peak smelling ability ranges from 5 to 10 years old**. During those years, we have the opportunity to experience many smells for the first time, and the luxury of time to revel in them.

Deploying Scent in the Marketplace

We make such immediate, deep, and emotional connections with the smells we encounter, it makes perfect "sense" to make scents available to delight and engage the brains of our consumers.

In *How Customers Think,* NeuroFocus Advisory Board member Gerald Zaltman notes that, "Olfactory cues are hardwired into the brain's limbic system, the seat of emotion, and stimulate vivid recollections." Once a scent is embedded in an individual's brain, even visual cues can cause it to be resurrected and even "experienced." According to Zaltman, "A TV commercial showing a person savoring the aroma of freshly brewed coffee can trigger these same olfactory sensations in viewers." (See Chapter 9 for more detail on how the Mirror Neuron System stimulates reactive motion in the brain.)

Zaltman sees scents shoring up marketing efforts in several ways. They can be "memory markers" that help a person recall familiar brands more than unfamiliar ones. They can also change the way we process information, for example, a lemon aroma can make us more alert. Zaltman speculates that scents of that type could be helpful when introducing a new product. Now with EEG testing, we can help determine which smells work best in which environment.

Olfactory Brand Marketing

Brands are probably the first and highest form of olfactory branding: Smell a Starbuck's coffeehouse with your eyes closed, for instance, and you know you can be nowhere else. Fall under the suntan coconut seduction of a Tommy Bahama store and you're halfway to the beach before you reach the cash counter. Johnson's Baby Powder carries powerful scents of soothing and comfort that cross many lines, and the smell of Gain detergent has a following of its own. Does your brand have a unique, iconic scent signature? Could it benefit from real, immediate, deeply embedded, and supremely emotional connections of fun and pleasure?

Olfactory Product Marketing

How many among us have wandered by a patisserie chicken roaster in our local supermarkets only to be seduced by the smell of grandma's chicken and potatoes dinner? Why do stores incorporate coffee grinders in their aisles to give us a fresh, unfettered access to the brand new blends? How might an apple spice cake smell resonate in a coffee shop or bistro or the bakery section of a large supermarket? Doesn't the smell of fresh linens make you feel more comfortable and more "tucked in" when you're abroad?

Always take into account the **smell of your offering.** Even if it's the best in its class in terms of taste, it will fail in the market if the packaging causes it to smell fake or plastic.

SEXUAL NOSES

Women have more sensitive noses than men, and are far better at putting words to olfactory experiences; men are particularly keen on the smells of their beloved.

Indeed, humans tend to prefer mates who have a slightly different genetic make-up than they do. This ensures a healthy, robust population, with a sizeable immune system.

Olfactory Environment Marketing

We know, for example, that the soft scent of lemon increases sales in seafood restaurants. The subtle smell of grass near the dairy aisle could take consumers back to a simpler, more carefree time, and subconsciously remind them of the fields the products come from. In high-end car or luggage stores, the rich, deep scent of polished leather calls to mind luxury, relaxation, and reward. In clothing stores, the invigorating scent of the sea or the romantic mix of roses and violets suffuses the experience and makes purchasing a product associated with those memories powerful. Realtors know that cookies baking seduce buyers into considering a "property" a home.

PROUST'S MADELEINE

Perhaps the most famous adage to memory from smell and taste comes to us from Marcel Proust, who experiences a soul awakening from a smell/taste combination he experienced as a child:

No sooner had the warm liquid mixed with the crumbs touched my palate than a shudder ran through me and I stopped, intent upon the extraordinary thing that was happening to me . . . And suddenly the memory revealed itself. The taste was that of the little piece of madeleine, which on Sunday mornings at Combray . . . my aunt Léonie used to give me, dipping it first in her own cup of tea or ti-sane. The sight of the little madeleine had recalled nothing to my mind before I tasted it.

TASTE

Breast milk is the first thing most of us taste and it primes us for a preference for sweet, warm foods. At the perfect temperature, accompanied by love, rocking, a sense of safety, stroking, smiles, and coos, it's a delightful debut into a world of senses that await us for the rest of our lives.

Every creature on Earth has a way to take in nutrients. In our case, it's the mouth, whose main job is to hold the tongue, a thick, mucousy slab of muscle. But, in humans and other higher life forms, the mouth holds an even higher charge—to bring us taste in all its symphonies, the revelation of a great wine, the paralysis that occurs after a bite of the chocolatier's best, or the face-contorting delight of a curry with just the right balance of spice. As with most of our other senses, taste is also a powerful deterrent, immediately laying down aversions to tastes that are against our better interests.

Taste and Smell

Although different, **smell and taste share a common goal** and often operate in synchrony. For example, like smell, taste is a chemoreceptor, meaning that both senses specialize in detecting the chemical scents and tastes we encounter. While they are separate senses with their own receptor organs, these two senses act together to allow us to distinguish thousands of different flavors.

The interaction between taste and smell explains why loss of the sense of smell causes a serious reduction in the overall taste experience, which we call flavor. Here's how those two senses combine to provide us the optimum experience of flavor.

Taste signals in the sensory cells are transferred to the ends of nerve fibers, which send impulses along cranial nerves to taste regions in the brainstem. From here, the impulses are relayed to the thalamus and on to the cerebral cortex for conscious perception of taste.

 We tend to smell something before we taste it. Often, mere smelling is enough to make us salivate. Of the two, smell is the first on the scene. Smell hits our brains very quickly. It takes 25,000 times more molecules of cherry pie to taste it than to smell it.

Desires

It may seem like it's all about ice cream, but really it's all about neurotransmitters. Some foods stimulate endorphins, morphine-like painkillers and mood elevators. These include salty foods, greasy foods, candy, and sweets.

Carbohydrate cravings are driven by a need to increase the level of serotonin in the brain and as such, they are sedating. By the way, your cravings may even be genetic. Identical twins, separated at birth, crave the same things, while fraternal twins don't.

Taste in the Marketplace

Taste stimulation is one of the senses most easily set off by the Mirror Neuron system.

Anytime you display an appetizing product, be sure the consumer can see it being enjoyed by another. This is the key to stimulating desire, and, most importantly, to moving to purchase. See Chapter 9 for the story of "Monkey See, Monkey Do."

Give food and beverages a visual "voice." Too often, we use words to describe, for example, "a tall, frothy beer" when a picture would say so much more.

Don't display obviously fake items, like miniature plastic tables in or around food items. They detract from the realism and, thus, the appetite the consumer generates for the product.

HEARING

Hearing gives us information vital to survival, for instance, by alerting us to an approaching car or fire engine. But, our sense of sound is more than perfunctory. Hearing allows us to generate deep, nostalgic memories associated with highly emotional moments accompanied by sound: Lullabies *do* lull babies to sleep. Even earlier, the mother's heartbeat and respiration soothe and calm the baby. Later, lovers celebrate their favorite song, the laughter of children delights any ear in range, the song of birds by your window, the rocking glory of a Rolling Stones concert, and all are extraordinary treats for our brains. We mark our traditional passages with music, for example, weddings, funerals, and graduations.

Our pupils widen and endorphins rise when we sing and there is a scientifically validated healing quality to singing. Comatose patients respond to music. The dying relax when music is played.

The sounds your product makes and the background "noise" of your shopping environment are a critical part of its **Neurological Iconic Signature (NIS).** When the Buying Brain hears the soda sizzle, the chip snap, or the coffee sipped, Mirror Neurons fire in some urgency: "I want that! Get me that!"

The sounds that accompany peak experience are critical to its enjoyment, and to its retention in memory. When casinos removed the tinkling of coins from one-armed bandits, I think they did a lot of damage to the fun of winning and being around winners in the coin machines. Which would you prefer: a joyous cacophony of nickels hitting the aluminum trays all around you, or a quiet prompt to insert your card to transfer your winnings?

TOUCH

If our predator's vision is a relatively recent development in human sense ability, and our primal sense of smell is the most emotionally direct of our senses, touch has the honor of being the oldest human sense, the most urgent, and the most integral to our survival and evolution. Every other sense organ has, well, an organ you can point to: nose, eyes, mouth, and ears. But, **our organ of touch is us**.

Think about it: If touch didn't feel good, we wouldn't sustain our relationships or produce offspring. But it does, and we do. Before he even hears his mother's heartbeat an infant feels her warm womb swaddling him, and her respiration soothes him. In his close, calming cradle, he sleeps and wakes, rocked by the gentle rhythms of her movements.

As you must now expect, early humans who did more touching produced lasting pair bonds and healthier infants who survived to produce offspring already trained in the healing power of touch. Not coincidentally, sex is the number one touch pleasure. And what a grand design that our species' goal is also our greatest pleasure!

Our need for touch soothing is so profound in humans, in fact, that touch-deprived infants often suffer some degree of brain damage. During even short separation of infant and mother, "changes occurred in heart rate, body temperature, brainwave patterns, sleep patterns, and immune system function," according to Diane Ackerman. When they're reunited with the mother, all psychological changes resolve almost immediately. But, physical distresses, susceptibility to disease, persist. "This experiment," says Ackerman, "concluded that lack of maternal contact may lead to long-term, systemic damage."

Our Largest Sensory Organ

Our skin is the barrier between us and everything else. It gives us our shape, protects us from invaders, cools or heats us, produces vitamin D, holds our body fluids, and mends itself quickly and constantly. At 6–10 pounds, **our skin is the largest organ in our bodies.** It is without doubt the key organ of sexual attraction. By combining eyesight and touch, primates like us excel at locating objects in space. Touch is, in many ways, the embodiment of sight.

Our fingertips and tongues are much more sensitive than are our backs. Some parts of the body are ticklish, while others itch, shiver, or get "goose-flesh." The hairiest parts of our body are the most sensitive to pressure, because there are many sense receptors at the base of each hair. The skin is thinnest where we have hair, too.

From mice to lions to humans, the whiskers around the mouth are exquisitely sensitive.

Different parts of the body vary in their sensitivity to tactile and painful stimuli according to the number and distribution of receptors. Our lips excel at touch discrimination, for example, and our forearms do not.

Pain produces the most urgent response. That's why many of our touch sensors are devoted to discovering and avoiding pain, key to our survival as a human, and by extension, as a species.

Touch in the Marketplace

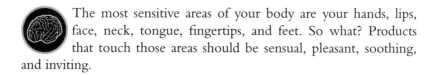 The most sensitive areas of your body are your hands, lips, face, neck, tongue, fingertips, and feet. So what? Products that touch those areas should be sensual, pleasant, soothing, and inviting.

As we discussed in the earlier portions of this chapter, your body has sensory receptors all over it, but they're distributed unevenly. Your tongue, for example, is covered with taste buds, but your back has relatively few sensory receptors. Your fingers can brush a jacket and know instantly what material it's made of, what shape the buttons are, even how warm it might be. Your buttocks on the other hand, provide gruff information on the hardness of the chair they sit on and that's about it. That's why your finger maps take up 100 times as much space in your cortex as does the map of your trunk.

Consider the sensory capabilities of the product or experience you're selling to the Buying Brain. If your experience is to be tactile, then infuse it with great fun for the fingers, great areas of exploration for the lips!

In this chapter, we explored each of the body's five senses to learn how best to use them to invite the Buying Brain in. We learned that:

- Vision is chief among our senses, and that our Buying Brains will discount information that is not in concert with the visual stimuli it receives.
- Our sense of smell is the most direct route to our emotions and memory storage. Being linked with a pleasant, iconic smell can significantly improve a product's success in the marketplace.
- What we hear is specialized and tuned to what interests us. The Buying Brain will easily ignore distracting or disturbing noises (along with any messages that accompany them).
- Tasting is one of the brain's great pleasures. Linked closely with smell, the taste of a product is influenced by the neurological iconic signatures that accompany it.
- Our sense of touch is the earliest of our senses. We are sensual beings and love to be touched. Any product or experience that is tactile **must** excite and invite the sense of touch.

- Sensory integration creates a richer degree of engagement with the consumer if you activate multiple senses that are synergistic/make sense together.
- Celebrate the body's movement through space by incorporating it in your messages. The brain loves to see and imagine peak sensory and motor experiences.

CHAPTER 6

THE BOOMER BRAIN IS BUYING

At the end of this chapter, you'll know and be able to use the following:
- How age affects the "hard-wiring" of the buying brain
- What strategies work best in targeting consumers over 60
- How the Baby Boom cohort promises to reshape the landscape of marketing
- New learnings that replace "conventional wisdom" with a new view of the over-60 brain in action

Age and gender directly affect the hard wiring of the brain. Background, education, culture, and experience all influence how we think and feel. But, they are learned. Age and gender are not. Since they have a great influence on how the buying brain works, it's important to look at them separately and in detail. We'll look at the older brain (defined for our purposes as 60 plus) here, and the Female Brain in the next chapter.

In all the years of human history before the great changes brought in medicine, nutrition, and hygiene over the last hundred years, **most people didn't age—they died.** Our society is still "learning" how to deal with what happens to a huge population, and to each individual, as we age. Until recently, studies of brain function, in particular, were focused primarily on disease and dysfunction, not on the natural changes that healthy aging brains undergo. More recently, within the past decade, neuroscience researchers have begun to explore real-time imaging of normal brains at different ages responding to many different kinds of stimuli, including marketing. Learning about these changes and the implications they have for testing your products and messages with the aging brains who buy them puts you a solid step ahead of competitors, who still have an outmoded idea of maturity. That's what we begin to address in this chapter and bring into full focus in Part 2 of the book.

In a very fundamental way, your brain is quite different at different times in your life. And, without debate, who you are and where you are in life makes a huge difference with regard to the "what, where, and why" of the messages to which you'll grant attention.

For the first few years of life, your brain undergoes such enormous changes that your entire way of interacting with the world is revised several times over.

From years 11 to 14, the brain undergoes massive growth and development. These changes continue to be incorporated and refined until about age 18, when the brain begins to settle down and assume a cognitive identity that will remain relatively stable for many years. American society offers a nod to this change in making 18 the age of legal adulthood. So when your teenager acts the way teens do, that means that his or her brain is developing appropriately, with vigor—and oftentimes, complete lack of forethought—but exactly as it should be.

From the early 20s until about 60, **the brain continues to change,** more slowly at first and then more rapidly later on. Again, within each gender, most brains are quite similar during these years, assuming all functions are normal. So, in reality, the key factor is not so much how your brain changes at, say age 60, as it is how much your brain has changed since it reached its peak performance at age 22.

For marketers, this distinction is important. We don't reinvent ourselves magically at age 60. Rather, our brains change over the years, sometimes quickly (as with childbirth or menopause), sometimes slowly, with a fair amount of brain-based differences evident by the age of 60 and above. So in constructing messages to adults, consider that they are still themselves, but, since they have changing, evolving brains, the way they process information can be quite different. I'll explain this in detail in the paragraphs following.

After age 60, transformations that have been slowly occurring become more apparent. Since the huge generational cohorts of Baby Boomers are now in their 50s and 60s, this change is of enormous consequence to marketers. The largest generational segment in human history is moving like the proverbial "pig in the python" directly into this life stage. Currently 46 to 64 years olds, **the 44 million Baby Boomers will all be evaluating your brand, product, package, message, and environment with mature brains in the very near future, if they're not already.**

As they've done with every aspect of American society they've passed through before, the Boomers promise to revolutionize the process of aging, and, thus, how we market to people over 60. When Boomers were babies, Dr. Spock emerged and parenting became a focus of our society. Then came Saturday morning cartoons, Hula hoops, rock and roll, Woodstock, war protests, yuppies, and now . . . empty nesters and retirees. Research suggests that these new mature consumers spend differently than their predecessors. For example, grandparents may outspend parents on toys for children. Who would market toys to 60 plus consumers? Savvy sellers who know about the priorities of the Boomer brain, that's who.

Importantly, the Boomer generation is also the richest generational cohort in history. More than two-thirds of them have at least some discretionary income, and they have the highest average disposable income of any group, at $29,754 in 2009. That amounts to more than ten trillion disposable dollars when we consider everyone together. **Boomers also control 77 percent of all financial assets in the United States.** They use about half of all credit cards, and spend about two and a half times the per capita average on discretionary purchases. So if you are not already marketing products and services to Mature Brains, perhaps you should be.

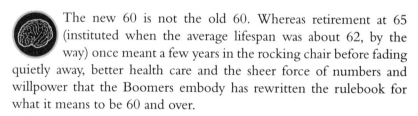

The new 60 is not the old 60. Whereas retirement at 65 (instituted when the average lifespan was about 62, by the way) once meant a few years in the rocking chair before fading quietly away, better health care and the sheer force of numbers and willpower that the Boomers embody has rewritten the rulebook for what it means to be 60 and over.

ATTENTION

Recent research has shed light on a problem that stumped neuroscientists for decades: Why do our memories get worse as we age? For years, the working theory was that there is simply a decline in the ability to store things in long-term memory. But, in 2005, Dr. Adam Gazzaley, Director of the UCSF Brain Imaging Center and NeuroFocus Scientific Advisory Board Member, performed a groundbreaking study that found a new explanation.

Our memory abilities are influenced by our ability to suppress distractions, and it is **this ability,** among other influences, that declines as we age. This means that people over 60 aren't necessarily more forgetful, but they are more overwhelmed by distractions. This new finding presents a huge implication, and a great opportunity, for marketers. Clearly, eliminating distractions is important when communicating with an older consumer. Keep the message obvious and direct and keep the copy and images clean and uncluttered. Let the message "breathe" with some white space around it. And avoid the impulse to "load up" messages with sounds, running screens, and quick-time animations. Not only are distractions detracting from your message to seniors, most of that content is not even making it past the brain "filters" of Boomer consumers. Teens will enjoy the multiple screens and a fast-paced experience. Grandmothers will not.

NEW LEARNINGS

We all have stereotyped images of what it means to grow older (that's also part of being human), but until very recently, we haven't had much science to contradict them. Just as it's done with every other aspect of consumer knowledge, thankfully, neuroscience has begun to unravel some of the mysteries about what happens to the brain as we age. We are now able to measure older brains' responses to stimuli rather than to rely on outdated notions that our grandparents might have held (or what we remember thinking we thought they thought—a very dangerous paradigm for developing brands, products, packages, messages, or environments!). While this is a rapidly evolving area of research—and there is much we do not yet know—what we do know and what we are finding out nearly every day indicates that **there are decided benefits to having an older brain** and yes, there are some deficits to consider as well. For example, a staggering 13 percent of Americans over 65 fall victim to Alzheimer's disease. However, in terms of healthy adult brains growing older, the news is far better than we might have presumed.

THE BIG (OLDER, HAPPIER) PICTURE

A growing body of scientific evidence supports the theory that, despite the top-of-mind cognitive and pathological declines that can appear as we age, normal, healthy adults have skills to help them manage their emotions in profoundly different ways than their younger peers. Not only do they experience negative emotions less frequently, they have better control over the negative emotions they do contend with. Equally as importantly, older brains also rely on a more **complex and nuanced emotional thermostat** that allows them to bounce back quickly from adverse events. Older adults, in fact, strive for emotional equilibrium, which in turn affects the ways their brains process information.

Functional reorganizing, enhanced compensation strategies, and effective intervention tools are among the most important benefits of having an older brain. As Patricia A. Reuter-Lorenz and Cindy Lustiz note, this combination provides older brains with a "more positive emotional bias than younger adults have." Put another way, this could be an empirical neurological basis for the idea of "wisdom" or "emotional intelligence." Older adults have the experience not to view every bump in the road as catastrophic, and they have the coping skills for modulating what they feel during the particularly bumpy portions of the road. What didn't kill us "then" probably isn't going to kill us now.

> The idea is that, when we market to the Boomer brains, it's not only appropriate but also **effective** to "accentuate the positive." Gloom and doom are **not** the way to reach an older audience, nor are portraits of a short, somewhat bleak future. Rather, focus messaging on the wit and wisdom of older consumers. Look, with them, on the bright side.

Studies have shown that the amygdala (remember, that's the brain area devoted to primal emotions like fear, anger, and happiness; see Chapter 4 for details) in young people becomes active when they view both positive and negative stimuli. But, in these new studies, **the amygdala in older people is active only when they view positive images.** They've learned to overlook the negative, at least when it's not impacting them directly.

Another way to look at this is that younger brains, unaware of what's ahead and how best to deal with it, cling to negative information, processing and reprocessing it in an attempt to predict and prepare for their uncertain futures. Older brains, on the other hand, have a lifetime of experiences, full of positive or at least nondisastrous events to help them. They no longer attend to the negative and may in fact "disattend" or avoid the negative. Seen in this light, the older brain's tendency to spin information positively is a hard-won life skill and age-worthy brain development, not a naïve perspective.

Another reason for the "positivity shift" that comes with aging may be that older adults put more emphasis on regulating emotion than do younger adults, and they do so with a greater **motivation** to derive meaning from life. To get to that point, older adults may focus on ideas, activities, and people that bring pleasant feelings and reinforce positive visions of themselves.

> So, in addition to presenting material positively to older adults, be sure you provide them with a positive spin on it that clearly relates back to themselves. Older adults like to feel good about who they are and how far they've come. They'll attend to your message with pleasure if you provide them with a way to relate that information positively to themselves and the positive self-portraits they've developed.
>
> On the flip side of this positive bias is an interesting quirk of the aging brain I touched on earlier—a tendency to overlook the negative. It's called "preferential processing," and several studies have highlighted it (see the Notes section for details). They indicate that, when presented with a negative message, as you might find, for example, on a warning label or some ad messaging, older brains can "delete" the **NOT** and remember it as a **DO** over time. So, "do not take with juice" might be recalled as "take with juice" after several repetitions, even if those repetitions are processed with relatively high attention.
>
> If you're thinking that this information is only relevant to caregivers, I'd encourage you to think again. "Do not neglect your IRA" could have the opposite of your intended effect, as could "Don't forget" the milk.
>
> Luckily, the fix for this bias is relatively simple: Craft messages for older brains in positive, not negative terms. Say: Remember the milk, the IRA, the brand, not "Don't forget" it.

Emotional Resilience

A related benefit to having an older brain is the resilience that comes with it. After all, by the time you've earned an aging brain, you've most likely seen it all—and have experience dealing with it. This doesn't mean you've triumphed over every adversity. Think back to a few things that caused you to lose sleep in your 20s (Does my boss like me? Should I have been more "visible" at the meeting?) and see what your gut reaction is to them now. More than likely, you've learned to "let the little things go." And, if you're an expert at resilience, you may have learned that "most things are little things."

> This "**don't sweat the small stuff**" idea can successfully underpin most of your marketing messages to older adults. They don't need to dwell on every tiny detail to embrace your product or service. They're far

beyond the need to rationalize their choices. Be broad and positive in your presentation of information, and remember that resilient brains do not respond—or perhaps even notice—scare tactics like "last chance to buy" sales techniques.

Broader Attention Spans

While an older brain may fall short in certain memory skills, including "**TOT**" or "tip-of-the-tongue" access to names and words, it excels in other areas of memory.

Studies suggest that older adults may have broader attention spans than their younger peers, so they can ultimately absorb more about a situation, message, or conversation. This may be another way of saying they have more patience. Their broader attention spans allow them to attend to more subtle and nuanced messages, and to give them the time and consideration they deserve. Once again, this brings us back to **the idea of "wisdom,"** meaning that older adults get more context out of their interactions, and then they combine that context with a greater store of personal experience to increase their ability to decode the situation and assess its relevance.

The flip side of this benefit is that these older adults may not remember the specifics—the TOT or tip-of-the-tongue—aspects of that communication. So they know what the overall message means, they know the context it fits within, yet they might not remember whether the story was about Mary or Terry. Fumbling with these details often wrongfully suggests to older brains that they're failing, when in fact they're operating in a broader attention span and in a context of a whole lifetime of experience. In reality, it's not such a bad thing to find one's keys in the freezer occasionally—if the trade-off means comprehending more of the big picture of one's interactions.

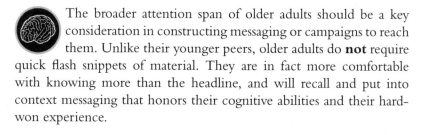 The broader attention span of older adults should be a key consideration in constructing messaging or campaigns to reach them. Unlike their younger peers, older adults do **not** require quick flash snippets of material. They are in fact more comfortable with knowing more than the headline, and will recall and put into context messaging that honors their cognitive abilities and their hard-won experience.

TOTs

As mentioned, one of the most frustrating brain changes for older adults is the difficulty in retrieving TOTs or tip-of-the-tongue facts. You've seen and probably have experienced the phenomenon. You remember the great movie you just watched, but can't recall the (household) name of its star. Frustrated, you stammer and search, "Tom, Mike, Brad?" before you sheepishly move on. Four thoughts on that very common occurrence:

1. You're not alone
2. It's completely normal
3. You get a broader attention span and a more positive attitude in trade
4. There's a fix

 To help your customers remember the name of your product or brand, try tying it in with a mnemonic trigger. When you see the star of the movie, Brad, think of cherry. Now you'll find it easier to retrieve the last name—Pitt.

 Taglines should work in the same fashion. What's the real thing? Whose good hands are you in? Are you lovin' it?

Familiarity Breeds . . . Belief

Another memory deficit that comes with aging is the tendency to consider *familiar* information to be *true* information. The way the brain interprets familiar information is, "I've heard that before; so it's likely to be true." This can be an obvious pitfall, of course, when the aging brain repeatedly translates what is untrue into true. That's one way a rumor can become a fact. Interestingly, warning older people about false claims can backfire: They hear the false version often enough and file it under *true*. David Richardson cautions against this tactic, in which addressing a false claim can inadvertently become "a recommendation." A much better strategy is to present the material you want remembered simply. Repeatedly, in a variety of formats: TV, radio, print, and banner ads. It's the frequency of exposure that matters in the aging brain.

 However, the **repetition reinforces belief** paradigm can be very useful to a brand that wants to keep a consistent story in front of its customers. If the story is repeated, the older brain will tend to see it as true. So keep your story out there, support it with messaging that lets older consumers feel good about themselves, and keep it positive to align the older brain with your brand.

THE BOOMER BRAIN: AGING POWER TO THE NTH DEGREE

As I mentioned at the beginning of this chapter, the fact that these natural brain changes are occurring in aging brains is only half of our story. The other half is the tremendous buying power of the generational cohort that is happening within. I cannot overstate the importance of maximizing your impact among **this game-changing group.** Perform neurological tests to assure that your message is on target. Listen to Boomer brains as they interact with your product. Find out how to make your brand a trusted advisor, an intimate friend and your in-store experience a positive, self-validating one. Conduct Brand Essence Framework studies to determine how your brand is perceived by the Boomer brain. Use Total Consumer Experience tests to identify the Neurological Iconic signatures that your product evokes in the older brain. Rely on Deep Subconscious Response measurements to isolate and quantify the key attributes that your brand or product is associated with in the mature mind. You'll learn much more about all these neuromarketing methodologies in Part 2.

The Boomer brain is waiting to hear you and demanding to be addressed in a new and unique way.

CHAPTER 7

THE FEMALE BRAIN IS BUYING

At the end of this chapter, you'll know and be able to use the following:
- The how's and why's of gender brain differences
- How to effectively address the female brain's special, hard-wired preferences
- The messaging elements the female brain loves
- Tactics the female brain rejects out of hand

One thing we can say with certainty is that, barring some kind of injury or abnormality, most human brains are very much alike. This was represented by the brain you met in Chapter 4, with the same functions, same speed of processing, and universal hard-wired reactions to primal stimuli available to any other, except for two important exceptions to the rule. First, the brain changes as it ages, as we learned in the previous chapter. Second, the brain of a woman is wired differently from the brain of a man. Let's look at this fascinating variation on the One Brain theme.

LEARNING ABOUT THE FEMALE BRAIN

Trust me; it's not chivalry that prompts me to provide the female brain with a chapter devoted entirely to her marvelous complexity. She's here because, in terms of consumer buying power and influence, she deserves to be.

For the first time in history, more women than men are working full-time. That's because the number of women working has remained fairly constant, while a full 82 percent of the layoffs from the recession of 2009 fell to men in depressed industries like manufacturing and construction, according to the *New York Times.*

In addition, single women now head almost a third of all households in the United States. In many cases women are the sole breadwinners and the

Figure 7.1
**Female income worldwide is greater than China and India's
GDPs combined.**

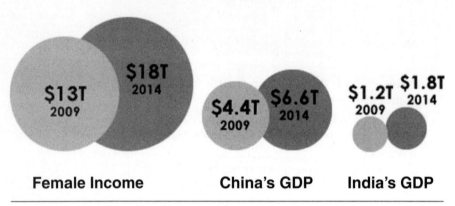

World's Largest Opportunity
A Growth Forecast (in trillions)

$13T
2009

$18T
2014

$4.4T
2009

$6.6T
2014

$1.2T
2009

$1.8T
2014

Female Income   **China's GDP**   **India's GDP**

Source: The Harvard Business Review, September 2009

decision makers for the products they buy. A recent study shows that **women worldwide have greater spending power than China and India combined** (see Figure 7.1), even though women on average are still earning only about 80 cents to a man's dollar.

Today's woman is, in fact, very different from her pre-recession predecessors. Like the rest of us, women have been hit hard by the country's economic crisis. As we'll see, women's brains are hard-wired to feel that anxiety more and to carry it with them longer, with deleterious effects to a woman's body, her psyche, her work, and her home life. Her world has changed, and the strategies she employs and the way she searches for and chooses her products and services will be changing for a long time.

Women control upwards of 80 percent of all of the discretionary income in the United States—and the decisions that surround them are as far-reaching as homes and cars, as indispensable as phone services and appliances, and as commonplace as food and clothing.

My company has for years conducted research on men and women and how their brains react to very specific elements across every category of consumer products and services you can imagine. **We performed literally thousands**

of tests and noticed distinct gender differences across 90 percent of the studies. In neurological testing for insurance, for example, we found that women reacted much more strongly than men to the character of the spokesperson, while men reacted to the price. In lighthearted ads for snack foods, men reacted to slapstick humor, while women ignored it. In automotive ads, men were all about the performance and women were interested in storage capacity and safety factors. In fact, after a time, our analysts became able to determine the gender of test subjects simply by their responses. So naturally, we followed the trail: Do male and female brains have different preferences, encode memory uniquely, and retain information in new ways?

CASE STUDY: THE BATTLE IN THE BEAUTY AISLE

Private-label brands have more than come into their own in recent years. This has been driven by a number of factors, ranging from heightened competitiveness between retailers and consumer products manufacturers to **changing consumer perceptions about a narrowed or nonexistent quality gap** to macroeconomic conditions compelling shoppers to search for better values across many categories. At any rate, store brand has gained in stature and is, in some cases, viewed on a par with national brands.

So it came as little surprise when a global retailer that has been making major pushes into revamping, upgrading, and marketing its private-label brands approached us about a category the company wanted to leverage: beauty aids—specifically, its brand of moisturizer.

The retailer presented us with a very interesting series of questions:

- How can we best determine the consumer's perceived points of difference between the leading brand of moisturizer and our private-label brand?
- Does our packaging convey the same attributes as the branded product?
- Can we identify how much the lower price point for our brand affects the consumer's beliefs about the quality and efficacy of the product?

Asking for women's articulated responses had created confusion in the product development and marketing ranks. The price issue had proved especially puzzling for them. It was unclear how far the price point could be moved before significant consumer reaction would be triggered.

The tools we used to discover the answers to these questions will be explained in detail in the chapters in Part 2, but I'll touch upon them here.

We ran two Total Consumer Experience (TCE) tests to tease out consumers' subconscious responses about the points of difference between the store brand and the leading brand. One test focused on women's actual use of the private-label product, and one concentrated on the competitor's product. The TCE examined the entire consumption process, segmented into individual steps, so it allowed our client to see a side-by-side comparison of exactly how consumers experienced the two products, across multiple senses, second by second.

Deep Subconscious Response (DSR) tests on both products evoked detailed data about how consumers perceived specific brand attributes. Coupled with the brainwave measurements and eye-tracking data obtained through the TCE, these tests provided clear and differentiated metrics for both products.

We also used the DSR methodology to determine price elasticity in the consumer's mind. The client came away with the exact parameters within which the company had some flexibility to adjust pricing without risking consumer perceptions about the private-label product and Purchase Intent levels for it.

The client was able to gain an in-depth understanding not only of how its own product was perceived—**the neurological high points** of the consumption process, the specific attributes of the package triggered in test subjects' subconscious, and the precise range of price points that formed the sweet spot in consumers' minds—*but also the same information for the leading (competitive) brand*.

Performing tests like the TCE between the two genders gave us plenty of electroencephalographic proof that the two genders did differ in their responses, but we needed to scan the medical literature to validate our assumptions. To our surprise, we found that the female brain was vastly understudied in the medical brain-related literature.

In fact, until the Right for Inclusion of Women in Clinical Research Act was passed in 1995, only 17 percent of medical research was conducted on women. The reason was that women's bodies cycle each month. They are never static, so it is difficult to establish a baseline. Because of this oversight, the female brain is now a prime area for new study and real advancements in marketing effectiveness. This area represents entirely new territory for companies with brands, products, or messages targeted to women. You can get ahead of this curve with the information you find here and in Part 2.

Before we delve too deeply into the Buying Brain of female consumers, a caveat: These figures represent average male and female brain tendencies.

They're not absolute and they don't accurately describe each and every individual. For example, I can tell you that, in general, men are taller than women, but we all know women who are taller than many men. In like manner, not all men possess a prototypical male brain, nor does every female possess a prototypical female brain. Still and all, men are most likely to have a male brain and women are far more likely to have a female brain. So let's begin from there.

MEET THE FEMALE BUYING BRAIN

Now that we've gotten the disclaimer out of the way, let's get to the gender differences. Like everything else that arose during the course of human (or any other) evolution, you may be assured that any changes we incorporate into our brain structures exist for one reason: to give an **advantage to our offspring** and thereby to help ensure the survival of our species.

So why did gender differences in the human brain evolve? The answer, quite simply, is because the two genders had two very different agendas. Primitive *homo sapiens* males and females faced entirely different selection pressures. (Read about the early evolution of the two sexes in Chapter 3) Men, for example, needed to hone—quickly—their systemizing and mechanistic skills because they were imperative for inventing, making, and using tools and weapons. Empathy, however, was not an important skill for males to master.

Better to kill your enemy swiftly and dispassionately than take the time to talk through his experience with him and try to comfort him.

The need for close social networking was also not a high-stakes skill for males, since they needed to be alone and focused for long hours on the hunt. Filial bonds with others were also not highly prized among primitive men, since confrontation and combat established their places in the tribal hierarchy. You never knew when you'd have to kill your BFF (Best Friend Forever) to protect your mate or your property. Instead, **the top male achievement was independence**: being able to act, mate, procreate, hunt, and live without relying too much on other males.

At the same time in our distant past, females became experts at empathizing, because those skills made successful mothering and caretaking easier. Highly **empathetic brains could anticipate and understand the needs of infants who could not yet talk**, and socially astute brains helped adolescent women make friends and allies in the new environments that became their homes after they mated (females left their tribes on taking a mate to avoid inbreeding, a critical threat to species survival). Multitasking and enhanced memory skills also served the newest tribe member well, as she learned to get along with the females in her new tribe, to practice their established rituals, and to remember the best places to find food.

Remember: The human brain hasn't changed much in 100,000 years. But society, particularly women's roles in it, has changed dramatically—even within this generation. From the right to vote and own property to the right to govern your own reproduction, to today's situation with more women than men in the workplace, women have stepped into a new role in the world in an evolutionary blink of an eye. As a result, their **hard-wiring is occasionally at odds** with the demands of the twenty-first century. Witness the rise of social networking sites for women to get a sense of how women, for whom community is most important, create their own families and virtual "over-the-fence" friends. Think of ways you and your brand, product, or company can align with this very real need by offering social media opportunities for your female consumers to meet others who are just like them. Consensus is a matter of survival both to the ancient and the modern female brain.

The worst possible scenario for an ancient human female would be ostracism from the group. She and her children would likely not survive. That same brain still functions in women today, elevating conflicts and disagreements to life-threatening emergency status in her brain. This emergency status causes the release of cortisol, a powerful stress hormone, which floods her system and prepares her to fight or flee.

> The levels of cortisol remain elevated and stay in her system much longer that with male brains. Unlike male brains, the cortisol pulsing through her veins actually impairs her performance (it enhances male performance). Women remember the stressor and the events immediately following it far better than men do. In terms of marketing mistakes, one may be all you get.

Women are supreme at creating their own families, either online, at work, or in the playground. These liaisons often last a lifetime.

It should come as no surprise, then, that the female brain reacts to details of life management as potentially catastrophic. Men reach that level of agitation only when there is a threat of immediate physical danger. So anything a marketer can do to lessen the impact of the life management hurdles she must deal with daily will be appreciated, remembered, and rewarded by the female brain.

ANATOMY OF THE FEMALE BRAIN

All brains are female from the very beginning; "baby girl" is our default setting. During the eighth week of gestation, a testosterone bath occurs in about half of all fetuses. If this powerful shower of testosterone happens, some communication centers in the brain shut down, while other centers for sex and aggression gear up, and a male brain is born. If no testosterone appears in the picture, communication centers continue to grow, complex pathways develop across the two hemispheres, centers that specialize in emotion bloom, and the brain remains female. Then, from the second month after conception to the end of their lives, the brains of men and women remain different (see Figure 7.2).

Do you want to know some more interesting facts? I just used a typically female tactic of inviting you into a conversation with me and seeking your

Figure 7.2
The female brain is fundamentally different from the male brain.

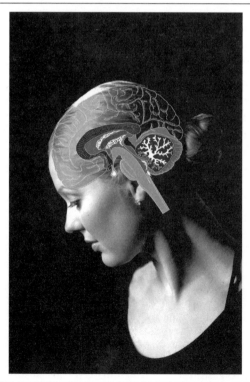

Source: Photo by NeuroFocus, Inc.

compliance. The male approach would have been more direct: "Here are some more facts." Did you know, for example, that preschool girls take turns during play about 20 times more often than boys do? Or that female babies make eye contact about four times more often than boys in their first three months? As adults, women continue to smile more than men, and to nod their heads in agreement with others far more than men do. Consider all of these traits and tendencies when you depict females using your product or package. *Use collaborative, reciprocal language—for example, "Let's put an end to boring dinners." "We support doing less laundry, don't you?"*

Show a woman engaged with others or, if she appears alone, make sure the female representing you appears open and caring, and that she is making eye contact with and even explicitly agreeing with your consumer. Comparing the typical male brain to the typical female brain, she has four times as many neurons connecting the right and the left brain (collectively, they're called the corpus collosum). This means that she processes information through **both rational and emotional filters**, unlike men, who use either one side or the other to process information. In constructing messages to her, always include some emotional component. Even if your positioning is based on hard, cold facts, she will process it more fully if her empathic, emotive brain is engaged.

This superior connection between the two hemispheres makes **the female brain the most highly-attuned multitasker of all time.** She accesses both sides of her brain quickly and easily, moving with remarkable dexterity between analytical and emotional processing. So, talk to both the emotional and rational sides of her mind. She relies equally on both and, in fact, filters rational messaging through her emotions. Engaging both rational and emotional circuits enables the kind of holistic, interhemispheric thinking that comes naturally to women. She is the ultimate holistic thinker and does not solve logical problems without emotional oversight.

Celebrate the superior ability to multitask in the images and messages you use to address the female brain. While males are more single-focused and can be shown honing in on the drive, for example, females are never doing just one thing. Show them using the cup holders, adjusting the seats, and talking to children or others in the car.

Acknowledge that she's integrating many goals with every purchase or shopping experience. By getting that meal, she's also saving money and spending more time with her family. She's a multitasker and likes being acknowledged for her abilities.

More interhemispheric connections also contribute to the female brain's superior big picture thinking—her ability to see situations and resolve them at the 30,000-foot level. As an executive thinker, then, the female brain will appreciate having all of the features and benefits required for her to make a decision laid out for her consideration. Let her know why a product or service makes sense for her and her family. Give her "big picture" reasons to choose you over your competitors, including, when appropriate, the message that your product or service is kinder to the earth or donates to a worthy charity. With men, the idea is to get to the point. And the point is, generally: "What's in it for me?"

It's easy and natural for the female brain to move from home to work, from clothes shopping to contract signing—even to combine these activities. Men compartmentalize and tend to focus on one thing—with one hemisphere—at a time. Consider all of these environments and her ability to move seamlessly among them when designing marketing campaigns for women. Reach her in every aspect of her life, not just in the kitchen.

The female brain is also programmed for more uneasiness and to do more planning than the male brain. That's because primitive and modern women needed to stay a step ahead in arranging for food, shelter, and care for vulnerable children. Today's female is equally adept and has an innate gift of remembering where the best deals are and how to find them. Use some caution before you rearrange her shopping world by moving things around in-store or online. And remember, she will always be interested in finding the best deal for her time, money, and effort. Find effective, efficient means of letting her discover where those are in terms of your brand, product, or store. Remember, too, that sometimes a best buy isn't enough. She will be willing to pay more if a product or service satisfies her requirements for her own or her family's well-being.

Appreciate the paradox: The male brain's highest goal is autonomy, whereas the female brain's highest goal is community.

Critical female brain facts for marketers:

 Rapid transfer of information between the hemispheres means she has the full resources of all of her brain at her disposal at any time and can move between hemispheres with ease and finesse. It also means women may have an easier time recovering from a stroke if damage is limited to a single hemisphere.

 Adjusting for size, women have slightly larger prefrontal cortexes than men. This helps allow them to control emotions during moments of peak anxiety. This extra restraint provided a moment to determine, for instance, if it was wise for a nursing mother to attack a predator head-on.

The female brain is smaller than the male brain by about 9 percent. Smaller does not mean lesser, however; both brains contain the same amount of brain matter; it's just packed more tightly in the female brain.

 Women have about 11 percent more neurons in the language centers of the brain.

 A woman has a slightly smaller amygdala (controls sex and aggression). Sex is emotional as well as physical for women, and the consequences of both sex and aggression are much, much higher—literally "life or death" for women.

Women have an eight-lane superhighway for processing emotion, while men have a small country road. Men, however, have O'Hare Airport as a hub for processing thoughts about sex, where women have the airfield nearby that lands small and private planes.

—Louann Brizendine, MD, Author of The Female Brain

147.8 MILLION

This is the number of females in the United States as of July 1, 2003. That exceeds the number of males (143.0 million). Males outnumber females in every five-year age group through the 35-to-39 age group. Starting with the 40-to-44 age group, women outnumber men. At 85 and over, there are more than twice as many women as men.

THE FEMALE BRAIN IN ACTION

As with every evolutionary benefit in every species, the female brain developed to help our species survive and thrive. Anything that can make her **a better parent or protector** will be incorporated as successful generations evolve. The female brain is specifically designed to nurture and protect. To meet those goals, their naturally empathetic, social brains encouraged our earliest mothers to form alliances that would allow them to find food while their sisters and cousins helped them care for infants.

In today's commuting, double-income world, women are actively seeking surrogate methods for forming deep connections with other women who share their interests. Blogging, Twittering, Facebooking, and other forms of social media help in this effort. Look for ways your brand or product can sponsor or promote opportunities for women to get together—either virtually or literally—in open forums that discuss, validate, and tie together all areas of their lives.

Today's new mother may not have the luxury of learning how to parent by watching her kinswomen. If your brand or product relates to child care, consider giving women and their children a way to interact with each other and perhaps with experts to satisfy this innate desire to watch and learn. Consider in-store seminars for new baby care, for example, or an expert discussion on excellent books for toddlers. Book clubs, play groups, and any bonding activity that has a link to you will be appreciated and remembered. The women involved will come to see you as a trusted ally, even a member of that treasured inner circle.

Emotional memories are paramount in her decision making and in her relationships. She will build close, life-saving social networks to surround her as she raises her children. She will remember with extreme accuracy whom she can count on, and whom she can't. These deep, trusting, reciprocal relationships will ensure that she has a reliable network to help her after childbirth, and later, with small children to tend to and feed. Your brand can become a part of her select personal network, a friend and ally she will rely on above all others. Because she is loyal and exclusive, she may shut out other suitors unless you violate her trust.

Because women remember stressful and negative experiences more than men do, do not disappoint or disillusion her. In the good old days, a bad product experience warranted 10 negative referrals. In today's Twittering, Facebooking, e-mailing, blogging world, that single bad experience can "go viral" and instantly be transmitted to 10,000 contacts.

Her larger prefrontal cortex came in very handy for our earliest mothers. Using these centers of reason helped her modify her responses, behavior, and emotional reactions. By not being quick to react to angry or aggressive behavior, she avoided, at worst case, a fight with a larger, stronger opponent—which could mean death to her and her infant. Her smaller amygdala has huge implications for marketers. Why is it that women don't react as strongly to the appeal of sex in marketing? While men may appreciate overt references to sexuality, women often do not. She may well find depictions of good fathers or men engaged in conversation far sexier than depictions that focus on the body alone. There's a reason men have a barrage of sexually graphic magazines to choose from, whereas women have chosen (with their wallets) to skip this avenue altogether.

Authenticity is absolutely **critical** when marketing to the female brain. Be honest. Be straightforward. Use models and spokespeople who look like they really use your product or service. The female brain can detect an imposter a mile away, and not only will avoid the suspicious message, but will tell her friends about it as well (remember that network!). Very recent studies show that females have a much larger and more integrated Mirror Neuron system (more on this fascinating system in Chapter 9). These special neurons allow her to excel at what's called "Theory of Mind," the gift of putting oneself in another's shoes. Women also feel events that happen to others as if they were happening to them. Men have highly functioning Mirror Neuron systems also, they just focus more on repeating an action observed.

Born empathizers, women have an innate and well-developed talent for seeing the world through others' eyes. For this reason, female consumers love to hear stories; they love to know how others feel; and, when it's appropriate and possible, they love to express their support. By being adept at reading faces and judging body language, our female predecessors could detect whether something was slightly amiss or a bit "off." Early human females needed to be able to read the literal or emotional landscape quickly and accurately to prepare for changes and to protect their children.

Her larger, more connected Mirror Neuron system also gives women superior recall of emotional events, partly because their amygdales are more easily activated by emotional nuance, which in turn leads to far greater memory encoding by the hippocampus. Do you ever wonder why your significant other remembers every word of a fight you had last Christmas? Blame it on her enhanced hippocampus.

Her greater language capabilities helped early females to communicate with each other as they went about their day, rearing children; gathering nuts, seeds, and tubers; and caring for the sick. They built powerful oral traditions of what works and what doesn't to guide them, and their society, away from dangerous options and toward time-tested opportunities. Each female didn't have to learn by trial and error which berry was poisonous, or which grain could be ground into a paste and carried for food for the day. Older females reassured younger ones that a baby's sickness would quickly pass, or that it required some interaction, or that the situation was dire. Women have a greater facility for the nuance of language, rely on it more, store it better, and use it three times as often as men do.

However, women no longer raise their children in a close and extended family. Some of that group's functions have fallen to friends met on Facebook or in playgroups. Still she longs for a feeling of connectedness.

The short story is: Tell stories to your female consumers. Don't be terse. While men appreciate "just do it," women appreciate the story of an athlete and how she came to get "it" done.

BEST PRACTICES FOR APPEALING TO THE FEMALE BRAIN

 Pay attention to facial expressions and tone of voice, not just text or spoken word.

 Because her hemispheres are so connected, and because she filters ideas through her emotions, present material with some emotional component. Make sure that the takeaway message is based in positive emotion. Factual/statistics memories don't stick as well, for example.

 *Allow her to show or experience **empathy**. That's her strong suit. Women recruit brain areas containing Mirror Neurons to a higher degree than males do.*

 Above all, be vigilant as to how you present the brand: It truly is like a person to her, and she will embrace or discard it passionately and completely, depending on how well your brand maintains your promise to her.

 Social connections are crucial—help her feel included; appeal to her through shared stories.

 Finesse your attention to detail and subtlety; don't be callous and overt. She appreciates and picks up on nuance. Don't challenge or threaten her with "Don't wait!" or "Call now!" messaging.

In this chapter, you discovered the richness and variety of the female brain. Hard-wired through eons of evolutionary selection, she is more:

Verbal
Empathetic
Resourceful
Able to multitask
Nuanced, subtle
Loyal
Altruistic

CHAPTER 8

THE MOMMY BRAIN IS BUYING

At the end of this chapter, you'll know and be able to use the following:
- The difference between a female brain and a mommy brain
- Why maternity enhances certain brain functions
- What specific consumer behaviors and preferences mommy brains share
- What entices and what repels the mommy brain

If marketing to Moms hasn't fully registered on your radar, consider this the next time you walk by a playground or school yard: From diapers to dinner, clothes to minivans, over-the-counter (OTC) medications to the parcel tax that paved the parking lot and the supplies and elbow grease that built the nontoxic play structure, the Moms there *made it all happen.*

Step into her circle and you'll hear Moms discussing in detail what products work, and which don't. In her e-mail box, you'll find Mom-to-Mom alerts on everything from the recall of strollers to endorsements of Old Navy to fierce political activism to calls to support sick girlfriends by organizing networks to provide dinner, rides, child care, you name it.

Should a suspicious visitor wander too near, you'll see immediate protective reactions, ranging from watchful waiting, to packing up the children and alerting the authorities, and, importantly, notifying the Mom network to stay away from the park.

These Moms, and the millions like them across the country, are an army—mobile, nimble, vigilant, and powerful.

If your product or message hits home with them, you have won over powerful allies who will support you through an enhanced network beyond anything you could create yourself.

Highly connected, super-effective tribal support is hard-wired into the brains of new mothers. They're predisposed to form communities, to exchange information, to protect and nurture each other and each other's offspring. So if they like you, you're in. If your product or message disappoints this important target group, be prepared to be shut out, and possibly even shut down. **Mothers are much less forgiving than other groups.** They are living out their ancient imperative to stand between their children and a dangerous world. Very few do-overs are available when marketing to Moms.

Please recall my previous caveat: I am speaking of "typical" maternal brain changes. We all know mothers who differ from the descriptions I'll present here. And we know Dads are also excellent primary nurturers (although our efforts to locate the Daddy brain are still underway!). But, in general, mothers who go through pregnancy and give birth experience the most significant brain changes of their adult lives.

We've been very fortunate to have a "front-row seat" into how new Moms react to products entering their new worldview. An example follows.

NEUROMARKETING AND BABY CARE PRODUCTS

A Midwestern consumer packaged goods company was wondering about one of its websites.

The product line featured was doing well—not great, but making its numbers. Still, given the growth potential for this market, and the corporate goal for increasing sales through the website, the lingering question was, **Can we do better?** If so, how?

Just from looking at the website, we believed the answer to the first question was a definitive "yes." We were confident that neurological testing would provide specific answers to the second. We had already developed a body of neurological best practices for presenting information and messaging on screens—so we knew going in that the website's performance could very likely be upped by applying those best practices. We also knew that we had the diagnostic tools—brainwave-based measurements—to identify specific new steps that could be taken to better attract, keep, and sell products to visitors to the site.

This particular client was of more than the usual interest to us because the product line was targeted to new mothers. One of the areas where we have done an enormous amount of neuromarketing research is the female brain, and a subset of that, the Mommy brain (reflected in the fact that you're reading two chapters on those subjects). Combined with what we know about marketing on websites, it was an intriguing proposition that appealed to both the brain scientists and the parents among us.

We measured Moms' subconscious responses to the website as a whole, and to the individual elements of the website. Eye-tracking gave us the necessary knowledge of what was attracting the strongest visual focus, and when we aligned that with the brainwave measurement data, we experienced what we frequently do when we conduct these studies. The answers and the solutions arise from the oceans of data and are distilled into very clear findings.

To cut to the chase, I'll reveal what we recommended, and what the client saw in terms of results after these changes were made to the website.

- Reorient visuals so that images are on the left, and semantics on the right.
- Feature Moms using the product, and *especially sharing the experience with other Moms*.
- Create a specific forum section where advice/tips are available from other website visitors.
- Rewrite key language to emphasize brand's understanding of the new mother experience, and offer "moral" support/basic tips on time/stress management.
- Reduce the number of placements of the logo on individual pages.
- Replace some key graphics with imagery that includes pop-outs.

There were more recommendations that got into detailed areas of the website, but some involve proprietary client information, so I'll outline what the top line results were:

- Website traffic spiked 26 percent in the first month following the redesign, and the growth curve continued ascending since (as I write this, the first full quarter's results are not yet complete).
- Overall time spent on the website increased by 14 percent.
- Number of pages visited (click-throughs) increased by 37 percent.
- Online product sales volume jumped by 24 percent.

The combination of neurological knowledge about how the Mommy brain is fundamentally different in several critical respects, and how best to appeal to new mothers' subconscious needs and wants, with the best practices we have for screen-based content and messaging enabled this company to restructure the website and exceed their earlier sales projections significantly.

Nothing is more important for a new mother than the health, happiness, and well-being of her family—especially her new child. Knowing how her brain functions at the subconscious level enabled us to respond to her in ways she finds relevant, useful, and worth her time and budget.

BUILDING A MOMMY BRAIN

Not so long ago, to be accused of having a "mommy brain" was something of an insult, a slang term coined as the surge of mothers flooded the workplace in unprecedented numbers in the 1960s. Perceived as forgetful and emotional, new mommies were derided at work and castigated at home. In fact, **best-selling author Betty Friedan once famously called homemakers with children "walking corpses."**

Today, those tides have turned. Scientists have argued convincingly that the "Mommy Brain" is largely responsible for our evolution and status at the top of Earth's food chain (as soon as the first reptile stayed around to guard and feed her offspring, we were off to the races). And economists have confirmed that the hands that rock the cradles truly do rule the world.

SPENDING POWER OF MOMS

Eighty-three million: The estimated number of mothers in the United States in 2004.

Two billion: The estimated number of mothers throughout the world.

Moms are **80 percent more likely to buy** a product from a **company that recognizes** the multiple roles she plays in her life.

Nearly **one in every five people online is a mother between the ages of 25 and 54,** with at least one child under 18 living at home.

Seventy percent of moms say "advertisers are not acknowledging or recognizing their needs as mothers" in ads.

Ninety-four percent of moms have purchased a product online.

Fifty-five percent of mothers with infant children are in the labor force.

Surprisingly little research has been conducted on "the Mommy Brain" to date. Most of the research on structural changes of "Mommy Brains" comes from lab studies of rats and monkeys, whose brains, it turns out, are very much like ours. The information provided here is new, relevant, and offers exciting possibilities for reaching the Mommy Brain.

Obviously, all mommies have female brains, but not all females have mommy brains. So when we look at these two spectacular organs, what marks the difference? Supercharged new neural networks lay down throughout pregnancy, labor, childbirth, and caretaking enhance and influence every lobe of the mommy brain, making it the ideal organ for child development, and, by extension, species survival. What this means in simplest terms: **The Mommy Brain changes to make her offspring her primary focus; she is no longer looking out for number 1.**

AVERAGE STATS FOR NEW MOMS

Diaper Changes: 7,300 by baby's second birthday

Sleep Deprivation: 700 hours in the first year

Giving Attention: One preschooler requires mom's attention once every four minutes or 210 times/day. Multiply by number of children until time required per hour exceeds minutes contained in twenty four hours!

Daytime Disruption: Brand new babies often have trouble with day/night distinction.

Sleep, eat, sleep, eat . . . : New baby's maximum sleep time is limited to the amount their stomachs can contain; most need to eat every three to four hours.

Baby Supplies: Cost of baby basics will run to $7,000 before baby's first birthday.

BRAIN CHANGES BEGIN IN PREGNANCY

Long before she holds her baby in her arms, a woman's brain begins a complex series of changes, preparing her for the new arrival:

- Progesterone can spike from 100 to 1,000 times its normal level; the sedating effects are similar to Valium.
- Cortisol levels will rise to make expectant mothers much more vigilant about safety, nutrition, her surroundings, and potential threats.

Thirst and hunger centers are activated as her blood volume doubles to support the growing baby. She finds it difficult to eat or drink enough and finds herself preoccupied with finding and consuming food and water. Distinct preferences and aversions also develop during this time, and can be long-term, lasting for decades. Strong aversions to nonfood toxins such as gasoline also work to protect the developing fetus. On the other hand, the diet of the pregnant mother will influence the dietary choices of the infant years after his or her birth. For example, infants who are exposed to mom's taste for garlic or apricots *in utero* often develop lifelong preferences for them.

Oxytocin production begins, making the expectant Mom sleepier, increasing her need to rest and eat more.

By the end of her third trimester, her brain goes through relatively large-scale changes, preparing to lay down a superhighway of enhanced neural connections. Neurogenesis—or new neuron creation—is enhanced and includes changes to portions of the brain that will last the rest of her life.

According to new research by Kinsley and Lambert:

"Mothers are faster, braver, and more efficient than other females. They have to be. *Achieving an objective such as providing food quickly allows mothers to return to and protect their babies.*"

NEW MOMMIES ARE MADE—AND "BORN"

While the effect of "mommyhood" is profound across most mammalian species, it's magnified among humans. That makes sense because **childhood lasts longer in humans than in any other species**. For a **decade or even two**, human mothers must use all of their resources to stand between a developing child and a dangerous world. As a result, caretaking—and the new neuron creation and connections it engenders—has more time to set down a permanent path in mothers' brains. A neuroscience adage ensures us that "Neurons that fire together wire together." Learning in the high-stakes environment of new motherhood is the most effective way to create new neural pathways. We don't learn if we don't care. And evidence and evolution clearly show that nobody cares more than moms.

Because of this high-stakes environment, changes occur in the maternal brain faster and with more permanence than at any other time of life. Of course, the ultimate reason Mommies' brains become different is the reason any evolutionary benefit occurs: Mommy brains increase the likelihood of survival of healthy babies and, through them, the survival of the species.

We all have or know mothers who are preternaturally intuitive, wizards at getting things done, and founts of fun and knowledge. That's because they undergo real, measurable, physical changes in their brains that enhance their performance in caring for their babies.

As neuroscientist Craig Kinsley says, "birth and caring for offspring literally reshape the brain [into] a more complex organ that can accommodate an increasingly demanding environment."

BENEFITS OF A MOMMY BRAIN

Childbirth is a uniquely powerful catalyst for brain changes. Neurogenesis occurs for the first and only time in an adult brain with a purpose other than to replace dying neurons. Mommy brains are enhanced: faster, higher-functioning than before. So marketing to mommies is a different prospect than marketing to any other group.

Each mommy will also form familial, life-saving social networks, remembering whom she can count on and whom she can't. She must develop trusting relationships in her "tribe" so she's covered after childbirth, with small children, and during times of sickness and stress.

Again, this is a prime opportunity for your brand, product, service, or store to become part of this powerful group. When my first children were born (twin girls), a local bakery invited neonatal care and lactation experts to speak to New Mommy groups. The mothers and infants who went to these fabulous meetings received real, valuable information, great food, camaraderie, laughs, and the tremendous joy of being among others with new babies. We still go to that bakery as often as we can and recommend the group to every new mother we know.

Her enhanced prefrontal cortex gives her the ability to control emotions. Early in evolution, mothers likely needed to appease groups, intruders, and the alpha male. This was a matter of life and death for her and her children. Modern mothers must navigate a similar, but less life-threatening labyrinth of work, home, in-laws, school, community obligations, and friends.

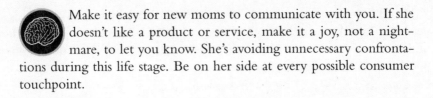

Make it easy for new moms to communicate with you. If she doesn't like a product or service, make it a joy, not a nightmare, to let you know. She's avoiding unnecessary confrontations during this life stage. Be on her side at every possible consumer touchpoint.

Her enhanced insula gives her **superior instinct and intuition skills.** Mothers are famous for it and here's why. If something's slightly amiss, or there's trouble brewing, females need to know so they can prepare and act with children and network in tow. She has the instinct to tell if you're drinking out of the milk carton, fudging on your homework, or embezzling from your company.

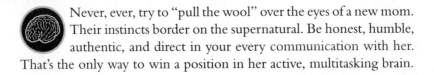

Never, ever, try to "pull the wool" over the eyes of a new mom. Their instincts border on the supernatural. Be honest, humble, authentic, and direct in your every communication with her. That's the only way to win a position in her active, multitasking brain.

Highly nurturing mothers are a key to species survival across all species. Consider the following examples: Sea turtles lay thousands of eggs, with a survival rate of <10 percent. Female elephants endure a costly 22-month pregnancy for a single birth, with a survival rate of ~87 percent (first year). But it's what happens after that costly birth that counts. Each new calf becomes the center of the herd's activity. If she's female, she will remain with mother and tribe for all of her 50–70 years. If he's male, he will stay with his mother until puberty, and then leave the herd for a solitary life, occasionally competing with other males for breeding females, living 50–70 years as well. These precious single births with long childhoods respresent both high individual investments and high individual returns, just like they do for us.

Of course, human mothers also **build networks** to support and bond with their babies. In humans, oxytocin cements human bonds and prompts mothers to nurture and protect. It also hooks pregnant and new mothers into the social world, causing her to crave community, companionship, sisterhood, and, particularly, other experienced mothers. This helps explain the wholehearted acceptance of social networking by moms. Any forum that encourages moms to connect will have great influence over that audience.

Oxytocin also causes new mothers to abandon personal fear and hostility responses to protect their offspring. As reflected by oxytocin levels in new mothers, there is much less "fight or flight" response—less amygdala involvement—but a great deal more "rest and recovery" time. Mothers must calm themselves down as threats develop, not rev themselves up, lest they leave a vulnerable child unprotected to join an unworthy fight. Fear centers in Mommy Brains become much less engaged than nonmothers. **Prolactin, "the parenting hormone," rises to eight times the normal levels in new moms.**

 Show plenty of relaxing, mom-to-baby interactions in ads targeting her. Grooming activities, in particular, still have a powerful hold on the Mommy Brain.

There remains, however, *marked* aggression against intruders. Motherhood is powerful assertiveness training. New ferocity lingers long after children are born. Show that you're protective of her child, too, by spelling out how your brand, product, service, or store keeps the child's safety foremost in mind, and the child's happiness closely behind. For example, one of our close friends drives past two grocery stores to reach one with sanitized shopping carts. A machine mists and sanitizes each cart, and a gloved store employee hands the cart to shoppers. You will see fuller baby seats in that store than in any others in this small town. The prices didn't get them there—the "baby first" action did.

Mothers also excel at **Theory of Mind,** the art of figuring out what someone else is thinking. Reading another person's feelings from nonverbal cues is a very high-order cognitive skill, and mothers excel at it. As with the Female Brain, allow new mothers to feel empathy toward those who represent your product, brand, or service. Enhance eye contact. Show babies. And present a few less-than-perfect/humorous scenarios (but nothing dangerous, of course).

Enhanced Emotional Intelligence: Mothers routinely exercise positive emotions, such as love and compassion, more than the general population, and they can summon these emotions more easily. With experience, mothers become masters of empathy, cultivating emotionally-smart techniques like self-restraint, conflict resolution, and reappraisal, or "spin control" to reposition life events in a positive light. Celebrate this delightful new tendency in all of your messaging to new moms. Look on the bright side. It's not a big deal. You don't have to comb the back of your hair. That sweater looks great with a little spit-up!

- **Self-Restraint:** exercised by brain's frontal lobes prevents moms from reacting, smacking, yelling, or abandoning.

- **Conflict Resolution:** helps moms repair relationships, helps kids resolve conflicts, keep life moving along.
- **Reappraisal or Spin Control:** This "learned optimism" helps moms make the best of things, to look on the bright side. Optimism is a great motivator, and a key part of emotional intelligence.

MOM AND BABY AS ONE

Dr. Mike Mezernich points out that breast-feeding is a temporary breakdown of identity between mother and child, which profoundly affects both of their brains. "It's a heavy dose of empathy and understanding that a male could never experience in the same way," he says, "a source of how women think about people in the world differently than men." Repetitive intimate experiences, such as cuddling, feeding, clothing, and changing, are a **crash course in human reactions** minute-by-minute. Moms learn the language of that person's changing thoughts better than they may know their own.

The mom–baby game of mimicking each other even has a sound evolutionary basis. Making faces and practicing coos makes you happy. Mirror Neurons are connected to the limbic system via the insula, translating imitation into positive emotion along the way.

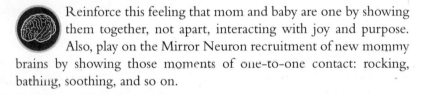 Reinforce this feeling that mom and baby are one by showing them together, not apart, interacting with joy and purpose. Also, play on the Mirror Neuron recruitment of new mommy brains by showing those moments of one-to-one contact: rocking, bathing, soothing, and so on.

BIRTH OF A MOMMY

Childbirth forges new neurochemical pathways in the brain that create and reinforce maternal brain circuits, aided by chemical imprinting, and huge increases in oxytocin. This results in a motivated, highly-attentive, aggressively-protective brain. It also forces the new mother to alter responses and priorities. Learning becomes a high priority because the stakes are high: life and death.

As it expands, the Mommy Brain is **specializing, exaggerating, getting more detail.** As Dr. Mike Merzenich notes, "Its positive plasticity is really quite stunning. Substantial brain changes contribute to the safety and wellbeing of the child and the mom as the birth experience becomes 'tattooed' or overlaid on the Mommy Brain." Within hours after birth, maternal aggression, strength, and resolve are well-established.

In her book, *The Mommy Brain: How Motherhood Makes Us Smarter,* Katherine Ellison puts it like this: "Like a human GPS [global positioning system], mommy brain has increased vigilance on all aspects [of mothering], including safety and stability of her nest." Parts of the brain responsible for focus and concentration become preoccupied with protecting and tracking the newborn.

Dr. Michael Numan, a neuroscientist at Boston College believes that medial preoptic area (MPOA) also becomes much more active in the mother's brains, following the influx of hormones during pregnancy. As a result, "neurons in the midbrain areas that are important in the feeling of motivation and reward, including the ventral tegmental area (VTA) and nucleus acumbens (NA)," often called the brain's pleasure center form a newer, larger "reward circuit that is important in feelings of motivation and reward. These stimulate new mothers in the same way winning the lottery or even using cocaine does. It keeps her coming back to nurture and protect her infant." So in a very real way, having a baby is like a drug—addictive and mind altering.

Celebrate! The new mom is, in a very real way, a new person. Her baby's birth is a rebirth for her, too. Revel in that baby love with her. Show pictures of beautiful babies, invite her to share her story and make new friends. Remind her of what a "superhero" she's become.

THE SUPER SENSES OF A MOMMY BRAIN

The innate brain wiring of all mammals responds to basic cues, growing fetus, birth, suckling, touch, smell, and frequent skin-to-skin closeness. These forge new neurochemical pathways in the brain that create and reinforce maternal brain circuitry, aided by chemical imprinting, and a **huge** remapping of neural pathways. In human mothers, neurogenesis occurs, "the first example of a body reacting to a physiological phenomenon [creating] new brain cells, which are linked to a new behavior," according to Samuel Weiss at the University of Calgary.

Major Multitasking Skill Improvement is perhaps the first improvement noticed. In rats and monkeys, new moms improve basic memory and learning skills, key strength for multitaskers of all species.

In Kinsley and Lambert's fascinating research, particularly when it comes to shopping-like tasks, like hiding food rewards (Fruit Loops) in different colored purses, Mom monkeys excelled, learning where the most Fruit

Loops were and retrieving them much more quickly than non-moms (in 17 seconds, in fact). In general and across mammal species, new moms have an enhanced learning curve, particularly when it comes to finding food, or any other activity that requires her to be away from her baby. Merchandisers: Do **not** waste her time. Put the milk up front, close to the diapers and the organic fruit. Consider a "pit stop" portion of the store for new parents, with everything they need in one spot. They'll thank you for it. And they'll tell their friends and return.

Why? Anything that **brings her back to her children quickly** is an evolutionary advantage. Parenting boosts a mother's brain to help her cope with maximum efficiency with the outside world.

Multitasking is also a great way to focus on the essential, and to ignore the rest: to accomplish the most possible in the shortest amount of time. It became a pure survival skill for ancient and modern moms and infants alike. As Patricia Ratey summarizes: "In evolutionary terms, you want a new mother to be as smart as she can be, to know the territory around her, to remember what her kids need, to pay maximum attention to the outside world."

Essentials of motivation also shine through in new moms: Suddenly they excel at taking task ownership, making split-second decisions and living with the consequences, they become more mature, and prioritize better.

Here is just a sampling of the other super senses new moms employ:

Smell: The brand new neurons of adult neurogenesis migrate to the mother's olfactory lobes to provide extreme subtlety in her sense of smell. Changes in the smell of baby, food, or environment will be interpreted and acted upon in milliseconds. Before the mother is even consciously aware of the change, she has monitored and made a decision on the source of the smell. This enhanced ability lasts through the remainder of the mother's life.

If you are marketing to a Mommy Brain, test her brain's response to the smell of your product, engage her Mirror Neurons by showing others enjoying great smells in your messaging, be vigilant about the smell of the environment you invite her into; consider using "scent marketing" to reach out to her through all of those newly-formed neurons.

Smell: New olfactory cells also help bond moms to their children. Mothers get a high from the smell of their babies and can easily distinguish their child's scent from a host of others from another just 48 hours after birth.

Smell: The sweet smell of an infant's head carries pheromones that stimulate the female brain to produce oxytytocin, a "love potion."

Sound: The female brain starts out more sensitive to sound than the male brain. Motherhood catapults these elite hearing skills into the stratosphere. After two nights, 96 percent of new mothers are able to distinguish their newborn's cry from other babies'.

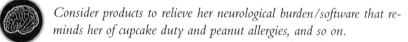 Indulge the Mommy Brain's superior hearing with pleasant sounds, laughter, children playing. Do not screech, scream, or offer other painful sounds, even in an attempt at humor. She will screen them and your message **out.**

Here are some other ways to reach out to the Mommy Brain:

Consider products to relieve her neurological burden/software that reminds her of cupcake duty and peanut allergies, and so on.

Don't change what's working. If she's taken you into her tribe, honor that relationship and celebrate the particular bond she has with you and with her children. One bad review of your brand, product, packaging, message, or environment can easily reach national, even international, proportions if it's broadcast to millions via mommy blogs and the abundant social networking websites. If you google "Mothers Against..." you'll find more than 80 million hits.

Trigger Mirror Neurons. Show activities she wants to engage in, particularly the one-to-one soothing activities she engages in with her own baby.

New mothers seek empathy and understanding. Show faces she can identify with, babies she won't be able to ignore, and experts and fellow moms who share her concerns and her lifestyle.

The more a new mother feels understood, the more likely she is to attend to/rely on you/your brand.

Emphasize safety in a positive emotional context, not through fear tactics. Talk about how your seat belts are advanced, but not about potential strangulation, stranger danger, or other primally fearful ideas.

Speak to the new Mommy Brain from a new perspective. She has new filters, new interests, and amazing new abilities. Any material that is irrelevant to them will be bounced back post haste, like a computer spam program. She simply doesn't have time to evaluate anything that doesn't obviously and immediately meet her needs.

THE GRANDMOTHER HYPOTHESIS

Human mothers are also rare in that they survive for decades after they are no longer fertile ("senescence"). Since survival of the species is all about procreation, there must be some *evolutionary benefit* to having women around after their childbearing years are past. The Grandmother Hypothesis argues that **senescent women are the cornerstone of successful tribes.** They make for better child care (including more food on the children's plates), healthier children, and a treasure trove of knowledge and wisdom to pass along. Many argue that grandmothers are, therefore, a key reason for our survival as a species (they also play a key role in the fitness of children in other highly-evolved, long-lived species, like elephants and great apes). Given that today's women have increased their lifespans into the 80s, many more children are also reaping the benefit of great-grandmother care. Grandmothers are also the most likely resource for children who can't be cared for by their parents. All that and cookies and milk, to boot. If you are fortunate enough to have a grandmother you can hug (your children's or perhaps even your own), be sure you do so.

CHAPTER 9

THE EMPATHIC BRAIN
IS BUYING

At the end of this chapter, you'll know and be able to use the following:
- Groundbreaking new research currently underway that shows how our brains react to or "mirror" what we see in others
- Ways to engage the Mirror Neuron System of your consumers to invite them to experience your brand, product, package, message, or environment "first-hand"

The quaint little town of Parma, Italy, is justifiably famous for its weather, architecture, culture, and food. Near the center of the top of Italy's boot, Parma is the sunny, warm home to Parmigiano reggiano cheese, Prosciutto di Parma, many medieval castles, and, of course, the University of Parma, founded in the eleventh century. I give you this little tour of a quaint Italian town, not because I am on their board of tourism (although I'd certainly like to visit), but because it provides me with the opportunity to introduce a bit of irony.

Our ironic story begins on a hot summer day in 1991, within the old stone walls of the university. Biding his time in the 1,000-year-old building sat a macaque monkey (see Figure 9.1), with an electrode implanted in his cranium, specifically in the areas that dealt with planning and carrying out movements. The monkey was calm and happy, quite accustomed to the electrode and to the staff and assistants in the lab, who treated him like a bright and amiable friend.

It was a hot day, so the monkey lulled in his chair, daydreaming. It was a nice day for the monkey, sitting in a university that was around when the British Isles were being invaded, and America was undiscovered, helping with twentieth century research on the deepest workings of the subconscious brain.

Figure 9.1
A macaque monkey helped with the discovery of Mirror Neurons.

Source: Photo courtesy of Dreamstime.com

Less ironically, given the day's temperature, a lab assistant returned from his break, eating an ice cream cone. The monkey's interest was piqued. Nothing to write home about there. But, remember, this particular monkey watching this particular ice cream cone being consumed had an electrode implanted in his cortex. As the staff member raised the ice cream to his lips, **electrical activity in the monkey's brain went crazy**—off the charts. That monkey, in his brain, was enjoying a delicious gelato, including all of the physical movements needed to make that happen. In concert with the ice-cream-eating staff member, the monkey's brain signaled its arms to raise foods to its lips, to salivate, to prepare for some major primate satisfaction. It was a true "monkey-see-monkey-do" experience, except the monkey wasn't actually doing anything more than watching. But to his brain—his Mirror Neurons, specifically—the monkey was in the midst of a salacious moment of pure primate gluttony. And so, by the way, was the lab assistant.

Giancomo Rizzolatti, a world-renowned scientist, was in charge of the monkey experiment happening in his laboratory. He wondered if the ice cream incident was unique, or had it actually uncovered a wonderful, previously undiscovered ability of the primate brain? So Dr. Rizzolatti did what great scientists do. He and his team developed a series of studies, recruited more monkeys, and the world's first work on Mirror Neurons began.

To no one's surprise, the monkeys had a similar response with peanuts. When a monkey saw another monkey or human eat a peanut, the neurons in his brain fired as if he, too, were shelling and eating a snack. In case after case, neurons in the prefrontal cortex reacted to the perception of the actions they observed.

In 1994, Rizzolatti published his first research on the newly-discovered area of Mirror Neurons. Found in two areas of monkey brains, the premotor and parietal cortexes, these Mirror Neuron networks also have important links to the superior temporal sulcus (STS), located above the ear toward the back of the head (in monkeys and in humans). The STS helps process facial and body movements and hand actions. **Mirror Neurons** in the STS track body movement like walking and arm swinging and are dedicated to detecting biological motion, a threat, or movement that might become either. They are a subset of our motor command neurons, representing some 20 percent of these. Research on Mirror Neurons is far from complete and represents one of the most exciting areas within neuroscience. There is so much more to be learned! In the following discussion, let's look at extending what we have learned from using the Mirror Neuron system to gain insights into the minds of consumers.

HUMAN SEE, HUMAN DO

Using a variety of brain imaging techniques, scientists went on to study Mirror Neurons in humans. Their results are remarkable, and ongoing. So by all means, stay tuned.

Basically, the Mirror Neuron theory says that when you watch someone perform an action, say washing a dish, **you automatically simulate** the action in your own brain. You have a template for dishwashing in your databanks, just as you have brain-wired templates for most things you do often. When you see someone throw a ball, your ball-throwing template is activated in the brain. The same thing with jumping rope, cooking a steak, and so on. What your Mirror Neurons are doing is adopting the other person's point of view.

Neuroscientist V. Ramachandran argues that the reason we have Mirror Neurons is to help spread useful information quickly. For example, at about 100,000 years ago, humans suddenly developed the makings of culture (tool use, fire, shelter, language, Theory of Mind, and so on). Dr. Ramachandran argues that, during this time period, we also developed Mirror Neurons to help us duplicate the actions of others. Instead of learning and relearning how to build a fire, for example, several people could watch a fire being built, and, as they watched the building, their Mirror Neurons caused them to feel as if they themselves were building the fire. As a result of this ability to **jump into another's experience,** key, species-enhancing skills spread quickly through the culture. Spreading both horizontally (teaching an entire tribe to build fire, and having them recall the steps immediately), vertically (teaching one member of a younger generation and having that person embrace and spread the knowledge), and, ultimately, exponentially (cooking shows today practice the same principle).

Activating the Mirror Neuron system is one of the most effective ways to connect with your consumer. Show products being consumed. Celebrate the effervescent sip of water, the sip of warm coffee. Let the consumer revel in the action being performed, for example, wince with the tart pleasure of a crisp green apple. When they are in-store, those fantastic feelings of desire will be subconsciously accessed.

Following is an example of how Mirror Neurons impacted one of our own studies.

MIRROR NEURONS AND MOTOR VEHICLES

There are an infinite number of ways that the Mirror Neuron phenomenon discussed in this chapter can be put to work, including for fun and profit and in marketing. Those miraculous "mirrors" in our brains are capable of mimicking just about anything that we can experience in our environments.

One of my favorite examples of how we applied knowledge of that amazing capacity is work we did for an import car manufacturer. We had completed neuromarketing research studies for this company on pricing and interior/exterior styling combinations, and they turned to us again when they were striving to increase the effectiveness of their in-showroom marketing materials.

Like many other retail businesses today, in-store video was proving to be an increasingly popular and useful marketing tool for this client. Their models ranged from sport utilities to minivans to performance-oriented sport compacts, but as has been true now for many decades in the automotive industry, the "sizzle" cars are what help to sell the more standard offerings. It's called the "**halo effect**," where the presence of a sexy sports car in the showroom serves as a magnet that can help attract prospects, who really end up buying the more practical people-mover they needed all along.

This carmaker had some beautiful footage of their particular hot model in full performance mode. The video was great to look at, and showed the vehicle off to real advantage as it traveled through scenic settings. Even if you were actually in the market for a more mundane minivan, the idea was that this presentation would capture your attention in the showroom and lend some of that sizzle to the sales process.

Except the video wasn't holding showroom visitors' attention long enough to have the desired result. The production values were certainly there, but the halo effect wasn't kicking in as expected in terms of retaining shoppers in the sales arena. Conventional research hadn't turned up any reason for this—focus group participants praised the content, which showed the car zooming here and there in alluring ways, so what was lacking?

Knowing what we know about the Mirror Neuron phenomenon, we decided to test a revised version of the video to determine if our theory about the solution was correct. We had the footage recut to incorporate scenes showing the driver actually piloting the car—swinging the steering wheel, rowing through the gears, opening the moon roof, operating the windows and sound system, and similar hands-on activities that demonstrated an actual human being fully enjoying the driving experience.

The results not only confirmed our hypothesis—**they sent the numbers off the charts** in terms of Attention, Emotional Engagement, Memory Retention, Purchase Intent, Novelty, and Awareness. Every single one of our primary and derived NeuroMetrics showed dramatic improvements over the baseline data recorded when we tested the original footage, which had shown mostly exteriors of the car, and almost no driver interaction.

The true test was back in the showroom. The company had told us that the average amount of time spent viewing the original footage in the showroom setting had been 87 seconds. The new version held shoppers' attention for an average of 143 seconds. Moreover, the client reported that the video was now attracting and holding visitors' attention far better across age and gender demographics as well.

The solution had been found by applying the Mirror Neuron effect—essentially, enabling passive observers to experience "driving" the car deep in their subconscious, while actually standing in front of a monitor in the dealer's showroom. We had purposely incorporated enough of a variety of activities, performed by a real driver, to trigger that response—and keep the viewers' attention long enough so that they might feel that residual glowing "halo" as they roamed around the more practical models on offer.

The discovery of the Mirror Neuron network for brain modeling of movements and biological motions made enormous inroads in the neuroscientific and the scientific community at large. Soon, however, another bombshell was ready to fall. Scientists lately have found **strong, pervasive mirror networks for emotions.** For example, when your friend chokes up when telling a sad story, your brain simulates a similar level of distress. You empathize with the story, precognitively and subconsciously. As Rizzolatti says, "our survival depends on understanding the actions, intentions, and emotions of others. We simulate these automatically, without logic, thinking, analyzing."

> If anything, the emotional Mirror Neuron system is even more powerful than the sensory/motor Mirror Neuron system. Use your consumer's desire to connect with each other by offering them chances to see and **feel** things as others experience them. This is most powerfully a visual/auditory effect, best suited for television, movies, radio, and print editorial. Even so, reading the word "sniff" in the proper context may cause you to do just that. Or "itch," "stretch," "swallow," or any of a hundred common activities you could perform while reading.

There is now considerable evidence that perceiving language activates corresponding motor and/or perceptual areas. For example, *He kicked the ball* activates the foot area of the primary motor cortex, while hearing the word "jump" activates brain areas related to leg movement.

> We've known for a long time that visualization (imagining oneself completing an important task, particularly widespread in sports coaching) improves performance. Olympians and professional athletes attest to the power of thinking through each stage of their performance before it happens. We're learning now that watching others perform the task you're about to undertake also improves performance. How this is done

is by recruiting the powerful Mirror Neuron system. When athletes or others who practice the sport or play the music watch a master in action, their performance actually improves. The more they watch their specific area of interest, the more they improve. The only drawback is watching virtuoso performances by Serena Williams or Michael Phelps improves performance only in bodies that actually DO similar activities, although all brains will fire while watching. Unfortunately, if "weekend warriors" watch Serena or Michael, the appropriate areas of the brain will fire, but, alas, there will be no improvement in performance.

MIRROR, MIRROR, IN MY MIND

Mirror Neurons operate in your subconscious. They absorb the culture, experiences, feelings, and actions of those around you—and you are changed. At the same time, your actions and emotions feed and change those around you—and they, too, are changed. Mirror Neurons for emotion reading and empathy reside in two areas deep inside the cortex: the insula and the anterior cingulate cortex. People with the greatest empathy have more gray matter in their right frontal insulas. The thicker this part of your insula, the better you are at reading feelings in yourself and others.

Your MNS operates all the time; you can't turn it off.

So when you see fear on another's face, you feel fear. When you see calm, you feel calm. When you see pain you feel pain, boredom equals boredom, yawn equals yawn, and so on. **Women have more active Mirror Neuron activity** in general than men do. (Greater empathy aids successful childbearing. See Chapter 8 for more on the Mommy Brain.)

The amazing and still-to-be-discovered facets of the MNS are not found in all species and appear to be related to those species with elevated consciousness: great apes (including us), elephants, and whales.

One spectacular variety, Von Economo cells, are highly-connected neurons that enable us to make fast, intuitive judgments for quick and ready insight. These are the neurons that are working when you don't know how you know, you just "know." These cells involved in helping you make snap decisions that are more than the flip of the coin. They come from judgment stored, but rarely accessed. Von Economo neurons are larger than most neurons and contain chemicals involved in social bonds, the expectation of reward, and detecting danger.

Mirror Neurons work all day, every day, in many ways you may not have noticed, for example:

- Seeing your child get a shot causes the parent to wince
- Watching a close partner handle a stressful conversation can cause your blood pressure to rise
- Seeing a bicyclist zoom down a hill will elevate your heart rate and give you a feeling of alertness and possibly even a mirrored endorphin jolt
- Helping an injured person can cause you to hold your own body as if it were injured
- Seeing a colleague win a deal activates your success and reward pathways, too

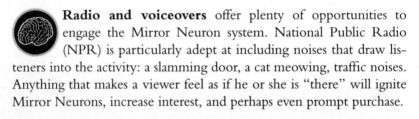 **Radio and voiceovers** offer plenty of opportunities to engage the Mirror Neuron system. National Public Radio (NPR) is particularly adept at including noises that draw listeners into the activity: a slamming door, a cat meowing, traffic noises. Anything that makes a viewer feel as if he or she is "there" will ignite Mirror Neurons, increase interest, and perhaps even prompt purchase.

This chapter introduces bright new research on the Mirror Neuron system. These specialized neurons are the markers of **great empathy** in humans and stimulate a "monkey see, monkey do" effect. Oftentimes, these neurons fire in the brain simply by watching, reading, or even thinking about an action. In the same way a yawn spreads around the conference room, think of the many ways you can use action and emotion to ignite the Mirror Neuron system in your consumer's minds and bring them subconsciously straight into the experience of your brand or product.

PART 2

ENGAGING
THE BUYING BRAIN

Source: NeuroFocus, Inc.

CHAPTER 10

NEUROMARKETING MEASURES AND METRICS

At the end of this chapter, you'll know and be able to use the following:
- The three primary NeuroMetrics used to assess the neurological effectiveness of stimuli, and how they combine to deliver an Overall Effectiveness Score
- The three Market Performance Indicators that are derived from the primary NeuroMetrics
- Why the Deep Subconscious Response methodology is such a powerful tool to identify and quantify brand attributes

In the chapters that follow, I am going to take you on an unprecedented tour into the five major areas of neuromarketing practice at NeuroFocus: brands, products, packaging, advertising, and in-store marketing.

In doing so, we are going to have many chances to talk about a toolkit of metrics—we call them NeuroMetrics—that we have developed to better understand how our brains process and respond to all these aspects of marketing. These NeuroMetrics represent the building blocks of our business and, as such, I would like to introduce them to you here.

My purpose is not to get into a deeply scientific discussion. I assume you are not a neuroscientist, nor do you want to become one just to understand how neuromarketing works. But, I do want you to appreciate that a tremendous amount of scientific effort has gone into the formulation and development of these metrics, and that they are based on established procedures, principles, and findings that have been honed in research labs around the globe and published in some of the most prestigious peer-reviewed journals in the world.

NeuroFocus has developed three primary NeuroMetrics, three derived NeuroMetrics, and one summary NeuroMetric. The primary NeuroMetrics measure *Attention, Emotional Engagement,* **and** *Memory*. The three derived NeuroMetrics measure *Purchase Intent/Persuasion, Novelty,* **and** *Awareness/ Understanding/Comprehension*. The summary NeuroMetric we simply call *Effectiveness.*

We are also going to discuss a more general methodology that you will encounter in the next few chapters: our *Deep Subconscious Response* (DSR) methodology.

We are developing new NeuroMetrics and methodologies all the time. These are the foundational elements underlying the work and insights I am going to share with you in the following chapters.

ATTENTION

The first question clients ask me about their ads or movie trailers or products on the shelf is: Are people noticing us? And this is exactly the right question to ask, because attention is the starting point of all marketing.

The brain is actually pretty amenable to letting you know when it is paying attention—provided you know where (and when) to look. As I've described in earlier chapters, the brain operates largely through electrical activity. As different clusters of neurons fire in unison, they create measurable electrical brainwaves at consistent frequencies. These electrical waves are the literal mechanisms of communication among regions of the brain. Electrical activity begins at particular frequencies; this excites other neurons, and the brain is soon humming along with coordinated patterns of oscillating electrical rhythms within and between different regions. All this activity shows up at the scalp and is picked up by our EEG sensors. Powerful analytical algorithms then process and decompose these signals into their constituent parts, and the logic of the brain's operations is revealed.

Attention is a fundamental function of the brain and produces a distinctive pattern of brainwave activity. Our Attention NeuroMetric is based on the moment-to-moment fluctuations of these brainwave patterns. The result is a relative measure that tracks how Attention waxes and wanes on a subsecond-by-subsecond basis.

People know when they are paying attention to something. They are actively "thinking about it." However, people do not have access to the predecessor processes that lead up to Attention. In other words, we don't know when we're about to become attentive to something, so we often don't know what stimulus has just caused us to begin paying attention. Only a brain-based NeuroMetric can pinpoint precisely what aspect of a message triggered Attention.

EMOTIONAL ENGAGEMENT

Emotional Engagement, like Attention, can **wax and wane** over time. Although our conscious perceptions of emotion feel consistent, at a subconscious level our brains are constantly updating our emotional engagement with the world around us.

So Emotion, too, as we measure it, is a moment-by-moment phenomenon.

Our Emotional Engagement NeuroMetric primarily tracks emotional arousal. This is the tendency of our brains and nervous systems to be more or less activated by the stimuli we come in contact with. Other words often used as synonyms for arousal are excitation, excitement, stimulation, or intensity of experience. These emotions are fundamental precursors of intentions, attitudes, decisions, and behaviors.

For stimuli like TV and print ads, or displays in a grocery store, Emotional Engagement represents **the connection we feel** toward what we are experiencing at a moment in time. How this connection plays out over time (is it consistently rising? consistently falling? fluctuating up and down?) is a key indicator of how a person is reacting to an unfolding story or message.

Emotional Engagement at this critical level is well below the threshold of conscious awareness. It is influencing our behavior in ways we cannot consciously track. If we did, we would react so slowly to the world that we would be at risk in a hostile environment like our ancestral homes. If a diligent market researcher tries to extract an articulated expression of Emotional Engagement, what he or she will get is a supposition or rationalization of that Engagement. The person having the emotion would be guessing just as much as the questioner! As many of our clients tell us, this is not the kind of data they want to rely on to make multimillion dollar decisions.

MEMORY

Memory is the third fundamental building block of responses to commercial stimuli, especially marketing messages in all their forms. It's obvious that if you can't remember it, it cannot influence you later on when you are in a buying situation.

Memory is one of the most deeply studied aspects of the brain in action. The mechanisms and structures by which the brain engages in both memory *encoding* and memory *retrieval* have been closely mapped and analyzed. As with Attention and Emotion, these Memory processes generate consistent and measurable brainwave patterns that indicate when memory processing is active. Researchers have been able, for example, to measure brainwaves during a memorization task and, by looking at those brainwaves only, predict with excellent accuracy the success or failure of a later effort to recall the memorized task.

Our Memory NeuroMetric builds on this research to identify markers of Memory activity as a person watches a message or engages in a consumer experience.

Memory comes in many shapes and forms, and although you would expect that a memory could only influence a person if he or she were aware of it, in fact the situation is much more interesting. There is a well-documented phenomenon called **implicit memory** that enables memories to influence attitudes, decisions, and behaviors without entering conscious thought. So measuring the likelihood that a persistent Memory has been formed at the moment of encoding is often the only way to determine whether that memory might have a later effect. Only a NeuroMetric indicator can identify such a memory-encoding event.

PURCHASE INTENT/PERSUASION

We now come to our three derived NeuroMetrics. Each of these can be thought of as being derived from a combination of two of the primary NeuroMetrics.

How can I possibly be so bold as to claim we can measure purchase intent? Every marketer knows that there are innumerable "intervening variables" between watching an ad and making a purchase. The answer is not so mysterious; it has to do with the concept of a **predictor variable** in contrast to an **explanatory variable**.

What we have found after analyzing thousands of ads and other marketing messages, including our ongoing program of analyzing messages that we *know* worked or didn't work in the marketplace (because our clients have shared their marketplace experience with us) is that a combination of two of our primary NeuroMetrics—**Emotional Engagement** and **Memory**—produce an extremely sensitive predictor of marketplace success. We know that a combination of Emotion and Memory while watching an ad does not *cause* someone to go out and buy a product. That would be what we call "the zombie reaction," and we know that normal brains don't operate that way. But we do know that high scores on our Emotional Engagement and Memory Activation NeuroMetrics do tend to be *associated* with increased purchasing. Thus, we can help our clients predict purchase behavior using this metric, even if we can't fully explain exactly why it works the way it does.

This is not to say that we don't have some ideas about why it works. Think about how an ad can make you more inclined to buy a product. If the ad is highly engaging, you are more likely to remember it. If your brain gets emotionally involved whenever you see the ad, and you reinforce your memory network for this product or brand every time the ad appears, is it so surprising that you might be more inclined to purchase the product the next time you have an opportunity to do so? You see the product on the shelf, this triggers the memory of the ad, that memory triggers the feeling of emotional engagement, and you say, "what the heck, let's give it a try."

Sometimes we call this NeuroMetric Persuasion rather than Purchase Intent, mostly when we are talking about a message that is not trying to drive a purchase. For example, in the broadcasting business a TV spot may be aimed at encouraging you to watch a particular show. No purchase is intended, but there is a definite persuasion attempt going on. We find that measuring Emotional Engagement and Memory during the spot is a good predictor of whether or not you will actually watch that show when it comes on.

Because it is composed of two moment-to-moment metric components, Purchase Intent/Persuasion itself has the useful property of being a moment-to-moment measure as well as a summary measure. This can be crucially important for pinpointing not only the overall persuasiveness of an ad, but the key moments in the ad that contribute most to that persuasiveness, and other moments that contribute least.

NOVELTY

The brain loves novelty, as we have seen, and advertisers and marketers often want to know if their message is perceived as novel or just as "more of the same." Millions of dollars may ride on the answer.

We have found that novelty can be inferred from a particular combination of the primary NeuroMetrics Attention and Memory. In explaining this metric, I often ask my audience to imagine a monkey swinging happily through the trees. Suddenly the monkey spots a new plant with a new kind of fruit hanging from it. The fruit may represent a new source of nutrition that could have great survival value for the monkey and his monkey troop. To take advantage of that new food source, he has to first notice it (pay attention) when he sees it, and second, he has to remember where he saw it. So it is not surprising that novel stimuli activate both attention and memory when people experience them.

Novelty is a valuable end in itself, and we suspect it is also a contributing ingredient in other aspects of responding to an ad or marketing message.

Novelty contributes to interest, surprise, and attraction, and can even contribute to a decision to purchase.

Novelty in advertising and messaging needs to be monitored over time, because novelty is a perishable good. Anything, no matter how original and unique at first, becomes familiar and commonplace over time. Advertisers need to know when novelty turns into boredom and ultimately into irritation, if they want to keep their messages fresh and interesting in the minds of their consumers. (This represents another advantage that neurological testing provides to advertisers: The ability to measure with explicit accuracy the habituation or "wear-in/wear-out" factor involved with television advertising.)

As with *Persuasion*, *Novelty* measurement can fluctuate on a moment-to-moment basis. It tells you not only an overall score for Novelty, but also which moments in an ad or message are most or least novel across the full experience.

AWARENESS/UNDERSTANDING/ COMPREHENSION

If I am an advertiser, I definitely want to know if my ad is Persuasive and Novel. But just as importantly, I want to know if people understand it. Do they comprehend the message? Is that message crystal clear or cloudy in its delivery? Are they confused or did they possibly misunderstand my message altogether? There's a NeuroMetric for that.

Understanding and Comprehension, we have found, are predictable from a combination of the primary NeuroMetrics Attention and Emotional Engagement. Why is this so? To illustrate this relationship when I am speaking to an audience, I often ask the audience members to try to recall the most illuminating lecture they ever heard in college, the one that really turned on the proverbial light bulb above their heads. What caused that lecture to imbue them with Understanding and Comprehension? Usually, it was because the lecture was emotionally engaging and captured your attention. The most profound lectures held my attention like a laser beam, and the professor was able to engage me emotionally in a way that made it impossible to look away. The net effect is deep and sustained understanding.

We have found in case after case that message Understanding is correlated with a combination of Attention and Emotion. We have fine-tuned that relationship in a formula, and today we can predict with great accuracy the degree of Understanding any ad or marketing message can achieve.

Awareness is also a moment-to-moment metric, allowing us to identify not just if a message achieves clarity, but exactly when it fails to do so as well. For messaging that depends on getting a clear message across, such information is invaluable.

EFFECTIVENESS

Our summary NeuroMetric, **Effectiveness**, is derived simply as a linear combination of the three primary NeuroMetrics. Since these three are already combined in the derived NeuroMetrics, these latter metrics are implicitly included in the equation as well (see Figure 10.1).

Figure 10.1
NeuroMetrics: Attention, Emotion, Memory
Purchase Intent, Novelty, Awareness, and Overall Effectiveness.

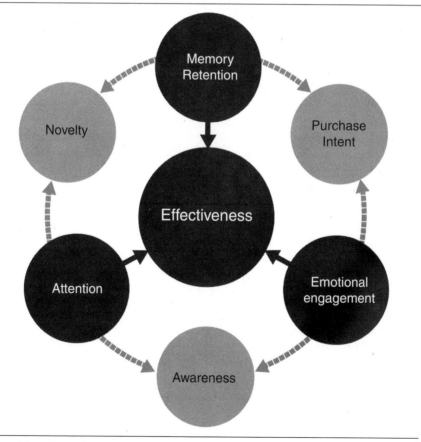

Source: NeuroFocus, Inc.

The exact equation that generates our Effectiveness NeuroMetric is, of course, a closely guarded secret, much like the Google Page Rank algorithm or the legendary Coca-Cola formula. But, as in both those cases, the value of the formula is apparent in its power to differentiate one result from another—for Google, a superior page ranking and for Coke, an unforgettable flavor. For NeuroFocus, the value of our Effectiveness metric is in its performance. It is a precise indicator and reliable predictor that is completely language-neutral and directly calculated from real-time brainwave measurements.

In the chapters that follow, you will see many examples of how these NeuroMetrics have revealed truths and insights that were previously inaccessible by traditional research techniques.

DEEP SUBCONSCIOUS RESPONSE METHODOLOGY

Our patented **Deep Subconscious Response** methodology is a clever use of a before-and-after Event Related Potential (ERP) design to compare precisely how a given experience, like watching an ad or engaging in a customer experience like using a product, affects the brain's receptivity to, or resonance with, a given process or design.

In a nutshell, what we do is first get a "baseline" measure of how receptive a person is to a set of concepts provided by the client. Then we **have the subject engage in an experience** like watching an ad or eating a food product. Next, we measure their receptivity to the concepts again after the experience. If a concept is reinforced by the experience, the "after" effect will be greater than the "before" effect—the subject will be more receptive to the concept and its association with the brand or product included in the experience. If, on the other hand, the concept is not reinforced by the experience, its "after" effect will be either the same or, in some cases, even less than the "before" effect.

Note that this is not a moment-to-moment measure, but rather **a summary impact measure.** Importantly, this task is entirely implicit. We never ask a single question. We take a snapshot, in effect, at two points in time, and measure the differences between the two. Since the only thing different between the "before" and "after" snapshot is the experience, we can attribute changes in the measures to the direct, subconscious impact of the experience itself.

Using this methodology, clients can rank-order concepts in terms of their affinity with a product or brand experience and determine which concepts are most associated with the experience and which are least associated.

As with our other techniques, a major strength of this methodology is that it is completely nonverbal and references true subconscious processes, not verbal reenactments or rationalizations. We have found this tool to be quite robust and able to tease out significant differences among concepts that on the surface might appear indistinguishable. Furthermore, we have found that applying the results of the **Deep Subconscious Response** methodology to new message copy can lead to large and surprising behavioral results. You will see some examples of this in the coming chapters.

PUTTING IT ALL TOGETHER

In the following chapters, I take you on a guided tour of the five major categories of NeuroFocus research.

We start out with Brands. Here you will meet the Brand Essence Framework. You will see how our suite of NeuroMetrics can be used to identify and classify the seven key dimensions of a brand: Form, Function, Feelings, Values, Benefits, Metaphors, and Extensions.

Then we will visit Products and see how our methodology can be used to highlight the **Neurological Iconic Signature** of a product consumption experience. Here we use both moment-to-moment and before-and-after metrics to chart out the implicit, subconscious meaning of a product, to determine how the product can best be expressed and marketed.

The next stop is Packaging, where we will see how eye-tracking and Deep Subconscious Response metrics can be combined to **understand where and how a package design** is working, and not working for communicating the essential features of the product within. We will also see how well a package attracts attention in the critical task of achieving shelf "pop out" and noticeability.

In the next chapter, we visit the In-Store experience to see how our metrics and measures illuminate the world of shopping and point-of-sale merchandising. Here we will see some new measures in action, including "walk around" in-store research methods and a unique alternative to Virtual Reality testing we call Video Realistic™ analysis.

Next, we take a detailed tour of Advertising. Here all the NeuroMetrics— primary, derived, and Deep Subconscious Response—are brought to bear to identify the strengths and weaknesses of various advertising concepts, strategies, executions, and mediums.

Finally, we take you into some related territory to share some path-breaking research we have done on how the whole marketing/messaging experience is subtly, and sometimes not so subtly, impacted by exposure on different sized screens—from large flat-screen high definition TVs to desktop/laptop computer monitors to the miniscule real estate of your cell phone or other mobile device's screen. Here we will see how our NeuroMetrics and related measures can be used to reveal surprising ways in which size really does matter. We will also see how neuromarketing can illuminate what happens to the brain as we engage with social media. Like our brains, social media is an entire world of communications and responses, all interconnected by a pulsating web of electrical signals.

With the great neuroscience and marketing teams I have been fortunate to surround myself with at NeuroFocus, and the world-class clients we partner with, our development of new metrics and measurement techniques is a never-ending process. It seems that every metric spawns an idea for two more, and every combination of metrics opens up an opportunity for delving deeper into the intricacies of how the human brain interacts with the flood of commercial stimuli it finds itself swimming in every day.

It is a "deep dive into the subconscious" that we enjoy taking each and every time we are privileged to do so.

CHAPTER 11

THE CONSUMER JOURNEY

At the end of this chapter, you'll know and be able to use the following:
- The seven steps that comprise the Consumer Journey Framework
- How it can be used to help marketing campaigns migrate consumers along a path
- How creative teams can use it to understand which components of the Brand Essence Framework to utilize for maximum effectiveness

A FRAMEWORK OF FRAMEWORKS

Throughout this part of the book I introduce a number of frameworks—nine to be precise—that we have developed at NeuroFocus to make sure that we are considering all relevant aspects of the various consumer "experiences" we study with our NeuroMetric measures. You can think of these frameworks as checklists of attributes or features that need to be considered to understand the full array of ways in which consumers can interact everyday with brands, products, packages, ads, and shopping.

To provide a bit of a preview, here are all nine frameworks we will be introducing in this and later chapters, what they refer to, and where to find them.

1. **Consumer Journey Framework:** how consumers relate to brands and products through usage and experience ... **p. 114**
2. **Brand Essence Framework (BEF):** the key attributes and features of a brand that makes it neurologically successful or not ... **p. 121**
3. **Total Consumer Experience (TCE) Framework**: how people interact with products as an embodied multisensory experience ... **p. 137**
4. **New Product Effectiveness Framework**: the key attributes of a new product that will determine its likely success or failure in the marketplace ... **p. 143**

113

5. **Pricing Framework:** the two dimensions used to determine optimal pricing ... **p. 151**
6. **Bundling Framework:** useful for analyzing the neurological effects of bundling options ... **p. 153**
7. **Packaging Effectiveness Framework:** the key attributes of a package ... **p. 157**
8. **Shopper Experience Framework**: the key attributes of an in-store shopping experience ... **p. 173**
9. **Advertising Effectiveness Framework**: the key elements of advertising that can be measured only by NeuroMetric techniques, not by people's self-reports or articulated responses ... **p. 193**

THE CONSUMER JOURNEY FRAMEWORK

The first framework I'd like to introduce you to is called the Consumer Journey. This framework helps us understand the phases of product or brand affinity in the consumer's mind. We have used it to measure and evaluate the impact of several types of marketing and advertising. Simply put, any consumer marketing effort has the purpose of migrating the consumer along a path or journey, and, therefore, should be measured using the appropriate NeuroMetrics for that step in the process. The framework can also be used to guide creative teams on what elements of the Brand Essence Framework to utilize to develop the most effective creative to accomplish this migration. We developed the Consumer Journey Framework based on our studies of advertising and interactive experiences among a variety of categories that successfully accomplished this migration.

The Consumer Journey Framework comprises seven steps:
1. Awareness
2. Information
3. Inquiry
4. Consideration
5. Purchase
6. Enjoyment
7. Advocacy

Awareness: Awareness is the first prerequisite for the Consumer Journey. This stage is where the consumer becomes aware of a product, its brand, and its category. Such awareness can be created either in the deep subconscious mind, or in the conscious, accessible, rational state of mind of the consumer.

Creating Awareness in the subconscious mind of the consumer can be achieved in many ways. Advertising, incidental exposure in articles and entertainment programs, and interactive marketing experiences are just some of the obvious ways to create Awareness.

Information: This is the point in the Consumer Journey where information about the brand, product, or service is **"pushed" to the consumer.** This information is not being requested by the consumer, but is being made available and accessible by the product or brand provider. Effective presentation of information is not about overloading the consumer with facts and figures, but basically providing the context and the associations inherent in the product landscape that makes them want to know more. The purpose of providing this level and type of information is to create in the consumer's mind a desire or need to know more. The purpose of Information is not so much to create purchase intent but basically to amplify on the Awareness already gained and nudge the consumer gently into wanting to know more.

Inquiry: Inquiry is a two-way process, primarily initiated by the consumer. This is the natural next stage after Information, in which the consumer begins instigating a discovery process to know more. This is the phase of the journey where the motivational need-to-know is transformed into a quest for facts and reason. It is very possible that the consumer has already made up his or her mind to acquire the product or service, and is engaged in a rational process of marshaling facts and figures to justify a decision that has already been made.

Inquiry is a consumer-initiated process, but it also provides an opportunity for the marketer to present facts and rationale that slake this thirst for information that is initiated by the consumer.

Consideration: This is the step in the Consumer Journey just prior to purchasing. This is where the consumer, after having Inquired, is now actively **considering** *purchasing* **the product,** and in doing so actively compares and considers the product or service to its possible alternatives.

To the extent you can facilitate and make the process of consideration easy and "tilted" toward your product, you are able to create a sense of goodwill and a sense of obligation deep in the subconscious mind of the consumer. When an insurance company, for example, helps consumers compare prices and other features readily, they are not only making an otherwise complicated process easy for the consumer, they are also displaying a core value that reinforces their brand image. Implicitly, they are communicating not only how they can ease the purchase process, but also how the consumer can expect the rest of the insurance coverage process to transpire as well.

In addition, they are creating a sense of goodwill and an implicit obligation in the mind of the consumer. **It is hard to say no** to somebody who took the effort to make it easier for you to compare and contrast products. This sense of obligation and goodwill in the deep subconscious mind of the consumer translates into loyalty and a willingness to be flexible with price.

Purchase: This is the most important and vital part of the Consumer Journey because this is where **the first interaction** with the brand or product/service offering actually happens. It is important to note that however wonderful the product or service is, the act of parting with money during a purchase is an implicitly painful process within the consumer's mind. In fact, brain-imaging studies have shown that brain activity during physical pain is similar to brain activity while spending money. To the extent that that pain can be minimized, it makes it easier for the consumer to appreciate the value of the product, and thereby justify the purchase.

As an example, stating that some percent of the proceeds will go to charity or another worthwhile cause enables the consumer to rationalize the act of purchasing in terms of providing pleasure and benefit to other people, thereby minimizing the pain in his or her own mind of parting with money. We have also found that at this stage of the Consumer Journey the pleasure of enjoying the product is "calculated" implicitly by the consumer, and must achieve a value that overcomes the implicit pain of the transaction if the purchase is to occur. Accordingly, an effective purchasing experience must overcome the transaction pain, for example, by communicating how close the consumer is to enjoying the product and deriving value from it.

When consumers bring a product up to the cash register and get ready to part with their cash, a neurologically-savvy management of this step in their journey will **remind them** once again of the enjoyment and the pleasure they are about to derive from this purchase. Doing this successfully not only facilitates the sale, but also provides another sense of emotional attachment in the mind of the consumer, who now feels more loyal and even thankful to the brand.

Enjoyment: This is where the consumer actively "consumes" and—you hope—enjoys your product. The consumer transports the package home, opens it, extracts the product, and begins the initial consumption experience. At this point, the consumer comes face-to-face for the first time with many aspects of the product and its package design that may not have been apparent before. Sometimes the product can be enjoyed straight out of the box, sometimes the product must be combined with other products to be enjoyed, and sometimes the product must be assembled to be enjoyed. In some occasions, there may be a set of rituals and/or a set of steps that must be taken in order to fully enjoy the product.

So **enjoyment of the product** requires the product provider to facilitate all aspects of these processes of usage, consumption, and enjoyment. As an example, if we look at how one enjoys wine, we can see the considerable effort winemakers have invested in teaching the general public how to successfully navigate a fairly subtle product enjoyment process. We can also see the important role of rituals and a sequence of sensory tasks that go into optimal enjoyment of the product.

Most modular furniture makers have difficulty in creating product enjoyment postpurchase, as the monumental task of taking the furniture home and assembling it can be frustrating and distressing for most consumers. It is equally distressing that many times the product is unavailable for enjoyment immediately after purchase, and must either be shipped or delivered to the consumer. Many computer makers have similar difficulty because the act of enjoying the product involves a level of assembly and connectivity that the consumer finds either frustrating or too hard to do. These are areas where **Enjoyment innovation could lead to big benefits.**

Ease of product enjoyment creates consumer loyalty to the product and to the underlying brand. Effective advertising needs to stimulate not only the purchase of the product, but also provide cues as to how it can be enjoyed once the product is acquired. We have observed in our research that strategically targeted and imaginatively executed advertising can facilitate a desire for immediate consumption and immediate enjoyment in the mind of the consumer.

Advocacy: This is the most "engaged" step in the Consumer Journey. It is also, not surprisingly, **the holy grail** of all product and marketing efforts. How can you get the consumer to talk about and actively advocate the product to friends, family, and peers? How can the consumer be brought to social networks, blogs, and other community groups to create extraordinary advocacy? Advocacy can trigger additional advocacy exponentially, and the viral power of such advocacy can create a tidal wave of consumer purchase intent. We have found that there are components of product design, interactive experience design, and advertising that create viral goodwill and a foundation for advocacy. Unleashing the raw power of social networks and associated advocacy in our connected society is critical to modern day marketing.

CHAPTER 12

THE BUYING BRAIN
AND BRANDS

At the end of this chapter, you'll know and be able to use the following:

- How brands can be measured precisely, accurately, and reliably across all of the seven critical dimensions of the Brand Essence Framework
- How that Framework can be applied to strengthen existing brands, significantly improve the success of brand extensions, and similarly enhance marketplace prospects for new brands
- How neurological testing provides previously unobtainable insights into and recommendations for core/critical brand elements including positioning and sponsorships

---

THE PROBLEM: UNKNOWABLE FEELINGS

At a recent marketing strategy meeting, one of our clients was reviewing his team's proposal for imagery for a brand relaunch. Spread out in front of him were four large mood boards with photos, images, logo concepts, and symbols. He is his company's Chief Marketing Officer, so a lot of people were in the room, anxiously awaiting his reaction. He viewed the mood boards for only a minute or two.

Then his fist pounded down on the table, punctuating his demand for answers.

"What does this have to do with my brand? How do you know this stuff has any relevance in the consumer's mind?" Each pound was accompanied by the scuffling of tabletop pens and phones—he was

(*continued*)

(*Continued*)

pounding that hard. The problem was no one had a really compelling answer to his questions.

For decades, brand managers and creative agencies have relied on a combination of their gut and consumer research to make multimillion dollar decisions about brand and marketing communications strategy. Sometimes the gut instinct is good, sometimes not. The research, however, has been asked to do something it simply cannot: provide precise, clear information about how a consumer genuinely *feels* about your brand on a deep, subconscious level. This is what our client was struggling with.

THE COMPLICATIONS

When our client was pounding his fist on the table, he was expressing his frustration that there were not clear and compelling indications of his brand's key attributes in each and every image and symbol he saw. Even more frustrating was that there was not complete agreement on what those brand attributes were in the mind of the consumer. There was some general agreement as to what his brand's key attributes were, and there were some disputed attributes. Plus, some hunches that there were **undiscovered** **attributes** that could expand their brand's reach into new markets. But, the traditional research had not brought clarity to this issue (again, because it could not access and measure at the deep subconscious level of the consumer's mind, where these brand attributes are formed and reside).

Your brand is the heart and soul of your business. Humans have a hardwired need to have relationships not only with other humans, but also with the functional and fun items and tools we use in our daily lives. The challenge is to present your brand as something your consumer can have and wants to have a long-term relationship with. **We love novelty and change,** but we also have a strong need for constancy and commitment. The brain has welldeveloped neural programs for connecting with the meaningful items in our lives. Learning and measuring the effects of these can provide guidelines for how you design, present, and communicate your brands to the people you want to reach.

From universal brands like Coca-Cola, to individual micro brands like your neighborhood coffee shop, the brands in our lives serve a vital human purpose: they give identity, meaning, and connectivity to our experiences and possessions. Humans have a basic need to organize our lives into the recognizable and the familiar. Learning about new things daily and constantly would quickly exhaust the mind. Yet the familiar can become the mundane. The recognizable can become the invisible. At what point does the brain thirst for a novel experience? To understand how and when this can happen, you must understand the foundational dimensions of your brand.

Foundational Brand Questions
- What is the deep, subconscious meaning of my brand in the consumer's mind?
- What is my true brand equity?
- How do I migrate agnostics to brand devotees?
- How do I track brand equity? How often should I track them?

THE BRAND ESSENCE FRAMEWORK—A FOUNDATION FOR NEUROBRANDING

There are many treatises written on brands: their archetypes, architecture, planning, strategy, and their activation. We have studied brands at the deep subconscious level across numerous categories, including automotive, financial services, fashion, health and beauty, Internet, consumer electronics, pharmaceutical, food and beverage, alcohol and spirits, fast moving consumer goods (FMCG), consumer packaged goods (CPG), retail, and many more. In each case, we studied what the brand managers believed the essence of the brand was and what the consumer's deep subconscious response to the brand was using the Deep Subconscious Response described earlier. Our observations of brands across categories have led us to decipher and reconstruct an explicit framework that operates both subconsciously and consciously in the human mind. We found a very consistent pattern that we have codified as the Brand Essence Framework.

We posit this Framework as the **core and foundation of neurobranding.** The Framework is easy to articulate and intuitive to understand. But at its core, it is the blueprint for gaining a deep and full understanding of how the brain creates brands at the subconscious level of the mind, and how to leverage that knowledge to strengthen existing brands, improve the performance of brand extensions, and create the most successful new brands.

The purpose of applying the Brand Essence Framework is to provide a very concrete way to build **brand passion**—a breathlessly romantic, yet thoughtfully loving relationship with the brand. Isn't it interesting that this complex relationship with the brand also mirrors our expectations in our lives with our significant others? In a way, this is a happy trade-off between the comforts and security of familiarity with a dash of novelty and newness to bring excitement into everyday life.

Of all the insights that neuroscience can bring to the business world, **this is perhaps the most powerful:** the ability to understand how a consumer truly connects various concepts about the brand at a deep subconscious level.

Importantly, the Brand Essence Framework can also be used to determine the effectiveness of both sponsored events and spokespeople. Both of these high-visibility corporate initiatives greatly influence how a Brand is received in the consumer's mind. For this reason, it's critically important to carefully match sponsored events and spokespeople with the objectives identified by the Brand Essence Framework. Using the Framework in the early stages of these campaigns ensures that the event or spokesperson reinforces the perception of the Brand in the marketplace.

When working to define a conceptual framework, it is wise to follow the brain's way of organizing the chaotic world we live in, from the specific/physical to the general/metaphorical. This seems to be the path the brain takes as it struggles to make sense of the world. It starts with the basic form of an object. Then it proceeds to larger and more abstract concepts. This is also how the brain comes to know your brand.

The Brand Essence Framework has **seven dimensions**. We define each dimension, provide examples of it, and explain its importance. Note that each dimension can be measured using a different combination of the NeuroMetric techniques outlined earlier, especially the Deep Subconscious Response methodology described in the last chapter.

Form: This is the physical manifestation of the brand. The **most tangible** sensory and physical connection the consumer has with the brand. In our testing, form attributes are deeply, but implicitly, recognized by consumers in their deep subconscious as being connected with the brand. We are biologically programmed to seek out and classify form. Yet, we may not be consciously aware that we are doing this. Many times we find that the formal elements consumers connect, recognize, and embrace in the brand are not easily described verbally, but can play a vital role in how the product is received, as we shall discuss later.

The formal elements of a brand that are more or less strongly connected in the subconscious might include logos, imagery, iconography, designs, and fonts associated with the brand. Connection could also be physical features of the product that include tangible elements, such as shape, size, capacity, color, or texture. Form includes not only visual elements, but also audio elements, such as tone, timbre, melody, beat, and harmonic qualities.

Think of the Form as the **face and voice of the brand.** In addition to the form attributes associated with the brand per se, it is also important to understand the form attributes of the *category* that seep into and become attributes of the *brand*. There is often a strong connection—brand and category—at the subconscious level. Therefore, it is important to ask three key questions:

1. What are the attributes of form that the consumer's subconscious mind connects to my *category*?
2. What are the attributes of form that the consumer's subconscious mind connects to my *brand*?
3. What are the attributes of form that the consumer's subconscious mind connects to my *competitors*?

The unique style lines and contours of the product personify the form attributes of some brands. A classic example is Porsche, which is personified by the unique styling of the front and the rear of the car. Gull-winged car doors scream Lamborghini, while the elongated hood, side coves, and quartet of round rear lights mark the distinctive styling of a Corvette. How long does it take one to recognize the unique shape of the bottle as belonging to brand Coke?

It is intriguing that the style of font can also serve to establish and represent iconic brands. While we can argue whether it is the color of the beverage, the condensation on the glass, or the bubbles at the very top that most quintessentially and best represent Coca-Cola, it is undeniable that the Spenserian Script of "Coca-Cola" does an instant and admirable job of representing Brand Coke. The choice of color and font (black and Spenserian Script) in the case of Coke Zero serves to represent it very well as a brand extension.

Since the individual formal elements of the brand that are connected in the subconscious mind of the consumer form the brand image, those elements are often the core protected intellectual property (IP) of the company. To that end, at the outset of neuromarketing research it is critical **to tease out the elements of Form** that are connected in the subconscious, and match those elements with the company's protected IP, trademarks, and copyrights to determine how best to protect them (and, ultimately, leverage them).

Here is something interesting we learned from our ongoing brand studies across numerous categories that has specific importance to the IP surrounding Apple. Brand Apple is represented not only by the Apple logo with a piece missing, but also by the distinctive candy-colored icon interface for the iPhone. We were surprised to find the strength of the subconscious connection of this user interface to the Apple brand. We are not surprised that Apple has filed appropriate intellectual property protections of this connection, which are now the subject of a legal issue between Apple and Nokia.

Function: The next dimension of the Brand Essence Framework is the function or functions provided by the brand in our daily life—not just any function, but those functions that are indispensable and unique to your brand. We emphasize *indispensable* as the critical distinguishing attribute for an important reason. In our testing on a variety of brands, the elements of Function that scored highest were the ones that consumers had at a deep subconscious level evaluated and rated as indispensable. These functional attributes provided a vital contribution to the identity of a brand.

Uniqueness is important because it differentiates the functions of the *brand* from the more generic functions of the *category*. The competitive differentiation of a brand, deep in the consumer's subconscious, provides the truest and most enduring barrier to consumer exit and competitive substitution.

In our testing of functionality, we have found it is important to distinguish between two categories, explicit and implicit:

Explicit Functionality: These are the Functions of the product that can be easily, and well, articulated by the consumer and implemented by the product designer. For an automobile, for example, explicit Functions include transportation and storage. But, in each case, NeuroMetrics can reveal a hierarchy in the consumer's mind—some explicit Functions clearly have greater personal resonance than others do. You need to be sure which Functions these are.

Implicit Functionality: These are the functions that the consumer finds valuable and indispensable, but **may not be able to articulate verbally,** or may be reluctant to articulate. For instance, for a family with children, the most important function of a DVD player in a car may be to provide babysitting on long distance trips, but parents may not be comfortable acknowledging this, as they may feel it reflects negatively on their parenting skills. But, it might still be an indispensable Function, one that might make the difference between purchasing one car over another.

As with Form, it is important to look at Function from three perspectives: your brand, your competitors' brands, and your category.

Feelings: These are the automatic emotional associations that arise at the mere thought or mention of the brand. They constitute the emotional archetype of the brand. Our testing across categories reveals that every well-known brand has a unique emotional identity in the deep subconscious. The activation of these feelings through appropriate in-store environments, aisle designs, and features and displays constitute implicit priming for the brand. Our tests have shown a measurable increase in Purchase Intent when the emotional archetype of a brand is displayed either through explicit or implicit priming.

Feelings can be thought of as a kind of **shorthand for a large network** of attributes and connections associated with a brand, including elements as diverse as facts, times, places, and people. Rather than requiring recall and a recitation of all the factors associated with a brand, the brain can just call up the summary Feeling that has been encoded from the larger underlying network. So, for example, the brain does not have to remember all the nutritional information associated with a product, it can simply access the good feeling it experienced when the nutritional information was examined. That Feeling then becomes an accessible shorthand summary of the nutritional information. It is important to understand the core feelings that have been tagged about the brand.

In exploring the landscapes of emotions associated with brands/products, I have found it useful to classify them under six broad categories:

1. Feelings associated with the **place, social setting,** and **occasion** of enjoying the brand/product
2. Feelings associated with the **act of preparing** to enjoy the brand/product
3. Feelings associated with **enjoying** the brand/product
4. Feelings associated **post enjoyment** of the brand/product (the "after-glow")
5. Feelings associated with the **larger cultural context** in which the brand/product plays a role
6. Feelings associated with the **live events** or **cycle of life** in which the brand/product plays a role

In each case, we gather the core emotions that could potentially be activated by the brand. This allows us to create a **comprehensive landscape of feelings** that are associated with the brand. Using the Deep Subconscious

Response technique, we can highlight a smaller subset of Feelings that represent the emotional core of the brand.

In considering Feelings, be sure to explore them from the three key perspectives: your brand, your competitors' brands, and your category.

Values: By Values, I mean the broader social and moral Values that a brand may be connected with, either explicitly or implicitly. Our studies of brands across categories has revealed that when brands resonate with a consumer's deep social, moral, or spiritual Values, the propensity for brand advocacy increases across both immediate and virtual social networks. Values strengthen the connection of feelings to brands. They reinforce and connect the brand to goals and objectives outside the self.

In exploring the particular values associated with a brand, it is important to note some Values endure over time, and others that become more or less prominent at different times. In our testing, we have found several categories of Values to be relevant to the essential character of specific brands: personal, spiritual, moral, communal, social, political economic, philosophical, historical, traditional, cultural, national, environmental, legal, or lifecycle-related.

Benefits: These are the personally meaningful rewards we expect to acquire by using brands. They are more general and run deeper than Functions. Benefits are usually articulated as statements and affirmations about what the brand can do for us, but they may be expressed implicitly as well. Our measurements across multiple brands reveal that stronger subconscious associations with particular Benefits tend to be correlated with the personal identity and Values of the consumer.

In fact, the Benefits of a Brand also serve as attributes consumers want others to know about them. For example, many of the benefits of Apple's iPad also serve as an aspirational description of the person who uses them. So the stylished and advanced technology of the iPad communicates to others that the user of the device is also "stylish" and "advanced." The iPad user has thus telegraphed important cues about how he'd like the world to see him, without ever having spoken a word.

In our studies, we have found the following categories of Benefits to stand out both implicitly and explicitly in associating a brand with a consumer's personal identity:

- Promoting physical beauty
- Representing intellectual accomplishment
- Improving sexual attractiveness
- Being fashionable and trendy
- Being "in the know," technically and intellectually advanced

- Achieving career and financial success
- Having pride in family and its accomplishments
- Being exclusive and elite
- Providing access to power and resources
- Reflecting genetic and racial pride
- Supporting uniqueness of personality

Metaphors: A metaphor is a larger-than-life concept that can be applied to an object—like a brand or product—with a paradoxical effect: even though it is not literally true, it somehow captures an essential quality of the object. For example, calling a truck "Ram-tough" is not a literal statement—how tough is a ram, anyway? But it represents an aspiration or ambition: it says this truck is dependable, strong, and stubbornly single-minded. Metaphors **often reveal larger than life expectations** that come to be consciously or subconsciously associated with a brand and its meaning to a consumer. The best brand Metaphors become synonymous with a promise or commitment made by the brand to the consumer. Our measurements reveal that the best communication strategies contain at their core a single Metaphor that is consistently presented and represented. The Metaphor stands for the brand ambition, which is to say, for a human ambition the brand embodies. These human ambitions provide the aspirational and inspirational architecture on which the brand builds its strategy. The Metaphor is **useless unless it is tangibly and consistently reinforced** through elements of the product, packaging, and communication design.

Not all Metaphors are positive, nor are they always generated internally by the branding team itself. We have found some Metaphors that were strongly associated with a brand *despite* the wishes of the branding team. We have found other Metaphors that the branding team did not even know were associated with their brands.

NeuroMetric measures like our Deep Subconscious Response technique are uniquely suited to identifying both implicit and explicit metaphorical associations with all kinds of brands. By focusing on how strongly a metaphor is implicitly activated after exposure to a brand, you can precisely measure the degree of association between the two. Given a choice of Metaphors to embed in an ad campaign, for example, implicit neurological measures can help you to determine whether a Metaphor connects naturally with a brand, or whether you are trying to "force-fit" an association that is unlikely to fit.

Extensions: The final dimension of the Brand Essence Framework is brand Extension. The consumer's brain may invite the brand to come and do more things, or it may not. How can you identify natural Extensions of the brand, those that will not produce an "expectancy violation" when compared to the core brand? Natural Extensions inherently make sense in the consumer's subconscious mind. Such natural Extensions are derived from implicit connections consumers make among any of the other dimensions of the Brand Essence. They may encompass Forms, Functions, Benefits, or other attributes of competitive brands as well as your own. Extending a brand is much more likely to result in success when the Extension is easily processed by your consumers, rather than requiring them to readjust their implicit associations to make a space for the new Extension.

Extensions can be achieved in many ways and forms. As we have measured brand Extensions across many categories, we found the most successful Extensions to utilize one of the following strategies:

1. **Functionality addition:** Extending a brand by adding functionality to it from observing how customers really use the brand, and the additional functions they perform with the brand
2. **Functionality merge:** Merging functionality from other brands, and, therefore, extending the brand by usurping functional territories previously owned by other brands
3. **Occasion merge:** Extending the brand by enlarging the number of occasions in which the brand is nominally used
4. **Interaction and interface merge:** Extending the brand by allowing it to combine and interact with other brands
5. **Technology merge:** Extending the brand by merging and integrating with related technologies
6. **Device merge:** Extending the brand by reducing the number of devices the consumer must carry, learn, and customize

The seven dimensions of the Brand Essence Framework encompass the entire spectrum of consumer experience of your brand. They truly represent the essence of your brand—the framework for your brand's identity and presence in the competitive marketplace.

Which of these dimensions are most important? Making a graphic of central dimensions as the brain interacts with your brand has, not surprisingly, **Feelings** are at the center (see Figure 12.1).

While the brain initially processes the simple, physical attributes of your brand, it quickly categorizes it based on extracted meaning primarily from the Emotions, Values, and Benefits of your brand.

Established Brands: Driving home the core feelings that consumers associate with your brand is key. What activates long-term memory for your brand?

Figure 12.1
The Brand Essence Framework Core and Outer Dimensions.

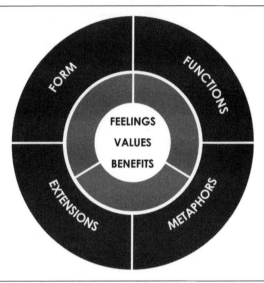

Source: NeuroFocus, Inc.

Is it the smell, the taste, a visual element? Focus on these so that the brain enjoys instantly placing this beloved friend in long-term memory repeatedly.

New Brands: Because a new brand is an unknown, focus on Benefits and Function if it is a new commodity brand and Benefits and Feelings if it is a new luxury brand.

Commodity Brands: Commodities should score highest on Form, Function, and Benefits. Commodities engage the brain on a practical level, stimulating a great deal of our rational cognitive processes. For commodity brands, the brain does not waste time evaluating nuances of style or engage in intensive neurological processes to assess how others in the social group would view the person using the brand. The brain asks, Is it useful? Practical? Does it meet my needs?

Luxury Brands: Luxury brands command premium pricing. In order for the brain to consider, rationalize, and commit to paying a high price, a great deal of *emotional* response is needed to enable the *rational* thought process that justifies such expenditure. Whether it's $25 for lip gloss, or $75,000 for a car, the brain must have a compelling emotion centered behind that purchase. Feelings, Values, and Metaphors are the brand attributes driving emotion. These must be strong to overcome the subconscious' initial reluctance/resistance related to price and facilitate a purchase decision.

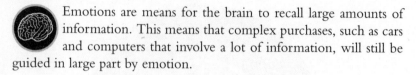 Emotions are means for the brain to recall large amounts of information. This means that complex purchases, such as cars and computers that involve a lot of information, will still be guided in large part by emotion.

APPLE

An exploration of the brain and a compelling brand often ends up with the Apple story. Why is Apple such a beloved brand? Is it because of its elegant logo? Its pretty colors? Its proprietary, tightly held operating system? It's all of these and more. Apple made an innately strategic decision a long time ago to help the brain do what it loves to do: identify and categorize. Apple focused on consumer ease of use, inherent fear/distrust of complicated and, therefore, intimidating technology, and designed beautiful products and packaging, which in turn gave the Apple brand enhanced meaning and an even stronger, consistent, and lasting identity. Apple also strictly controlled distribution, giving their product an identity that was separate from other computer brands. And they adhered to price points above the category norms, imbuing the brand and the products under that umbrella with the aura of desirability.

It didn't hurt that they chose a universally recognized symbol of the natural world—friendly, delicious, attractive, and organic, that could be stylized and still retain its subconscious attributes—as their logo.

What sets Apple apart is this beautifully consistent brand strategy, where every consumer touchpoint expresses the same brand attributes, making it delightfully easy for the brain to assign meaning and significance to this brand. The effect on the subconscious is near irresistible, and the price is "justified" as reasonable because it's such a clear, direct, consistent reflection of inherent value.

Context has a huge impact on how the brain processes an experience. Apple understands this, especially in their retail operations. If you shop a store aisle, where everything is piled up or kept in bins, your takeaway is a perception that all is cheap. Implicitly, if it's of value it won't be piled up in the corner. On the other hand, this can also work to some brands' advantage; a bargain retailer deliberately stacks things up to give you the view that you are getting a deal.

For luxury brands, of course, the opposite is the case. When you go to a Rolex store, your watch is displayed in a locked case. And when they bring it to you, they polish it and present it on an elegant padded case. The unspoken but clearly communicated message is that this brand is inherently precious, highly valued, and valuable, and, therefore, worth the price. The feeling of desire is actually heightened by this air of exclusivity, reinforcing the individual elements of Rolex's Brand Essence Framework.

Context for a Brand

How important is context to the brain? Just how important is revealed in a fascinating experiment involving a violin and the Washington, DC, subway:

One cold, winter morning in Washington, DC, a solitary violinist played Bach and Schubert for about 45 minutes in the corner of a Metro subway station.

About 1,000 people walked past him as he played. Every few minutes, a person might stop for a moment or toss in a dollar or two. Other than that, no one paid much attention to the violinist.

One young person stopped, very curious. He tried to stay, but his mother pulled him along. He was three years old.

After 45 minutes, the violinist packed up his instrument. No one applauded, no one spoke to him, and no one noticed his departure.

His take? $32.

The violinist was Joshua Bell, one of the world's most famous musicians. He played on his Stradivarius, one of the finest (and most rare and expensive) violins in existence. The previous night, Joshua Bell had played to a sold-out concert in Boston where the seats averaged $100.

The *Washington Post* organized the experiment as a study in context, perception, and priorities. The results speak for themselves.

Note that one of the people who was most interested in listening to Joshua was a child. As we mature, our brains learn to categorize an experience based on context. Children are less prone automatically to assign meaning to an experience based on context, and are able to perceive that some wonderful music was to be heard, despite the subway platform setting. For the adults, in that context Joshua Bell playing in the Washington, DC subway was worth $32. In contrast, in another context, Joshua Bell performing at Boston's Symphony Hall was worth approximately $220,000.

Humans develop the frontal lobe well into our 20s. Frontal lobe development enables contextual processing.

So what? So, because teenagers and young adults' brains are still developing until their 20s, greater care must be taken to develop brands and brand messaging that take that malleable state of mind into full consideration.

Let's get back to our client who pounded the table about mood boards. He was seeking symbols that expressed his brand's best attributes. How can a symbol embody so much meaning and emotion? Some symbols become so iconic that they can single-handedly impact an experience to a significant degree. Let's explore one such symbol, the ultimate international logo of competitive sports, the Olympic Rings.

During the 2008 Olympics, there was the usual onslaught of high-profile advertising, with a coterie of top brands paying substantially for the privilege of being an official Olympic sponsor. At a price tag of $40 million, such Olympic sponsorship was a global strategic marketing play and a huge investment, but one for which there was little means of directly, accurately, and reliably measuring any resulting brand lift.

NeuroFocus conducted a DSR study to tease out the potential impact of Olympic sponsorship on consumers' subconscious perceptions of brand image, versus the effect that only running advertising during the Games had for other brands. The Olympic brand itself has a brand essence, with "Achieve" being the leading attribute we studied.

The result: We found clearly **stronger brand lift** for ads by official Olympic sponsors compared to ads by nonsponsors. Our findings finally confirmed, in scientifically valid statistics, what earlier conventional research had only been able to intimate.

How does a brand develop such deeply resonating symbols? The Olympic Rings have been in use since 1920. Almost 100 years of exposure has been a significant factor in this symbol's ability to evoke a deep response. Other than decades of use, how do you develop a logo and brand symbology that the brain likes to remember and become attached to?

THE RESOLUTION: THE SYMBOLOGY OF A BRAND

To help our table-thumping client and save his fist (and the furniture) from further abuse, we devised a study to find out which of the myriad symbols on his mood board resonated deeply with his consumer base. The problem that he had faced was the **inability of traditional research to uncover clear consumer preferences.**

This is an ever-present and critical issue in marketing. There are two obstacles to perfectly predicting consumer behavior through traditional means. First, conventional methodologies cannot provide the same level of scientifically precise information about how and what consumers notice, feel, and remember, and what will motivate them to action, as neurological testing can.

Second, we don't have perfect information about events that will happen in the future that will impact behavior. Fortunately, for the human race, we cannot and likely will never be able to predict behavior perfectly all the time. Thank goodness we can't—life is much more interesting this way. However, we can use neuroscience to get closer to the truth of how people will feel and behave prospectively. That's what we did for this client and the following is how we did it.

Brand Essence Study Synopsis

This particular brand is in the insurance field, a category with its own challenges. Consumers are averse to change and value security and trust above most other attributes. This is how the brand had appealed to their consumer base: as a very secure and trustworthy caretaker of one's money and well-being. But their focus group findings hinted that there might be other attributes that consumers associated with this brand, attributes that were more personal and friendly than just security and safety. Even more important, several people who were close to the pulse of the consumer, especially the Chief Marketing Officer, had a gut feeling that this was true. But there wasn't enough clarity or organizational alignment to move forward with a high degree of assurance into this new territory.

"Let's do a neuroscientific study of our consumer's reactions to these mood boards. And let's do it in five key markets around the world," our client decreed. Two weeks later, we did just that. We found that in addition to "safe" and "secure," consumers associated "friendly" and "supportive" on a deep, subconscious level with this international brand.

This was a huge finding. Because it was **determined neurologically,** by extracting information captured and processed at the precognitive stage, there was strong corporate alignment with the research results, and these additional attributes were featured in all marketing campaigns going forward. Understanding that "friendly" and "supportive" were strong brand attributes allows this company to construct strategies, select symbols and imagery, and formulate language that are better synchronized with consumers' true, but unarticulated (and inarticulable!) core feelings about this brand.

Takeaways:
- The seven dimensions of the Brand Essence Framework
- Key neurological best practices for brand positioning and marketing
- Context is critical for the formation and recognition of brand identity at the subconscious level

CHAPTER 13

THE BUYING BRAIN AND PRODUCTS

At the end of this chapter, you'll know and be able to use the following:

- The specific processes that the subconscious goes through when a product is consumed or experienced
- How the neurological high points of those processes can be extracted and leveraged for maximum product design, performance, and marketing effectiveness
- How to apply neurological testing to significantly improve the success rates and avoid the potential pitfalls of new product introduction
- How to determine the appropriate price for a product and the bounds of price elasticity and reasonability within the deep subconscious mind of the consumer
- How the principals of product feature bundling work from a neuroscientific point of view

---

THE PROBLEM: ALTERING A "SURE THING"

The Brand Manager and the head of Consumer Insights sat across the conference table from me. In between, atop the polished mahogany, sat their product.

The Brand Manager explained, "We already know what the top attractors are—what we'd like to get is additional data on how our customers would respond if we alter the formulation." The confidence

---

(*Continued*)

in her voice bespoke her long tenure at the helm of this well-known brand. "Slightly," she added, with a note of reassurance for my benefit, I guessed. "We're not going to mess with a sure thing."

"Well, we know from *focus groups* what the attractors are," the Consumer Insights chief quickly interjected. "But you're saying the test you do may produce something else?"

That conversation from 3 weeks before now rang in my mind as I sat across a different table in a different room with these same two executives. This time, what lay before us was a stack of paper.

"Your research has pegged the consistency as the key trigger of consumer satisfaction," I offered. "There's very little variation in the studies you gave us. They convey just what you told me in our first meeting."

There wasn't much reaction from my small audience. No wonder—I was confirming what they already knew.

Or so they thought.

"But we found something different."

As the lights dimmed, the image of an iconic consumer brand glowed on the wall screen.

THE PROBLEM: THE PRODUCT INSIDE THE BRAIN

The brain has a seemingly endless supply of surprises in store for us. Even when logic and experience and, yes, traditional consumer research tell us convincingly that something is true, the brain may know differently. So we ask it. Because it doesn't volunteer that information—the deep-seated data residing in our subconscious has to be sought out, in true scientific fashion, with true scientific rigor and standards.

But, you can't just put a NeuroCap on someone and wait for the brain to reveal its secrets—you have to prompt it, trigger it, and cause it to react to a specific stimulus. Only then does the brain talk back to you about what it really thinks, feels, and remembers. Only then do you discover what consumers really notice . . . what they genuinely feel . . . and what they hold onto in their memories about your product.

CAPTURING THE TOTAL CONSUMER EXPERIENCE

When we test products for clients, we get the brain talking with something we call the Total Consumer Experience (TCE). This is such a powerful and versatile neuromarketing tool that I'm going to go into some detail about it. The TCE measures a consumer's brainwave activity step-by-step as he or she approaches and proceeds with the consumption or other use of a specific product. The TCE measures a test subject's subconscious responses to anything the five senses can register. So it's applicable to virtually any consumer product.

The Total Consumer Experience is a methodological framework with which we measure the consumer's brain responses as they continuously interact with the product. It literally measures the **totality** of the consumer's interaction—all the way from examining the package to enjoying the product.

Its value lies in helping companies identify the Neurological Iconic Signatures (NIS) that are the highpoint of their interaction with the product. Emphasizing these peak moments tends to increase both sales and consumption of the product. Activating the NIS at the point of sale increases purchase. In addition, ads that focus on the NIS score higher in both Purchase Intent and overall Effectiveness than ads that do not feature the NIS.

TOTAL CONSUMER EXPERIENCE FRAMEWORK

Typically, a TCE comprises the following steps:
1. Visual examination of the package
2. Handling the package with the anticipation of product use
3. Extracting the product from the package
4. The multisensory perception of the first moment of contact with the product
5. Multisensory neurological perceptions and responses as the product is consumed
6. Either enjoying the product for a second time or putting the product away
7. Postproduct consumption rituals/bliss

As we measure the brain's response through this continuum of consumer experience of the product, **we're able to isolate precise points** of this experience that are extremely evocative for the brain. We call these points the Neurological Iconic Signatures (NIS) of that particular TCE. These are the points of the consumption experience that become the true representations of the product and most deeply encoded in the brain. We have also found that reminding the consumer through these iconic signatures creates a natural desire in the mind of the consumer for the pleasure of these experiences. It "primes" them to desire and seek out the product between uses.

Another fascinating observation has been that while we have outlined the macro stages of the consumer experience above, many times the most evocative high points—the NISes—are the unarticulated micromotions and microstages. As we continuously measure the entirety of the experience, we can isolate and tease out those unique Neurological Iconic Signatures.

Of Spoons, Signatures, and Synapses

If you can touch it, taste it, smell it, see it, or hear it, we can measure your brain's reactions to it. Coming back to the example I started with, that is why we applied the TCE methodology to our client's leading brand of yogurt.

Now, you may be wondering: what is there to know that's so complex about eating a simple thing like a container of fruit-flavored yogurt? You put a spoon in it, you stir it up, and you eat it. Simple, right? But for your brain, it isn't at all a simple process.

First, all five of your senses are involved. Nothing unusual about that from the brain's point of view—but it might not have occurred to you when thinking about enjoying a package of yogurt.

Next, from a neurological perspective, there actually are several distinct steps involved. We identify and isolate those steps, and measure them independently of each other. (That said, your brain doesn't start and stop in neatly separated steps—so please understand that we measure the TCE on a continuous basis, from start to finish. But we're able to isolate individual components of the overall product consumption/usage experience as well, as we go—and that's what we do in a TCE study.)

The end goal of the TCE is twofold: first, we want to gain a comprehensive understanding of and insights into how a consumer responds to a product at the subconscious level. And second, we want to identify the specific high points of that experience—the NIS I already described above.

What triggered the most significant brainwave response? Which features, which parts of the consumption experience elicited the brain's attention, sparked emotions, and were retained in memory? What are the identifiable "hallmarks" of this product, as registered in the consumer's subconscious?

The answers to those questions are in the product's Neurological Iconic Signatures.

Neurological Iconic Signatures

Neurological Iconic Signatures are just what the phrase implies: they're the brain's high-water marks, the unique imprints on the subconscious that are made when something causes a significant neurological response.

Their value to marketers lies in the fact that, when we identify an NIS, we gain an unprecedented picture—in precise detail—of **what is most powerful about a product** from the standpoint of the consumer's subconscious.

Equipped with that knowledge, smart marketers can devise means, methods, and materials designed to convey those NIS' back to consumers outside of the actual consumption/usage process, through advertising, packaging, in-store marketing, and a host of other avenues.

More on NIS in just a bit.

THE RESOLUTION

But, first, let me get back to our yogurt package, because it's illustrative of how an NIS can and very often does escape notice by our rational minds. Let's examine what happens when you consume a container of yogurt, from both the physical perspective and the neurological one. (There's a surprise waiting at the end.)

First, you **see** the package. Synapses in your visual cortex fire as nerve endings in your retina capture and transmit signals. Your prefrontal cortex calls the shots, directing muscles around your eyeballs to focus your vision on the target. Your brain simultaneously decodes color, shape, size, and location of the container. This data is matched against information stored in your memory, and at the same time is matched against all the data streaming in from your other four senses.

The supercomputer spits out the answer in an infinitesimal fraction of a second: *yogurt*. That known, the prefrontal cortex proceeds to order the muscles and ligaments in your arm and hand to extend toward the container. Your brain calculates the distance and amount of time to target, and adjusts actions accordingly. Your fingers form the correct shape to grasp the container.

As you grasp the round plastic, your brain modifies the amount of pressure required for your fingers to hold onto the container, as it receives data about the resistance of the package and its weight. Temperature and surface texture information are transmitted as well.

(continued)

(*Continued*)

Time to proceed to the next step: lifting the container and opening it.

Now the nerves and muscles coordinate anew, driven by the master control center in your prefrontal cortex. Then another sense kicks in: as you remove the plastic top and then peel the metal foil back, you **hear** the sound at the same time as you sense the slight resistance of the adhesive on the top of the container.

And yet another sense floods data into your neural networks: you **smell** the contents. Now we're approaching what everyone would consider the Moment of Truth: tasting the product.

Next, of course, because it's a fruit-based yogurt, you pick up a spoon, insert it downwards, feel the consistency of the gelatinous content as the spoon encounters slight resistance due to the semithick texture . . . and you stir. As bits of fruit surface and swirl, your senses of sight, smell, and touch actively process new streams of data.

At last: time to **taste**.

You collect a puddle of the creamy substance on the spoon and raise it to your mouth. Once again, whole batteries of nerve endings, muscles, neurons, and synaptic networks within the brain interact, enabling the motion and anticipating what concerted actions are required to get the spoon and its contents safely and intact into your mouth.

Before it even gets there, though, your sense of smell is heightened as the yogurt approaches your face. Both your nasal cavity and your mouth receive the scent. Once inside, your mouth and tongue experience the flavor, texture, solid contents, and temperature of the yogurt, signaling your brain with the information that it is (1) delicious, (2) cool, (3) somewhat thick, (4) contains semifirm bits of an identifiable fruit, and (5) is OK to swallow, which you proceed to do.

And that concludes the typical yogurt consumption process—and therefore, by definition, our TCE.

There's nothing new or surprising in this series of steps. As you read through them just now, your brain was recognizing them and registering nothing novel or worthy of extra special attention.

So where's the special power and value of the TCE?

It's hidden in the information above. But you won't possibly guess it until I tell you what it is. Neither did our friends the Brand Manager, the Consumer Insights (CI) head honcho, or the rest of the brand management and CI departments, along with the marketing group, sales staff, ad agency, supermarket chains that stock the brand, and on and on.

So, what would *you* guess would be the biggest, most prominent Neurological Iconic Signature embedded in the simple process and pleasure of consuming a container of fruit-laden yogurt? Would it be feeling that cool, slick surface of the plastic container? Sticking the spoon in? Maybe stirring up the fruit? (Hint: that's usually the choice most people make when I pose this question.) Or actually tasting the yummy stuff itself? Which one do you choose?

The correct answer is **none of the above.**

Nope, the real standout Neurological Iconic Signature that arose, clearly and unmistakably out of the billions of bits of brainwave and biometric data that we collected in this study was ... wait for it ... *grasping and removing the foil covering over the top of the container.*

As it turns out, the brain loves that action and the multitude of sensations that it produces. Places it above all others in the hierarchy of subconscious preferences. Why, we can only conjecture. But there is no mistaking that something about the tactile, auditory, visual, and olfactory sensations involved in peeling off a foil barrier atop a container of yogurt brings the brain great satisfaction. Remember: it's 100,000 years old. It knows what it likes, even if our conscious sense of our own brains can't tell us what that is. And that is why we invented the TCE.

Spoon-Fed Surprises

We discovered some other surprises along the way in this particular test (as we do on many).

The client hadn't specified which type of spoon to use in the TCE. Truth be told, we hadn't thought much about it in advance either. But, as we began the TCE sessions, we decided to test two different types of spoons, just to see if the brain would differentiate and rank one higher over another.

Sure enough, it did. Somewhat to our surprise, the **TCE turned up plastic as the preferred utensil material, rather than metal.** Something about the texture; or perhaps that it was a warmer material than the yogurt (and warmer than the metal alternative); or maybe the light, matte color; or the slight but unmistakable flexibility of the plastic

(continued)

(Continued)

handle ... honestly, we don't know, nor can we query the brain to find out for sure.

All we know is that the brain loves fiddling with the foil ... and prefers plastic over metal.

But if you're the yogurt marketer managing a major brand, that's **important and valuable** to know. Because that's *actionable* information.

If I, Master Yogurt Marketer, know what the brain loves and prefers, I can apply that knowledge to my packaging, to my advertising, to my in-store displays and product demos ... the list goes on. I have a fundamental competitive advantage, because I have detailed, scientifically proven, actionable steps that I can take to leverage that knowledge.

Fast forward: while I can't disclose client trade secrets, I'll just say that armed with those two key pieces of brainwave-based insight, our yogurt manufacturer is hard at work developing novel ways to leverage the foil-peeling experience. And exploring ways to signal to consumers that the plastic they prefer in their yogurt-spooning utensils is heard, understood, and answered.

I'll add that our postresearch recommendations included specific ways in which the company can leverage their new NIS knowledge across their advertising, marketing, and retail activities.

We put the brain to work by asking what it likes—and then listening to the whispered answers that guide us to the truth about how best to package and sell something like yogurt.

Notes for the Practitioner:

1. The TCE study is done for one product experience at a time.
2. The TCE study can be done in two modes:
   a. **Self experience**—that is where each consumer goes through the entire experience himself or herself and we measure his or her brain throughout the continuum of the experience.
   b. **Observed experience**—that is where consumers watch a video of someone else going through the same consumption experience, and we capture their brains' responses during this viewing.
3. It is wise to perform a Deep Subconscious Response test on brand/product attributes prior to the consumption experience and perform another deep subconscious study after the experience. This differential

enables us to track how experiencing the product transforms perceptions about the product. This helps companies determine the individual critical elements of the consumption experience and how each affect perceptions of the brand/product.

A company that exemplifies this superior grasp of consumers and their involvement and engagement with the actual product is Apple. In their retail outlets, you can find most Apple products readily available to be experienced firsthand by the consumer. All Apple computers are fully loaded with all software available for use. iPods and iPhones are present so their full functionality can be experienced. As consumers experience the product, any preconceived notions are dismissed and the brand attributes that Apple wants them to take away are reinforced.

NEW PRODUCT LAUNCHES—INNOVATION

What other roles does neuromarketing play in the product category? The answer is plenty. For many companies, new product introductions are a fresh source of oxygen. But the cost—in time, corporate resources, dollars, and sometimes reputation and brand image—can be substantial. The failure rate of new products in the marketplace is daunting.

Estimates hold that anywhere between 70 and 95 percent of all new products fail, depending on the category. Even skewing toward the low end of those figures, the picture is clear. Hundreds of billions of dollars are spent, and lost, on product launches that nosedive, leaving a wreckage of budgets, and sometimes careers, in their wake. One projection has it that just under half of all corporate resources dedicated to new product development and launch end up having been devoted to marketplace failures. Fewer than 10 percent of all new products and services survive their three-year birthday.

The obvious thing to ask is, couldn't that money be better and more wisely spent?

Of course, corporations plan for some failure; they have to. It is in the nature of new product introductions that some will miss the mark, for a wide variety of reasons, some of which are beyond the control of their creators. But that said, it is a brutally expensive experiment. The good news is it doesn't have to be.

NEW PRODUCT EFFECTIVENESS FRAMEWORK

While no one can guarantee 100 percent likelihood of success in this sector, neurological testing can improve the success rate considerably. It enables companies to understand in advance, before major sums are expended, several key elements of the new product experience:

- How consumers will respond to a new product **concept**
- How they will react to the product's **formulation or function**
- How they will process the proposed **positioning** for the product
- Whether the **packaging design** will trigger the critical NeuroMetrics of attention, emotional engagement, and memory retention
- How the product will stand up against the current competition in the real-world **retail environment**
- How consumers will connect and value **new product extensions** against the existing **brand**
- Which **features** consumers value most highly, and which the least
- Which **bundles of features** will carry the highest valuation in consumers' minds
- Which new product **names** will trigger the strongest subconscious response
- Which **price point** will strike the elusive but prized "sweet spot" in buyers' brains

All these and many more questions can be answered simply by asking the brain and listening to its replies. Gaining that knowledge in any one of these categories can **reduce risk;** enhance the chances, even the likelihood, of marketplace success; and improve the ROI on new product launches.

We utilize neurological testing to determine the effectiveness of various innovation concepts. But, the power of the method is that, as we continually analyze brain responses, even if the concept at the overall level is not particularly effective, we can tease out the pieces of a concept that had high levels of effectiveness. This allows us to salvage the high points of a concept even if the overall concept did not resonate with consumers. This also allows us to combine the high points of various concepts and create newer, much more effective variants and hybrids. Quite literally, we involve the consumer's subconscious to help design the final concept, thereby ensuring in advance the strongest likelihood that it will be embraced by that same subconscious when it actually reaches the marketplace.

There are two methodologies we use here: the first is creating a neuroscientific version of the traditional test. The way that the concept is positioned and shared with the consumer follows the accepted product innovation framework. We gather NeuroMetrics for every element of this framework as it is being presented to the consumer.

The methodology is that every concept is represented through the following core elements:

1. **Name with Headline (2–5 words):** the name of the concept with a few words that form the core headline associated with it.
2. **Consumer Insight (2 sentences, 3–8 seconds/sentence—basic human truth):** this represents a basic human truth, desire, or need that arises from a deep understanding of human nature.
3. **Consumer Benefit that supported the Consumer Insight (1–2 sentences, 8 seconds/sentence—what the product brings to the consumer that fulfills the insight):** the consumer benefit is more than the provision of the desired function, but it is also the satisfaction of a deeply felt social and emotional need.
4. **Product Descriptions to reinforce the Consumer Benefit:** the product description is a statement of the value proposition and the proof points that confirm it.

The second methodology adopts a slightly different view of how a concept might be presented. Based on our studies of how people recall products and services, we found a hierarchy of how a product or service is naturally experienced:

1. **With whom** the product or service was experienced
2. **Where** the product or service was experienced
3. What was the **occasion** of the product or service being experienced?
4. Salient **attributes** of the product or services

With this hierarchy in mind we created a description of the product or service that would follow suit with the following scenario: imagine you are with [blank] at this beautiful place [blank] on the occasion of your [blank] enjoying an experience that [1, 2, 3 attributes of the product or service].

We have found that creating these social/spatial/emotional landscapes is a prerequisite to stating the purported functions and benefits of the product. The product lives in an ecosystem dominated by people, places, and feelings. Providing those contexts is necessary for evaluating the inventiveness and innovation associated with the product.

In either methodology, the innovation concept is created as a radio ad and the consumer listens to the verbalization of that concept. Brain responses are continuously recorded and the features or descriptions of the product that generate the greatest levels of Attention, Emotional Engagement, Memory,

Purchase Intent, Awareness, Novelty, and Overall Effectiveness are highlighted. We have found this neurological highlighting and scoring of innovation concepts can minimize and reduce the risks of marketplace failure.

Capturing the NeuroMetrics data serves another important purpose. There is a traditional fear in the mind of marketers: if a product seems too new, it may not do well in the marketplace. We have found that for new products, there is a need for balance between high levels of novelty and high levels of purchase intent. If one were to assume the classic four-box with purchase intent along the X axis and novelty along the Y axis we would see products or services that have both high levels of novelty and purchase intent. These become the natural first tier of products for innovation.

Many of our clients have also performed traditional research that includes surveys and focus groups on the effectiveness of these concepts. Consequently, we have created a very interesting resonance and dissonance matrix where the X-axis represents the neurological effectiveness and the Y-axis represents the articulated effectiveness. See Figure 13.1.

The northeast corner is a quadrant that represents the greatest level of cognitive response. That is to say, the items in that box are the ones with the greatest neurological and articulated effectiveness. The concept resonates in the subconscious and the conscious. **We consider these "the next big idea."** The concepts in the box to the left of that, which are concepts with low neurological effectiveness and high articulated responses, are usually red flags. These are ones that enable people to confirm something they either want to believe or already know about themselves but are deeply emotionally opposed to. These concepts, while apparently having a level of marketplace appeal, are eventually doomed to fail in the marketplace through a lack of genuine deep consumer acceptance. We urge our clients to be wary of these prophets bearing false success, because they require major surgery on the concept.

The third box is the one with high neurological effectiveness and low articulated enthusiasm. These are concepts that people truly enjoy but are reluctant to admit openly that they enjoy them. In these cases it is vital (and easy) to fine-tune the concept by changing the packaging. The clever change of the name, making it more socially acceptable, will result in easily fine-tuned marketplace success.

In the last quadrant are the concepts that have poor neurological effectiveness and articulated displeasure—these are guaranteed marketplace failures, to be avoided entirely.

Our application of neuroscience to test innovation concepts has yielded remarkable success, leading to both the methodology and the neuroscience

Figure 13.1
When neurological and articulated responses are high,
look for a big idea

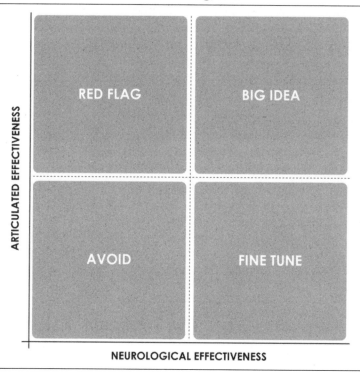

Source: NeuroFocus, Inc.

becoming part of the innovation pipeline and new product tollgate process in a number of companies.

In addition to identifying innovation concepts, this method of benchmarking and creating the overall NeuroMetrics for innovation serves yet another critical purpose. Many times the **translation of the concept into a product is flawed.** That is to say, a great and brilliant concept eventually was stripped of its brilliance, its features warped, and its objective destroyed through the process of execution when the concept came to life as a product or service. Many companies have started using our NeuroMetrics throughout the process of innovation to ensure that the same level of effectiveness defined through NeuroMetrics scores, which mark the birth of a concept at its inception, are not degraded throughout the process of translating the concept into a product and its associated marketing. The consistent use of the same set of Neuro-Metrics from the inception of the concept through the various stages of the execution into a product or service guarantees that the original intent and novelty of the concept is not lost but maintained throughout the process.

The chapter on Advertising outlines the power that neurological testing can bring to that branch of marketing. Given how critical advertising is for the introduction of new products into the marketplace, it merits special mention here.

If you know the features that appeal the strongest . . . if you know the optimum positioning . . . the best-received packaging design elements . . . the highest-scored name . . . the price that consumers will find most acceptable . . . if you know, with scientific precision, how your customer's brain will respond *before* you create the ad campaign, **you go into that process with a distinct competitive advantage.**

If you're going to make the kind of major investments in any or all of the above categories that most new product launches demand it makes the most business sense to optimize your chances for success. Knowledge is not only power—in the case of new product introductions, it also means cold hard cash and, nine times out of ten, life and death.

FAILURE ANALYSIS: SIX REASONS PRODUCTS FAIL

We have been called in many times by companies to investigate why a new product launch failed. Sometimes it was the result of the product itself, its packaging, its ad campaign, its in-store execution, perhaps competitive action, and sometimes several of these factors combined. In each case, *there are as many lessons to be learned from product launch failures as there are to be learned from product launch successes.* When we have used neuroscientific analysis to study product launch failures we have come across certain specific criteria:

Failure Reason #1: the concepts were chosen based on articulated intent rather than consumers' deep subconscious responses.

Failure Reason #2: the appropriate trade-off between novelty and purchase intent was not made.

Failure Reason #3: NeuroMetrics of the marketing campaign revealed that the deep emotional benefits of the product were not successfully articulated through the campaign.

Failure Reason #4: NeuroMetrics of the execution of the product concept through the product itself and its associated packaging were substantively lower than the NeuroMetrics of the concept. In other words, the loss of concept innovation in the process through to execution noted above.

Failure Reason #5: product features and packaging did not present a substantive competitive barrier, which in turn, enabled launch of competitive products that were better from a NeuroMetric standpoint.

Failure Reason #6: the Deep Subconscious Response to the product or service was disconnected from the subconscious response to the core brand attributes. In other words, the product or service was emotionally disconnected from the brand.

It is, therefore, important not only to understand how to launch products successfully but to look at the litany of woes associated with poorly launched products and services and reexamine them through the lens of neuroscience to see what was successful and what was not—**and why.**

When a new product fails, sophisticated companies conduct a marketing postmortem to determine why. Learning from failures is, obviously, an excellent way to avoid them in the future. But, it is devilishly difficult after the fact to deconstruct all of the individual components that go into the conceptualization, development, production, and marketing of a new product, and have confidence in the accuracy of the results.

By probing the subconscious for answers, **you add an entirely new source of insight and understanding.** It is the commercial equivalent of trying to comprehend the cosmos through a land-based telescope. Peering through our layered atmosphere that necessarily distorts the image, versus soaring high above the Earth and gaining as clear and unobstructed a view into the depths of space as can be had by the human eye.

In the book *Fundamental Neuroscience*, Floyd E. Bloom said, "As we begin the twenty-first century, the Hubble Space Telescope is providing us with information about as yet uncharted regions of the universe and the promise that we may learn something about the origin of the cosmos. This same spirit of adventure is also being directed to the most complex structure that exists in the universe—the human brain."

I posit that neuromarketing is to marketing as the Hubble telescope is to astronomy: a quantum leap forward toward far greater knowledge and insights attained with scientific precision and certainty.

You cannot achieve this knowledge to the same high standard of accuracy through conventional market research methodologies. Throughout this book, you will read the fact that the human brain is structured, and functions, in such a way that relying on its articulated responses, as compared to its earlier registration of information at the deep subconscious level, produces inherently and unavoidably flawed results.

By asking for consumers' articulated responses as to why they didn't favor a new product with their pocketbooks, you are by definition accepting the fact that the responses are going to be distorted. In contrast, when you "ask" the brain, measuring neurological responses at the precognitive stage, you are gaining access to the very source where the most accurate answers are originally formed.

Neurological testing offers consumer products manufacturers a powerful tool to analyze product failures because the methodology allows the "cause of death" to be pinpointed much more accurately. Measurement of consumers' responses can be made to:

 *Specific **components** of the product itself, such as taste, texture, ingredients, color, sound, scent*

 ***Packaging** elements including artwork, photographs, logos, fonts, placement and content of nutritional information, and warning labels*

 ***Ease** of opening/use*

 ***Pricing** "envelope of reasonability"*

 *For brand extensions, the **carryover value of the parent brand** (or lack thereof)*

In the In-store Marketing chapter, you'll learn about how mobile EEG testing and Video Realistic technology enables us to study consumers' subconscious responses within actual retail settings, or in virtual ones. In regard to assessing product failures, this capability offers marketers the means to measure the effects of shelf placement, product displays, competitive product presence, and on-shelf/in-store merchandising and promotional elements.

Rather than second-guessing the reasons why a particular product failed, or attempting to glean that critical insight by asking consumers to try to recall, after the fact, what they liked or didn't like about the product, relying on neurological testing can produce the answers straight from the source: the consumer's subconscious, which is the ultimate arbiter of product selection and purchase.

MAKING CHANGE? ASK THE BRAIN

 If you want the best data, the best solution is to ask the brain for it.

Before undertaking a fundamental change in something as basic and essential as a familiar brand/product's familiar packaging, it's advisable to have a very clear and exact understanding of the individual elements that make up consumers' *existing* subconscious perceptions of the brand/product. Only then can you navigate something as potentially treacherous as a package redesign with the utmost confidence that your customer will approve it with her selection at the shelf, and the opening of her purse.

The best that all of the advertising, couponing, merchandising, publicity, slotting fees, and trade promotions you've invested in can do is get her to pause at your placement on that shelf. Your package can either push the process to completion, or hinder it at the crucial final stage. Neurological testing offers the means to know—in advance, with clarity, precision, and full assurance—if your package design will stand in the way of sales success, or deliver that ultimate purchase stimulant.

PRICING FRAMEWORK

Many companies spend resources and energy toward gaining a better understanding of the two components of the Pricing Framework:

1. **Sweet Spot**. That certain price that appeals to consumers and makes the product or service seem like a bargain, a good deal, and is also comparable to what other competition offers. We call this the sweet spot.

2. **Envelope of Reasonability**. This "envelope" offers a way to push the limits, safely. How far can the price be pushed before the consumer believes that the price has moved from reasonable to unreasonable? This represents a categorical shift in perception.

Price is an ephemeral quantity; in that, consumers have little idea what it costs to make a product and the associated margins. Consumers do not know what the margins associated with an automobile versus a fragrance are. It is, therefore, seemingly unreasonable that the consumer would make the determination of what price is adequate. However, whether we like it or not, such determination exists. Not only is there a "valid" price, but there are limits of price elasticity in the consumer's mind. Once again, though, it is very difficult for that consumer to articulate what those exact pricing parameters are in a way that can assure a marketer of the validity and accuracy of that response.

We have found the best way to capture and understand "sweet spot" is to look through the lens of the **Deep Subconscious Response test.** We showcase products and associated prices to consumers while giving them an explicit task that has nothing to do with the associated product or price. We then look for both the high and low ends of a novelty response; that is to say, we look to see when the prices appear ridiculously low or ridiculously high to them at the subconscious level of their minds.

Both of these points, representing the outer and inner limits, are the "stretch" of price. We note that if the price appears artificially low, notions of a good bargain usually accompany it or that something is wrong (poor quality). We also note that if a price is unreasonably high, it triggers incredulity and the associated categorical shift toward unreasonableness. Now you have identified your **price elasticity** and how much you can stretch it.

In addition to spotting the inner and outer bounds of the extent of pricing reasonability, we also perform minor variations from a price to figure out whether the appropriate changes in the subconscious response are minor or great. Simply put, a sweet spot of pricing is defined as a point in the pricing continuum where minor deviations in price do not produce substantive deviations in the associated subconscious neurological response. That is to say, it is a stable point. Price points that are not the stable point, in that minor deviations from prices produced major deviations in subconscious responses, represent a price point that is not the sweet spot. We calibrate the price point continuum to figure the points of stability and points of instability. Points of stability—our sweet spots—are like a valley floor; you always roll toward the valley floor from the sides of the surrounding mountains. Points of instability are like the top of the mountains, where a minor shift in one direction or the other moves you away from the price points. This is how, using the methods of neurological equilibrium, we determine the sweet spots of pricing.

THE BUNDLING FRAMEWORK

There are many kinds of product bundles. We have found it effective to measure them through the Bundling Framework:

- Based on product features and characteristics
- Based on product shape and size
- Based on product consumption occasions
- Based on segments of the population that use the product
- Based on the product's quality, price, handling, and storage

So the real question is: How will consumers perceive a product bundle? How will this product bundling affect or impact the notion of inherent value associated with the bundle? When the consumer subscribes to or buys a product bundle they are hoping that it provides more than the sum of the parts. Instead of buying each of the product items one at a time, a bundle provides value. That value may have nothing to do with the product itself, but it may have to do with the ease of product storage, carrying the product, accessing the product, restocking the product, and the variety of ways in which the product lives with the consumer for the rest of its life cycle.

The consumer perceives **value in the product items being together** and presented together by the manufacturer rather than buying them one at a time. This is a very deep subconscious perception of inherent value, and can rarely be articulated logically and rationally by the consumer. Many times we find that the act of picking each product, while apparently an act of eminent ease, may appear difficult to the consumer in the store; and thus, the minor act of making things comfortable through bundling may provide a level of value that is not apparent to logical and rational reasoning. However, we know that there is a deep subconscious connection to the ease and simplicity associated with bundling and the perceived inherent value of the bundle. The subconscious feelings are rarely articulated and, therefore, we evaluate product bundles through the means of the Deep Subconscious Response Test.

Takeaways:
- Neurological testing can illuminate exactly how consumers respond to products at the subconscious level, along the entire product consumption/experience pathway.

- The brain actually "marks" the high points of these experiences. These Neurological Iconic Signatures can be leveraged in product design and packaging, across the full spectrum of marketing materials, and in the retail/point-of-sale (POS) environment.
- Brainwave activity measurement can be applied to gain a comprehensive understanding of consumers' subconscious responses to a planned new product introduction *before* substantial investments are made in product design/formulation, naming, pricing, and marketing campaign concepts and materials.
- Neurological testing can reveal the core reasons why a new product or brand extension failed in the marketplace.

CHAPTER 14

THE BUYING BRAIN AND PACKAGING

At the end of this chapter, you'll know and be able to use the following:
- How well-understood and marketplace-proven neuroscientific principles can be put to use to create the most effective new package designs, or improve existing ones
- The set of specific Neurological Best Practices to apply during the package design process
- How neurological testing enables companies to perfect the use of package design as a core element of brand positioning—especially in highly competitive categories

THE PROBLEM: DECLINING MARKET SHARE

It's about the most frustrating thing that can happen to a brand: launch a new product that establishes a new subcategory, watch sales shoot up, only to watch them drop down as your largest competitor launches a similar product that eats up your market share. Needless to say, our client was not pleased.

Since these were similar products with similar market share, the client decided to focus on an area they could change quickly: the package. Besides, they suspected that the competitor's package was better, more appealing at the shelf and with better messaging about the new product. Their question: How did the brain view their package next to the competitor's?

YOUR BRAIN IS A HUNTER

It is, in fact, a highly trained hunting machine, the likes of which the world has never seen. Hundreds of thousands of years and countless trillions upon trillions of evolutionary advances have honed the organ inside your skull into an ideal pursuit device.

"Jaws" is a squeeze toy compared to what you carry around in your cranium.

Improvements in brain structure and functions enabled early humans to learn the patterns of the world around them, for example, to identify the best berries, single out the most desirable prey, shape the weapons that would secure food—survival. Even though we no longer have to skulk through the jungle or pace the Serengeti in search of sustenance, the brain has lost none of its exquisitely developed skills.

In the midst of the modern neighborhood grocery store, it is still the world's perfect hunting machine. And hunt it does, avidly, continuously, and relentlessly.

You are blissfully unaware of that fact as you stroll the aisles—your prefrontal cortex ensures that you devote conscious resources to cognitive puzzle solving and price comparing and choosing between the regular Oreos and the Double-Stufs. But all the while, the hunter deep below the surface is scanning.

What is it looking for? The answer for starters is the familiar. For male minds especially, **landmarks in the immediate environment** are a critical component of the shopping experience. For females, **the overall context matters more.** Both facts are reasons why effective packaging is not only at the core of successful product marketing in the retail setting, but is also one of the single most important elements of neuromarketing.

Others have opined about how the package is the face of the brand, theorized about the proper proportions and relationships of fonts and logos, pondered the appeal of economy-size versus standard-size, labored over shapes, and on and on. All are valid and certainly worthwhile and necessary. But to fully grasp how consumers really respond to packaging, we must dive deeper, to the place where data about your package design arrives and is examined, dissected, analyzed, and judged.

The Subconscious

Last night I was at the grocery store, and I caught myself scanning the shelves along the chips and dips aisle. I suddenly realized (this is the penalty of being so fully immersed in neuromarketing) that I was actively searching, and I thought about what my brain was actually doing right at that moment. Your brain, and every other consumer's, does exactly the same thing.

We seek the familiar, pleasing, and reassuring. We seek the connection that we have had before, because we anticipate the rewards that we know that connection will bring.

But . . .

> The brain also values and seeks the new.
>
> In addition to the search for what's familiar, **our brains are also drawn to Novelty.** Because of evolutionary forces that drove developments in brain structure and function, we have learned—through a whole lot of trial and error, a good deal of which involved life and death—to search out new experiences, because ultimately they can be rewarding to both our physical and our psychological selves.
>
> When you look at the sheer number of brands, products, and packages just along one aisle of your average supermarket, or wall-to-wall at Wal-mart, it begs the question (a critical one for every marketer): Does my package stand out against the clutter and especially the competition? If it does, why does it? Could I make it work even better? And—forbid the thought—if it doesn't, what do I do about it?
>
> Finally, thanks to neuroscience, we have the answers to those questions.

PACKAGING EFFECTIVENESS FRAMEWORK

In analyzing neurological responses to packaging across a variety of retail environments across multiple categories, we found a number of common threads. Based on these neuroscientific observations we created a Packaging Effectiveness Framework (PEF) that allows us to evaluate, from a neuroscientific standpoint, the key elements that make a package stand out and optimally represent the product within.

This also helps answer the three vexing questions that confront every marketer:

1. Does my **product pop out on the shelf?** This determination is made using the NeuroMetrics of Overall Effectiveness and Novelty.
2. Will she select my product and take it home? This determination is made using the NeuroMetrics Purchase Intent and Awareness/Understanding.
3. When the product is in the pantry, will she use it? How soon? This determination is made using the NeuroMetrics of Immediacy of Consumption and Novelty.

The difficulty for marketers is that if you ask a consumer "what makes a package really pop out?," he or she will be hard-pressed to recall, much less articulate, all of the packaging components that had an impact on them. The Packaging Effectiveness Framework incorporates the best practices we use in evaluating any given package and its pop-out potential. The individual elements of the PEF are:

Imagery and Iconography: Our studies have consistently confirmed that choice of imagery and iconography are key drivers that impact the pop-out power of a package at the subconscious level. The primary NeuroMetrics we track to evaluate imagery and iconography are Attention, Emotion, Memory, and Novelty. In the store, imagery and iconography need to create a tremendous amount of emotional appeal. While attention is important, the amount of emotion created by an image and the icons associated with it are very critical in the aisle. Our neurological observation has been that a store environment resembles a vast array of numbers and letters. It is as if the consumer just tapped into an Excel spreadsheet full of unrelated numbers and words.

As the consumer navigates through this ocean of numerical and semantic meaning, s/he looks for emotional landmarks—what we call an **"oasis of emotions"**—where reason can take a break. The imagery and iconography in a package provide these emotional oases. We have found that imagery and iconography that are emotionally evocative provide very natural pop out for a package.

Another noteworthy finding is that the imagery that pops out is usually that which the consumer has seen before. We found that packages that represent scenes, images, or icons featured in TV advertising the consumer has seen resonate extremely well and pop out in the consumer's mind. A classic example of this phenomenon is a face shown on a package that is also shown on TV. This facial recognition, which reminds consumers of something they have seen before, brings a degree of **implicit familiarity** to the package, even if that familiarity is not recognized consciously. From the neuromarketing perspective, the reason this is important is because the brain will focus first on what is familiar. Survival of the species has compelled and enabled our brains to possess this extraordinary capacity. Using imagery and iconography that is familiar yet connected to the brand makes a package visible in an otherwise cluttered environment.

As noted elsewhere, our own research and much of academic literature has found that the human brain is uniquely poised and positioned to recognize faces. So to the extent that the image or icon on a package can be represented by, or include a human face, that package tends naturally **to stand out from the clutter.** Because our brains are biologically programmed to scan for and identify faces in a sea of clutter, especially seeking some level of familiarity, it is strategically and tactically useful to leverage that fact in packaging design.

Imagery and iconography also work well when they are very relevant to the category in question. Across all categories of products, we find some common themes; one is an attentional and emotional boost from depicting the *source* of the product on the package. For example, on milk cartons we like to see cows. On orange juice containers, we like to see juicy oranges. On health and beauty packaging, flowers and dew drops. There is a natural attraction in the mind of the consumer for a depiction of the source of the product. We have found in numerous cases that packaging that uniquely positions and identifies salient aspects of a product's sources turns out to be more effective than packaging that does not convey this information.

Font Structure: We have observed that font structure plays an important role in a package's pop-out propensity. Packages that have interesting, unique, or **"funky" fonts** convey a sense of whimsy and a sense of the product. The primary NeuroMetrics we use in analyzing font structure are Attention and Novelty. Some fonts appear to be implicitly aligned with a product or brand. They contribute to stand out by enabling rapid decoding of the product's identity, even before the text is read and interpreted in the language centers of the brain. The distinctive script of Coca-Cola is an excellent example that expresses the brand even from a distance.

Another finding about fonts is: The **overuse of fonts creates clutter** and turns off attention and emotional engagement. Our findings reveal that packages using more than two kinds and three sizes of fonts suffer precipitous drops in effectiveness versus packages with fewer fonts and font sizes.

Finally, we have found that even the directionality of the font on a package can be important. The eye and brain usually perceive things better from the outer edges to the center. They pay less attention to things that move from center to outer edges. From an evolutionary standpoint, therefore, objects, fonts, or words that appear to run from the periphery to the center of focus catch more attention. Text that creates the impression of moving away from the center toward the periphery appears to be retreating, so they are accorded less attention.

Numerosity: Simply put, this is a computation of the number or groups of information that must be processed or understood on a package. The primary NeuroMetrics for assessing the impact of numerosity are Attention and Awareness. Numerosity relates to a phenomenon called **"fluency of processing,"** which is impacted by the number of clusters of objects or images shown. When a package consists of five or fewer distinct image groups, it is much easier for the brain to process than when more groups are present. That range enables greater fluency of cognitive processing and greater subconscious "enjoyment" of the package. Moreover, there is considerable neuroscientific evidence that an even smaller number of images, closer to three, may be even better for ease of processing.

Spatial Arrangement: We have found that the arrangement and relative spatial positioning of imagery versus semantic content (words and numbers) has a huge impact on the overall effectiveness of the package. The core NeuroMetrics are Attention, Effectiveness, and Awareness. Some spatial arrangements seem to work better than others. For example, we have found that placing images on the left and words on the right is superior for rapid processing by the brain. This is because items in the left visual field are perceived by the right frontal lobe, whereas the right visual field is perceived by the left frontal lobe. Since the left frontal lobe is specialized in most people for interpreting semantics, while the right frontal lobe is specialized to process imagery and iconography, this **speeds up processing** and contributes to a positive emotional impression. So, when you have imagery and iconography on the left and words and numbers on the right, a package design will be generally more effective, other factors being equal.

Colors: Our studies have confirmed what is widely believed: Colors impact packaging in a deep way, akin to how music impacts the brain. Colors, like music, appear to provide an unarticulated emotional response to the package. The primary NeuroMetrics we use to study color are Attention and Emotion. While it is useful to study the package in isolation, we have found that lighting in the aisle also impacts the neurological effectiveness of the package. It is very important and useful to study the package with the right parameters of lighting; specifically, those that most effectively simulate the shopping experience.

Our research shows that **cultural differences impact responses to color** in a significant way. In conducting global studies, we have discovered intriguing correlations between colors with strong cultural connotations within a society, and the colors common in nature surrounding that culture. The Deep Subconscious Response technique enables us to determine the subconscious impacts of different choice of colors in different cultures.

Shape: We have evaluated **the shape of packaging** to determine if and how it contributes to the pop-out power of the package. We have found that the shape of the package creates more than a simple visual appeal—it can actually reinforce the brain's natural proclivity to simulate holding the package and enjoying the product. The primary NeuroMetrics we use to study shape are Attention, Emotion, and Novelty. We also monitor the level to which different aspects of shape—lines, contours, and/or unique features—attract attention and emotionally engage the brain. To the extent that the shape of the package draws the consumer's interest, eye gaze will follow the curves and the primary outlines of the most novel design components. We have found that packages with unique and novel features that stimulate tactile contact work better than packages without such features.

Also, packages that facilitated **a comfortable fit in the hand** presented the greatest stimulation and trumped those that did not. We, therefore, monitor carefully the extent to which a package or product design accommodates a comfortable fit in the hand, as this seems to contribute to attention and emotional engagement.

Size: We have consistently observed across categories a deep subconscious **connection between size, perceived value, and price acceptability.** Simply put, the higher the price paid, the bigger the expected package. The more valuable the product is perceived to be, the bigger the package is expected to be. Even for products whose value is represented by its "smallness," the packaging is expected to be "bigger." The core NeuroMetrics we use to evaluate size are Attention and Purchase Intent.

The strength of the correlation between price and size creates interesting opportunities for manufacturers. Varying the size of the package provides room for price flexibility. We have found it useful to evaluate the Deep Subconscious Response connection between price points and packaging size to find the boundaries of price reasonability, and then reverse-engineer the optimal package size to match the optimal price. In cases where the product package will spend its useful lifetime in a particular location (for example, laundry detergents), size must also be aligned with the spatial dimensions of that location. We have found that consumers automatically and implicitly estimate the "fit" of such packages with their expected locations, and summarily and instantly reject the package when there is a perceived mismatch.

Interplay of Imagery and Semantics: Many times, we find that packages with very poor responses in terms of neurological effectiveness have one thing in common: words are written over interesting image backgrounds. Anytime you have important and relevant semantics overlaying an interesting image background, the brain appears to ignore the semantics in the forefront while taking in the imagery in the background. The brain evidently views the overlaid semantics as "distraction," and tries to suppress them. Subsequent testing reveals that the distracting semantics had poor recall and weak memory processing associated with them. NeuroMetrics we have used to study the interplay effects of imagery and semantics are Attention, Effectiveness, and Memory.

Patterns of Eye Movement: While I have focused primarily on brain responses in this discussion of the Packaging Effectiveness Framework, and not on peripheral physiological measures, there is one interesting physiological correlate worthy of mention. In our analysis of packaging, we have found that placing imagery, iconography, semantics, and branding elements in a pattern that naturally facilitates a **curvilinear eye gaze path** is superior to those that are strictly linear across the package. Our observation has been that when the same creative elements are arranged in a curvilinear pattern, packages achieve superior effectiveness scores compared to packages where the same elements were arranged in a linear pattern. Similarly, we have found that arranging elements to stimulate *clockwise* eye movement is more effective than arrangements of the same elements with *counterclockwise* eye movement.

Product Reveal: In our testing of packaging across categories, we have found another interesting phenomenon: Packages that reveal the actual product **perform better** than packages that do not reveal the product. By "reveal," I mean the variety of ways a product can be seen or experienced through the package—sight, sound, taste, smell, or touch. Packages that enable a sensory interaction with the actual product performed better uniformly. The core NeuroMetrics that we use to compute the product reveal factor are Attention, Emotion, Purchase Intent, Novelty, and Awareness.

Aisle Connect: How well the packaging connects with advertising and displays surrounding it in-store has been found to be an important component of effectiveness. When packaging is designed in isolation from advertising and display design, the results are rarely connected. But we have found that when the elements of the packaging and surrounding displays connect in a meaningful way, **package effectiveness increases,** especially in cluttered aisle contexts. The primary NeuroMetrics that we use to analyze the level of aisle connect are Memory Retention and Awareness.

Messaging Congruence: This is a vital component of the Packaging Effectiveness Framework. Implicitly, the package must convey the essence of the product and brand to the consumer explicitly stating that message **in words** on the package. We use the Deep Subconscious Response technique to test the extent to which this congruence is occurring. To do so effectively, the package must reinforce the key elements of the Brand Essence Framework. It is vital that the package has a very significant match with the Brand Essence elements of Feelings, Values, Benefits, and Metaphors.

Neurological testing in the packaging category reminds us that the brain absorbs fully the entirety of the world around it but, also, simultaneously captures and processes the tiniest details in that world. That ability is one reason why humans stand atop the food chain. We see, recognize, react, and adapt to the big picture. At the same time we live amid the endless details that comprise that picture. Packaging is a good representation of that duality—the brain absorbs the package as a whole, but at the same time breaks it out into individual elements and assesses each both independently and as a part of the whole.

Neurological testing functions in very much the same way. Effectively, we mirror the brain's own mode of operation, capturing consumers' subconscious responses to the **macro and the micro.** I want to stress the importance of that approach, because there are so-called "neuromarketing" companies that purport to capture brainwave activity, while in reality they are either relying entirely on biometric measurements, or only measuring a very small area of the cortex.

Sometimes science allows us to make definitive statements, and this is one of them, which every marketer considering using neuromarketing needs to know: **Only full-brain EEG-based measurement can capture the necessary broad scope of brainwave activity occurring across multiple neural networks** that leads to accurate, in-depth, and actionable research findings. Don't be fooled by anything less. If in doubt, ask a leading neuroscientist about that fact.

When you consider how many opportunities there are to make a misstep and to inadvertently create something that jars the brain and causes a disconnect or otherwise negatively affects the subconscious's perceptions of a package, the significance of full-brain EEG testing of package designs becomes clear.

When it comes to products that you put in or on your body, the brain activates a different hierarchy of the senses than it does with other products.

These are very often highly competitive and sometimes low-margin categories, where a significant/unique marketplace advantage can result in outsized rewards in terms of market share and profitability. Neurological testing provides that advantage, by measuring what the subconscious responds to best. Marketers can leverage that knowledge to improve the effectiveness of their packaging.

Neuromarketing is still new enough that the occasional misconception can surface, and size is one of them. The thinking along these lines is that only large companies can afford or could benefit from brainwave measurement of consumers' subconscious responses.

Allow me to burst that bubble with another case study. One that underscores how asking the brain directly for its take on a critical element like package design, for a new small company that is truly rolling the dice by rolling out a new brand in a mature category, populated by long-established traditional brands, with strong brand loyalties, where perceived major product differences are relatively scarce, can make a big difference.

Olive Orchard Options

California Olive Ranch is a young company founded with a single-minded focus: create and market a premium olive oil that consumers would love. Creating the product itself was something that they were well suited to do. It's delicious and admirably high in quality; in fact, California Olive Ranch leads the development of a new way of harvesting olives that results in the freshest oil. But, making a superior product is one thing. **Launching a new brand** into an already-full category is another. California Olive Ranch knew that the most effective marketing they could muster was core to their business strategy and goals.

The brain responds to food marketing in some specialized ways. Mirror Neurons, which I explain in Chapter 9, play a key role. When observing someone else consuming a food, the brain actually experiences the same sensations itself, as if it were consuming the food as well. As mentioned above, products that you ingest or apply to your body invoke different sensual hierarchies than other products. Another key point is that the brain prefers to see presentations of "natural" images associated with food; and there are more such distinct neurological characteristics that can improve the effectiveness of food marketing efforts.

Figure 14.1
California Olive Ranch

Source: Photo by The Olive Board

Being the savvy business people they are, the California Olive Ranch team sought to leave no potential advantage unused. In a category like theirs, with long-established and entrenched competition, and retailers for whom shelf space is some very valuable real estate, launching a new product presents stiff challenges.

California Olive Ranch had developed two different package design solutions. One we'll call "Map," because the labeling featured a stylized map of California, and the other "Orchard" (see Figure 14.1). (That one's so obvious as to need no explanation.) Diving to the deep subconscious level of the mind would uncover the neurological effectiveness of each of these two options.

We devised a neurological testing scenario that would plumb those depths and discover how consumers would respond at retail to this new olive oil. The first phase would explore consumers' subconscious responses to the package design. The second phase would tease out those deep-seated, precognitive responses to the new brand itself and its perceived attributes.

Test Variables: Two different package designs for California Olive Ranch. There were four fundamental objectives for the testing:

1. **Determine** each package's ability to score well in our three primary NeuroMetrics: capturing consumers' Attention, engaging their Emotions, and stimulating Memory Retention.
2. **Evaluate** how the packages scored in our derived market performance metrics of Purchase Intent, Novelty, and Awareness.
3. **Measure** how well the packages conveyed the intended messaging.
4. **Compare** the packages' performance to two competitors.

While I go into the methodology in more detail in the Brand chapter, I want to take a moment here to touch on the framework that we employ to identify and quantify brand attributes. The process is instructive for a good understanding of authentic neuromarketing and the neuroscience underlying it. See Figure 14.2.

Figure 14.2
The Deep Subconscious Response (DSR) test measures subconscious resonance in the brain.

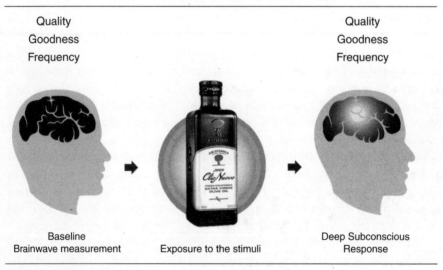

Quality		Quality
Goodness		Goodness
Frequency		Frequency

| Baseline Brainwave measurement | Exposure to the stimuli | Deep Subconscious Response |

Source: NeuroFocus, Inc.

Baseline

First, we conduct neurological testing to measure the brain's responses to, in this case, three brand attribute words. This measurement establishes a "baseline," giving us a clear picture of how the brain reacts to these specific stimuli. The chosen words are inserted among other "distracter" words, so no special attention is paid to them during this phase of the test.

Brand/Product Presentation

The next step is to show an image of the brand or product. In California Olive Ranch's case, we had bottles with the two different label designs on them.

Message Resonance

The third step is to repeat exposing the words, intermixed with the distracters.

Comparing the neurological results of the first baseline test with the results from the second "resonance" round, after exposure to the brand/product, reveals the degree to which the subconscious mind associates those attributes with the brand. From a scientific perspective, this process produces unequivocal evidence—there are no other variables involved, so the results are clear and reliable indicators of the brand's attributes.

In this California Olive Ranch example, the results of the neurological testing of the overall package design, coupled with the brand attributes study, **gave the company detailed knowledge** of how consumers would respond to the two different labels. The savings that can be realized at this stage of a new product launch are considerable, when you factor in the expenses incurred in the conventional model of having to conduct focus groups, test-market two different bottles, and so on.

In comparison, neurological testing cuts right to the central issues and delivers precise, concise answers, in a fraction of the time at a fraction of the cost of traditional methods. What did measuring consumers' subconscious responses to the two different package designs produce for California Olive Ranch? How did this new brand measure up against two existing brands?

Here are some top-line findings:

"Map" versus "Orchard"

Ladies and gentlemen, we had a winner. It was "Orchard."

Consumers' brains preferred that label design in every one of our six metrics: Attention, Emotional Engagement, Memory Retention, Purchase Intent,

Novelty, and Awareness. In five of the six, the margins were significant—sometimes major. In memory retention, the two designs were close enough to be called even, although there was an identifiable edge for "Orchard."

When we developed an overall Neurological Effectiveness score for both bottles, "Orchard" notched significantly higher than the "Map."

Brand Attributes   Both label designs attained positive rankings for the brand attributes studied. "Orchard" gained the upper hand in two-thirds of the target messages.

Competitive Products Comparison   Both California Olive Ranch package designs fared well against the two competitors that were tested. While there was more variance across the six individual NeuroMetrics than in the head-to-head comparison between the two California Olive Ranch bottles, the net outcome was:

- "Orchard" scored higher than the competition in overall Effectiveness (by as wide a margin in one case and even greater in the other as it had against "Map"), as well as in Emotional Engagement, Purchase Intent, and Awareness.
- "Map" also scored well in these categories, with rankings greater than or equal to the competition.

Why Use Neurological Testing for Packaging?   Scores and other statistics are excellent objective quantifiers of a packaging design's performance. But, as central and useful as they are, they only reveal the results of any market research methodology, including neurological testing. Discerning the broader, underlying **strategic reasons** for the results are where neuromarketing really adds critical value. Being able to offer specific, highly actionable recommendations on how to improve package design puts neurological testing ahead of the pack.

In California Olive Ranch's case, here's a small sampling of what we deduced from the brainwave and eye tracking measurements we conducted. Consider these as Neurological Best Practices for packaging design and execution:

Clutter-free is a decided plus. Both competitors' packaging is very cluttered, and the fact that both of California Olive Ranch's designs were markedly less so gave the brand a clear competitive advantage.

Going natural scores points. *California Olive Ranch had already made good use of "natural" imagery, which the brain prefers in association with food products. We counseled that what would likely improve scores even more was to incorporate more realistic "natural" imagery (for example, the olive and orchard trees).*

 Off-center is a good thing. *Our studies have shown that the brain prefers an attentional focus that is slightly off-center. California Olive Ranch already had imagery at the center of the label, which is basically pleasing to the subconscious. But shifting the central imagery a little to the left—because the brain prefers images on the left side of the visual field—might further spike effectiveness.*

There were additional specific recommendations made, ranging from ideas for improving effectiveness using the top of the bottle to the application of certain design elements such as color and text in other locations.

THE RESOLUTION

Coming back to the client package study I addressed at the outset of this chapter, for our client's product and the irritatingly similar competitive product, we tested the two package designs. Sure enough, the competitor's product scored significantly higher on all measures of Attention, Emotion, and Memory. It also fared a bit better on Deep Subconscious Response to messaging. Here's what we found:

- Imagery and Iconography: Competitor had better product feature-related imagery
- Font Structure: Too many fonts, hard to read
- Numerosity: Too many image groups, hard to process
- Product Reveal: Competitor product easier to see—more effective
- Messaging Effectiveness: Competitor scored higher on key messages such as "new" and "tasty"

A few months later, a new package design rolled out. What did it look like? It was cleaner, more in resonance with the product, and overall a more pleasing design. All of this is all well and good, but most important of all, sales are up.

Takeaways:

- Strive for clean, uncluttered package designs; the brain prefers them
- Highlight what's new; the brain seeks out what is novel
- Use the specific Neurological Best Practices outlined above to stimulate better receptivity by the brain, and, therefore, higher Attention, Emotional Engagement, and Memory Retention
- The smallest details in a package design can have outsized effects on the subconscious. The brain takes it all in; neurological errors subtract from overall package design effectiveness

CHAPTER 15

THE BUYING BRAIN IN THE AISLE

At the end of this chapter, you'll know and be able to use the following:
- What the brain avoids in the retail environment
- The essential framework the brain uses to organize the shopping experience
- Best practices for retail environments
- How to activate Neurological Iconic Signatures at the store

---

THE PROBLEM: HOW TO ROCK THE AISLE?

A cookie and cake mix manufacturer was going around and around with focus groups on how to design a new concept for a product display that would appeal to shoppers as they approached the end of the aisle. Focus group results kept coming back consistently conflicted (yes, that's an oxymoron, but apt). Should they try the new design or stick with the known way of doing things? The time and financial investment involved was significant, and as we know, shoppers don't want to learn a new aisle configuration unless there is a good reason for it.

It's a jungle in there. Literally, from your brain's point of view, when you walk into a store—let's say, your typical supermarket—regions of your brain react the same way that they did when our ancient predecessors made their dangerous progress across the Serengeti.

For example, what would you guess would alarm your subconscious, setting off a 100,000-year-old internal warning system as you wander the aisles?

171

The answer is something as common as an end cap (that's the display area at the end of most supermarket aisles). It triggers what neuroscience describes as an avoidance response deep within your subconscious. The sharp edges of the metal shelves pose a potential threat to you—just as the sharp tip of a branch would in the jungle. You could be blinded, cut, perhaps bleed to death, right there amid the Cheerios and Cap'n Crunch.

Ridiculous in today's world? Of course, but your brain still registers the danger and responds accordingly. It alerts your body to the subconsciously perceived threats and directs you to avoid them, and get out quickly.

Your brain is geared, from evolution's millennia, to seek out and protect you from the dangers that lurk around you. That sharp corner—of the end cap or your kitchen cabinet—represents just such a threat, and your brain cannot help but react instantaneously, and subconsciously, to avoid it.

 The brain dislikes straight lines and sharp edges. Where possible, avoiding incorporating sharp lines in a store setting makes the experience much more pleasing to the brain.

In many studies across categories and retailers, we have found display devices with rounded edges to have greater levels of neurological effectiveness, and shelf dividers known as "blades" with rounded edges to outperform regular linear dividers. The lesson here is to remove the perceived threat that sharp edges present, and the uber-watchdog, that 24/7 sentry sitting atop your shoulders—your subconscious mind—will relax and be happy.

This principle was confirmed in a recent study for another food manufacturer. Here's what we did, and what we discovered:

Variables tested: three aisle designs (one with rounded edges)
Gender map: 50 percent male and 50 percent female
Findings: the design with rounded corners significantly outperformed the other two designs. Rolling this out in test markets resulted in a significant increase in sales—15 percent. That's how much the brain likes rounded edges.

What else prompts your subconscious to respond when you're roaming the retail range?

Our in-store studies have revealed another intriguing fact. It appears **the brain prefers natural textures**. The exact same aisles with the same products and features with alterations in textures performed significantly differently, the key learning being natural textures seem to evoke a deep emotional response in the brain. We humans are creatures of nature, and as such, we are neurologically oriented to find the sight, feel, scent, and even the sound of things like wood, grass, leaves, and water familiar, comfortable, and inviting.

The subconscious can be "fooled" to a limited degree, though. For example, plastic representations of wooden surfaces can substitute for the real thing, if executed authentically and plausibly.

Are You Experienced?

The brain thrives on new experiences. But experiences, as we have all learned in various ways living our lives, come in all sizes, shapes, and levels of success.

Retailers strive to make the shopping experience positive, fulfilling, and entertaining. For market research purposes though, with a thousand sensory inputs at each turn, shopping can be nearly impossible for humans to distill and describe in clear and useful terms. In the retail sphere, what from a neurological perspective makes for a positive experience? What are the pain points of purchasing for the consumer?

1. Navigating through the ranges of pricing and array of features
2. Having to make a choice between options
3. Parting with cash to make a purchase

Entertainment can act as an antidote to these pain points. More on that in a few paragraphs. Let's examine the basics from the brain's point of view.

SHOPPER EXPERIENCE FRAMEWORK

How can we quantify and compare superior experiences in the retail environment?

We have found in our research a number of elements that give an edge, that separate out one purchase enjoyment experience from another. Studies across categories, retailers, and the globe have revealed startling commonalities we have incorporated into a framework to analyze and evaluate in-store shopping experiences.

The Shopper Experience Framework comprises seven critical elements. Like the Brand Essence Framework, the Shopper Experience Framework encompasses an entire experience, categorizing the process the way the brain does, from the simple and personal to the complex and metaphorical.

Resonance in the consumer's mind to the Shopper Experience Framework's dimensions are measured using both continuous EEG measurements and the DSR technique discussed earlier.

The seven dimensions of the Shopper Experience Framework are:

1. Information
2. Environment
3. Entertainment
4. Education
5. Simplicity
6. Self-Worth/Social Worth
7. Community

Information: The person immersed in a shopping experience must find it rich in information and informational relevance. Information is intimately related to "findability." Being able to find what one wants easily is a hallmark and crucial benchmark of a superior experience. The NeuroMetrics we use to evaluate information are Attention, Memory, and Awareness. We typically evaluate the organizational design of the categories in the store for ease of use and intuitiveness. We evaluate displays, promotions, and product information for clarity and understanding. We evaluate menus and menu boards for comprehensiveness. It's useful to measure the Deep Subconscious Response to the following key categories: **findability, ease, simplicity, discovery, and pleasure.**

Enabling information search without the use of words or numbers can work wonders in the in-store environment. Our studies have found that effective in-store environments creatively use imagery and iconography to enhance emotional processing and avoid taxing the memory with words and numbers.

From the sales consultant in a store's fashion and beauty departments to the technology sales representative in a computer store, **human beings play a vital role** in providing information to the consumer. As an integral component of in-store analysis, for stores where humans primarily provide information, we record and analyze these conversations to evaluate them for their neurological effectiveness. This technique is particularly useful in the pharmaceutical industry to analyze the neurological effectiveness of sales representatives whose role, and challenge, is to provide information to physicians who on average have less than 90 seconds to devote to this process.

When it comes to new products or features, humans hunger for knowledge and information. We subconsciously seek information as we forage down the aisles: *what's new?* Was it there last time or is it really new? Neurological testing is designed to reveal if there is a manageable amount of information that the brain can absorb in the retail setting, or is it too overwhelming, causing the subconscious to "shut down" the attention devoted to individual stimuli. Recent neuroscience research is indicating that the older we get, the harder it is to suppress distractions. This has huge implications for the retail industry, especially with the increase in aging populations in many countries around the globe.

Environment: Environment refers to the physical context of the shopping experience. This context is by definition multisensory and provides numerous opportunities for implicit priming to set the shopper in the right frame of mind, motivate purchasing, and imagine enjoying the products relevant to their life. The core NeuroMetrics of environment include Attention, Emotion, Memory, Purchase Intent, and Novelty. Across categories, retailers, restaurants, fast and quick service outlets, malls, and even websites, the multisensory environment triggers multiple subconscious associations the consumer has formed with brands, products, occasions, and life events. Our studies have consistently shown that environments that mimic the consumer's natural environment for product consumption create superior Purchase Intent compared to environments that do not.

Environments that prime the occasions or life situations in which the consumer uses or experiences the displayed products and services create significant Emotion, Purchase Intent, and Novelty. A large company making baby foods and baby products asked us for recommendations on idealized environments for moms who shop for babies and very young children. Based on our research on retail environments, we proposed creating a separate room (similar to the high-fidelity rooms within retailers that sell high-end home audio and video systems) with padded floors, softer lights, and a quiet atmosphere with a lullaby playing. The goal was to recreate an environment that was a noise-free sanctuary for the mom. Our neurological studies revealed that this multisensory sanctuary contributed to high levels of Emotion, Purchase Intent, and Novelty.

Environments are also created by the creative use of merchandising features, displays, aisle designs, signage, and end-caps. These elements play a vital role in re-creating natural environments, but we have also found that too many elements can compete with each other, lowering the effectiveness of all. Thus, while it is important to study these elements individually to understand their distinctive Effectiveness, Emotional Engagement, and Purchase Intent levels, it is also important to study them together.

We have also found that different display elements serve different purposes at different locations in the store. An end-cap in an aisle serves primarily to generate Attention, whereas Novelty is more likely to be generated in the lobby of the store. But when the consumer approaches the aisle from the lobby, the end-cap can begin to generate Emotional Engagement, and significantly contribute to Purchase Intent by defining a suitable physical context as the consumer enters the aisle.

It is also very revealing to analyze the Deep Subconscious Response of the consumer to different designed environments. Instead of finding whether the shopping experience was "pleasant," "comfortable," or "exciting," we have found it more productive to look at the Deep Subconscious Response to aspects and truths of the environment that pertain to the consumer's life, such as "homelike," "genuine," and "dinner time."

We have also found that "implicit environments" can be created through category and product adjacencies. That is to say, placing selected products next to each other can create an implicit environment without explicitly labeling it as such. Another kind of implicit environment can be created by placing categories together that are emotionally or logically related in the consumer's mind. These "microenvironments" can create high levels of Emotional Engagement and Purchase Intent that exceed levels each product can attain on its own. It is our observation that a linear warehouse-like placement of products in stores is much less neurologically Effective than environments that create a superior shopping experience with an environment that is natural, effective, and intuitive in the consumer's mind.

Entertainment: A huge benefit of modern life is the luxury of being entertained while we shop. This is such a compelling feature of the experience that we seek it out whenever we can. What a joy to be able to delight in the perusal of edibles, rather than constantly looking over one's shoulder for predators! We are thrilled by it every time. The combination of shopping (which the brain more or less equates with hunting and gathering) and entertainment is enormously powerful. That's why shopping has become a national pastime.

As I pointed out earlier, shopping to the subconscious is often akin to wading into an ocean of numbers and words. This sea of information can be effectively navigated through emotional cues that guide the shopper through islands of entertainment. We have found that **entertainment provides emotional relief, minimizes the pain of purchase, and increases overall shopping time.**

Entertainment also seems to proffer the side benefits of converting the goal-oriented shopper into one that browses and is generally more relaxed. The consequence of this transformation is that the shopper becomes more open to considering categories and products that were not originally under consideration. The primary NeuroMetrics of entertainment are Emotion and Novelty. While there can be considerable entertainment value to features and displays, we find larger increases in Emotional Engagement and Novelty when entertainment involves interactions with humans, animals, or technology.

When we explicitly isolate and test the individual aspects of the in-store environment that are meant to entertain the consumer, rating them on entertainment value and potential, we have consistently observed that a higher entertainment value is highly correlated with better ratings of the overall shopping experience. Worth noting here is that personnel in the store, be they clerks, waiters, or floorwalkers, play a vital role in providing an entertainment boost for the consumer. To this end, we have found it useful to evaluate the scripts and delivery performances of personnel to analyze the neurological Effectiveness of their typical interactions with shoppers.

Education: Superior shopping experiences are those that enable consumers to walk away not only having absorbed a lot of information, but having **extracted insight** that becomes part of an education experience. Education is more than information. It is distilled insights that can be used on an ongoing basis. As discussed earlier, the human brain seeks to categorize, organize, and make sense of the chaotic world we live in. The insights gained could be human, cultural, about oneself, about life or society, or perhaps about the future.

The brain conducts a constant quest for knowledge and facts, from trivia to major insights. To cite a specific example of the importance and relevance of this neurological tendency in the retail field, we have analyzed aisles in a category that we prepopulated with the usual mix of display exhortations—promotions, price points, and calls to action. We computed the Effectiveness scores for the overall experience and the Deep Subconscious Response for these aisles. We then replaced the usual materials with small signage presenting facts, insights, and trivia that had educational value. When we re-analyzed the same aisles, we found a significant jump in Effectiveness.

We find that **displays emphasizing educational value are processed differently** in the brain than displays that have purely entertainment value. Displays with insights and educational value are processed more "rationally" and prime shoppers to conduct more "considered shopping." Consumers engage in more price comparisons and feature comparisons than when exposed to more entertainment-oriented displays.

We have also noticed higher levels of brand loyalty shifts when educational materials are presented at the point of purchase. Similarly, for a new brand that is attempting to penetrate a space owned and dominated by a category leader, educational displays can prime the consumer to engage in more rational decision making and potentially weaken the more emotional hold of brand loyalty on the consumer's mind.

Simplicity: Simplicity improves the shopping experience. Whether it understands the basic purpose of the product or service in the first place, finding additional information, streamlining the purchase experience, transporting products to your home, opening the package, or fixing a problem, simplicity must be a core component of the consumer's experience. This is why a new aisle design in a familiar store is almost universally disliked, no matter how beautiful or functional it may be. Once the brain has become comfortable with a store layout, its sense of simplicity is upset by the new layout because it requires energy and cognitive resources to master. If the new layout is well designed and pleasing, then the rebellious brain will learn it more quickly, eventually coming to enjoy the shopping experience even more than before. NeuroMetrics of simplicity are Attention and Memory. As things get simpler, less explicit attention is required and the consumer can navigate primarily by accessing memory, often implicit memory. Walking the aisles becomes a similar experience to driving home from work.

We have found that simplicity is often associated with numerosity, color, taxonomy, and the fluency of processing. When we measured the Deep Subconscious Response to shopping environments, we found, not surprisingly, that fewer objects in the environment contributed to a sense of simplicity. But we also found that too much environmental simplicity could become perceived as a lack of choice. In our studies, we found simplicity turning into lack of choice in different ways from category to category in the store, on an aisle-to-aisle basis. Our studies have led us to conclude that there is no general principle that can be applied uniformly to determine an optimal level of simplicity in a shopping environment.

The **intelligent use of color** also contributes to a sense of simplicity. We have found that aisle designers can intelligently use color to separate and highlight, thereby creating greater simplicity of navigation. Taxonomy is another key dimension of simplicity. The choice of words, categories, and subcategories create logical hierarchies of information that can significantly impact findability, and thereby become a core contributor to perceived simplicity.

Self-Worth/Social Worth: An experience that enhances one's self-worth might transpire in a store when the salesperson compliments you on how amazing you look. Or perhaps as you walk out of the store with your purchase, the sales clerk says, "that was a very good deal you got!" Self-worth arises from an experience in which shoppers come away feeling good about themselves.

Social worth arises from an experience in which shoppers come away feeling good about their contribution to society. "I am a smart shopper and I provide environmentally-conscious products for my family on a tight budget" brings a sense of both self-worth and social worth. Our brains are hard-wired to balance our individual and group needs. When both needs are met by a shopping experience, we are most satisfied. Self-worth and social worth both help us withstand the pain of parting with cash. The primary NeuroMetric of self-worth/social worth is Emotion.

We have found a number of elements in the in-store environment that can naturally enhance self-worth. According to our studies, signage in the store that stimulates an affirmation of one's worthiness increases perceptions of self-worth. Signage in the store that proclaims that the "**consumer is deserving**" increases self-worth. Shopping trips where some percent of the overall trip purchase is donated to a worthy cause of the consumer's choosing enhances self-worth. In studying coupons, we have found that **coupons that include an act of charity** can produce a significant rise in Purchase Intent. Given that most corporations engage in corporate charity, we have seen that contributing to charitable causes in a way that includes the consumer in the process, thereby increasing the consumer's self-worth as well as supporting the charity, can be a doubly beneficial effort.

In one study, we tested the impact of charitable giving at the point of purchase. Consumers were asked to choose one of four deserving causes to receive a percentage of what they spent. We found that this simple gesture resulted in a huge increase in Emotional Engagement, as well as much higher Deep Subconscious Response scores for words relating to the "pleasure" or "satisfaction" associated with the shopping experience.

Community: **People want to belong.** It may be a car club, sales club, club of people who love panda bears or a group of people who believe in green products. Whatever it is, humans are hard-wired to want to *belong* as part of a community.

In our early hunting and gathering days, the community literally helped ensure basic survival. As we evolved, the conscious and subconscious rewards of community became more subtle, but nonetheless deeply valued and, therefore, consistently sought after: companionship, personal fulfillment, shared cultural experiences, "tribal status," and more.

A community serves a larger purpose. The explosion of social networks on the Internet today is just the latest example of that fundamental fact. Digital communications have provided a way for people to pursue their true niches and find or form communities to which they want to belong. From a neurological perspective, people value a shopping experience that automatically enlists them as members of an exclusive and unique community.

The subconscious seems to assign superior value to an experience that combines a sense of exclusivity, on the one hand, with a sense of belonging on the other—a difficult act to balance.

For the subconscious, exclusivity and belonging are not inconsistent; quite the opposite, they can and do coexist comfortably together. The NeuroMetrics of community are Attention, Emotion, and Memory.

Community can have many foundations—geographical, lifestyle-based, age-based, ethnic, preference- or interest-based, or purpose- or passion-based. We find that communities **fulfill deep emotional needs,** so naturally when we analyze retail environments, we specifically seek elements that are intended to showcase a sense of belonging, or affiliation with a community of choice. We then analyze those elements to find the level of attention the community generates in the consumer's mind: the emotional engagement of the community and the memorability of the community. We then measure the Deep Subconscious Response to community-related themes by analyzing resonance between the shopping experience and words like "belonging," "affiliation," and "community."

Sorting Through the Stimuli

Your brain is subject to an onslaught of stimuli in the shopping environment and it's becoming more cluttered all the time. You may feel fully assimilated to the in-store cacophony, but your prefrontal cortex is firing in high gear as you stroll the aisles, simultaneously processing all the sights, sounds, smells, and tactile sensations you're subjected to . . . even tastes, when you stop and sample the occasional product offering.

Your neural networks are sending and exchanging data at blinding speed, correlating all these incoming sensations, and the prefrontal cortex is orchestrating the entire process, sorting through the coursing streams, assigning priorities, calling on stored memories, and blending the symphony of stimuli in order to make sense of it all.

"The music of merchandising" plays in your head as an ever-changing melody, rising and falling in tempo and intensity as you stroll down the aisles. Your brain collects data from the visual cortex, processing what each of your eyes are seeing, turning that information into three-dimensional, stereoscopic imagery and simultaneously matching that with data streams flooding forth from the auditory, olfactory, and tactile centers. In turn, it's doing the same thing with the "lead information" streaming in from your ears, fingertips, nose, and mouth.

And all the while, your brain is reminding and enabling you to breathe, blink, swallow, walk forward, turn your head, focus your eyes, and countless millions of other activities that are largely and often exclusively the purview of your subconscious mind.

Subconscious Signals

Ever stood in front of a whole drugstore shelf full of toothpastes and felt a certain ennui? Pondering which to choose: paste or gel, whitening/brightening/cavity-preventing, mint or wintergreen-flavored, white, striped or aqua, seemingly ad infinitum? If you have, it's because of a fascinating neurological phenomenon called repetition blindness.

Your mind checks out when confronted with too much of one thing. (Even a good thing!)

So, what does this mean? This means that your product's visual appeal when stacked adjacent to your competitors is critical, especially for categories where product sizes, shapes, and packaging tend to be very similar. Find ways to stand out for the subconscious, and it will reward you with its attention.

Repetition blindness occurs when your frontal cortex has to process an array of similar visual images all streaming in from the visual cortex. Coming back to our dental health example, when your brain "sees" box after box of identically-shaped toothpaste packages, lined up in row after row, many sporting very similar colors, logos, words, and images . . . well, your brain takes a kind of mini-holiday.

"Too much, too identical, can't differentiate, where's the novelty," it tells itself. And the result is that your subconscious perceives it as a sort of big blur.

We're neurologically programmed to search for differences. To seek out things that enable us to make sense out of the environment we find ourselves in and to navigate our world safely and productively. When the brain is presented with a series of repetitive images—even if there are some differences among them—repetition blindness sets in. The brain no longer "sees" each individual image as it would if that image stood alone, or with only a small number of similar/identical images.

Ultimately, of course, the brain reasserts itself and makes sense out of what it sees—if it didn't, we might all be stuck in the health and beauty aids section forever, staring at the sea of Crest and Colgate before us. As it does in so many other instances large and small, critical and minimal in scale and importance, the frontal cortex takes command, and we reach out, pluck the toothpaste of choice off the shelf, and plunk it into our cart.

 The solution is to stagger carefully your displays, both in depth and height.

We were blind, but now we see.

How does that three-pound mass of neurons, water, chemicals, and electrical signals perched atop you manage the in-store product selection process? By calling upon a mix of memories stored in your subconscious.

What did you choose last time? Do you favor mint over regular flavor? Does your subconscious recall preferring the tactile sensation of gel versus paste? Did the combination of colors on the package trigger an appealing response? Was your brain primed by something to default to your brand of choice?

But memory isn't all that's at work in the aisle.

Marketing Magnets

Has a clever personal products company realized that your brain is drawn, magnet-like, to human faces? If so, is there packaging or a piece of merchandising material nearby that depicts a friendly visage?

Bingo! Advantage, neuromarketer.

 Neurologically, we are designed to focus on faces. They are our windows into what may lie in store for us, danger or affection, trust or treachery. A face nearly always ranks highest on the brain's list of things to monitor.

So what? So, feature faces every way you can, because by doing so you are playing directly into something very central to the brain, and it will reward you with its concentration and the precious gift of assigned cognitive resources.

But that face-featuring shelf talker is just today's neuromerchandising method. Effective, but there are other "tricks of the trade" that can be applied to win your attention, break through the blindness, and attract you to choose a certain product.

COMING SOON TO A SUPERMARKET NEAR YOU: NEUROLOGICAL ICONIC SIGNATURES

Remember the Neurological Iconic Signatures that were discussed earlier? The brain's high points achieved while actually experiencing a product? Here's where the brain would love to be reminded of them: in the store.

To see how that might work, let's place ourselves behind a shopping cart, wheeling our way toward the wine aisle (hey, watch out for that end cap! This store obviously hasn't done all of its neuromarketing homework).

What's happening to you as you go? As we described earlier, tens of billions upon billions of neurons are firing away, actively processing the sheer floods of data coursing in from all five of your senses. Your conscious mind is unaware of all this activity, but your subconscious is not only smoothly accommodating all this information, it is also simultaneously coordinating it all together and matching it up against earlier data stored in your memory.

Meanwhile, it's also telling your legs and feet to move in rhythm to enable you to walk forward and keep your balance. It's also telling your auditory system to pay attention to the announcement of special savings in the produce section. It's triggering your visual system to track what's ahead and alongside you simultaneously. Lastly, it's registering all the cans, bottles, logos, colors, signs, shelving, lighting, the cool round metal of the cart handle in your fingers, and the textures of the tile on the floor below your shoes, and so much more that this book couldn't possibly relate it all.

And it's scanning for the familiar, the target, the light green bottle, and the parchment-tinted label.

Now, imagine that as you approach that section of the store and turn down the aisle your subconscious is met with something wholly unexpected and seemingly out of place: a **Neurological Iconic Signature**.

Let's say as the leading edge of your cart crosses an invisible infrared line, triggering a tiny unseen sensor on the nearby shelf, you suddenly hear the unmistakable "POP!" followed immediately by the equally familiar "glug-glug-glug" of a wine or champagne bottle opening and being poured.

What does your brain do? It **reacts** big time. Almost exactly as it would if you were holding a bottle, opening it, pouring it yourself, and hearing those identical sounds. Suddenly, your brain is experiencing essentially the same neurological responses as it would if you were about to actually consume a glass of wine for real. (Read more about Mirror Neuron activation in Chapter 9.)

Do you think that, upon encountering this powerfully resonant audio stimulus, the consumer's subconscious would respond with a stronger indication of Purchase Intent? Next time you're in a supermarket, just for fun (and profit) think about how many different opportunities exist for NIS marketing, and how many different brands and products it could benefit. Think about what individual NIS' might be for those brands and products, and how different senses could be reached and appealed to with NIS stimuli.

Sight, sound, taste, touch, smell: Imagine a shopping environment that elevated the experience into something surprising yet familiar, stimulating, and pleasurable. Imagine having many billions of neurons firing with recognition and gratification subconsciously as you shop, subtly enriching the experience.

If you don't drink wine, it's highly unlikely that encountering an NIS related to the core experience of consuming it would cause you to buy it, and the same with any other product. We're not mindless sheep, strongly susceptible to seduction against our basic wishes and will, our ingrained preferences and prejudices. The brain is far too sophisticated and powerful to be so easily moved. NIS' are themselves powerful, to be sure—but they're not *that* powerful.

On the other hand, if you enjoy wine, and your subconscious is presented with a familiar, engaging stimulus that reminds you how pleasant, enjoyable, relaxing, and rewarding a nice glass of Cabernet can be, or a celebratory flute of champagne—in the middle of that supermarket aisle!—well, that's neuromarketing.

THE SUBCONSCIOUS SIGNIFICANCE OF SIGNAGE

One of the more important changes that has occurred in the retail industry in recent years is the proliferation of in-store signage, specifically in-store video displays.

As in-store signage has multiplied, it has brought with it a set of questions and challenges that confront consumer goods marketers and retailers. Foremost among them is how much is too much. A corollary is what works best and what works least effectively.

Once again, here is where neurological testing can provide answers that no other research methodology can offer.

Let me start with the answer to the question, how much is too much? The fact is there isn't one correct, one-size-fits-all solution. The reason for that lies in the human brain. We are capable of taking in and processing vast amounts of data. Since our survival depended on being able to monitor our environment constantly, using multiple senses simultaneously, we are very well equipped for the modern supermarket jungle.

But, there is a limit. The frontal cortex is continuously monitoring what we are taking in in the way of stimuli, and it discards data just as continuously, making split-second decisions on what is important and what isn't, what is interesting/potentially useful and what is not, and what to transfer to memory. That subconscious mechanism operates automatically.

But overload the visual cortex with too much similar or identical data, and as I described before, repetition blindness sets in. For our other senses as well, the subconscious selects what it will allocate our Attention, Emotional connection, and Memory Retention to—and what it will overlook or ignore.

A Sea of Orange Amid the Shelves

Case in point: A major European retail chain wanted to know how the visual environment in its stores might be affecting shopper attitudes and behavior.

So one evening after closing time, we went in with a full production crew and shot eight hours of high-definition video, documenting every bit of signage in one of their stores. Then we went back to the lab and analyzed every bit and byte of it.

The evidence was right there on the screen: their stores had experienced a literal *explosion* **of signage.** In addition to the normal store branding, directional, and departmental signage, there were signs atop individual racks of goods. There were overhead signs featuring seasonal sales messaging. There were, of course, hang tags everywhere. End caps boasted multiple signs, almost from floor to eye level. And on and on.

But amid this ocean of promotion, one feature especially caught our eyes. Along the aisles, the shelves were peppered with orange "money off" talkers. Depending on the particular department, there could be dozens of these little items, boasting multiple price points. They stretched from low shelves to high ones, one end of the aisle to the other. Frequently they were lined up in an almost-seamless stream, taking up a good portion of the edge of each shelf.

We knew the effect on consumers without having to run an actual neurological test—because we had already done so much work in the retail category that we understood the neurological impact of such price-promotion proliferation.

Confronted with this colorful assault at a point the brain becomes unwilling to devote the additional cognitive resources to attempt to decipher the commercial cacophony. Such a surplus of salesmanship results in a subconscious "tuning out" on the part of the consumer.

In addition, it creates confusion in the subconscious as the brain attempts to reconcile the concept of "sales/money off" with existing notions of brand image and value. The brain is geared to operate as efficiently as possible, conserving its energies for its constantly evolving hierarchy of needs, assigning cognitive resources to the functions that will result in the best return on that investment.

Sorting through a sea of shelf stickers, attempting to make sense out of them, quickly drops in the brain's ever-changing list of priorities—and the result is, at a certain stage we may walk right past them without even really seeing them.

HIDE AND SEEK

We discovered other neurological obstacles as well. For example, we saw numerous examples of **occlusion** occurring.

The occlusion phenomenon is one of the neurological "best practices" that we advise companies about. In comic book parlance, it can be used for good or evil.

In simple terms, occlusion is when something is partially obscured by something else (see Figure 15.1).

In this particular circumstance, occlusion was happening to the signage on some end caps. Products on the shelves were stacked in such a way as to hide a portion of the signage behind them. This was especially important because in many cases the signage was offering valuable information to the shopper—sales prices, "two for one" offers, rebate information, and so forth. You already know from reading above in this chapter about the important role that information plays in creating a superior shopping experience.

Figure 15.1
Occlusion

Source: Photo courtesy of Adsoftheworld.com

As I said, from a neurological perspective, **occlusion can actually work to intrigue the brain.** It's a simplified visual puzzle—and the brain loves solving simple puzzles, especially visual ones.

For certain signage—such as that in quick service restaurants' menu boards—partially obscuring one product behind another can not only save precious messaging space, but it can attract the brain's interest. The eye might linger just a little bit longer, trying to uncover the partially hidden image. When it does, there's a small neurological reward—we applaud ourselves for solving the mystery.

But in other situations, such as the ones discovered in our midnight video expedition, occlusion can work against everyone's best interests. If you make something too difficult for the brain, you run the risk of causing the subconscious to rule against the further expenditure of precious neurological resources in an attempt to sort it all out to our satisfaction.

In a quick-service restaurant setting, the subconscious can fairly readily infer from the partial product seen what the actual product is. There are enough clues to enable that. But in another retail setting, the brain may be unable to decipher easily what the remainder of the partially occluded message is, especially if it's to do with numbers. In that kind of circumstance, the brain simply writes off devoting any extra effort to attempt to figure it all out. Your expensive, time-intensive signage efforts were just for naught.

VIDEO HERE, THERE, AND EVERYWHERE

It's now a cliché to talk about the universality of video in our lives. We're living that reality daily. And, as noted, it's become more commonplace in the retail world. Screens are surfacing everywhere from shopping carts to shelves and escalators to checkout counters.

So the questions arise: **how effective is this medium in this medium?** And what are some neurological best practices that marketers can follow to maximize their investment in video messaging?

Starting with the "big picture" and moving on to more specifics: as a neurological rule of thumb, simply running existing TV commercials on in-store screens is generally not as effective as conventional wisdom would have it. In-store video should be developed to stimulate purchase and consumption.

Unlike your living room, the retail environment is already saturated with stimuli for the subconscious. Your body is in motion, all five of your senses are in more active modes (although sight and hearing are certainly stimulated watching TV at home), there are multiple competing sources of incoming data (other shoppers, and the PA system, squeaky cart wheels, and so on). The net effect is that apportioning/rationing of cognitive resources as have been discussed. The brain budgets.

TV commercials usually demand that we follow some sort of story line, often with multiple characters. They are designed and executed with the idea (the hope!) that the viewer will be devoting most or all of their attention more or less continuously to the message. They frequently depend on our witnessing specific scenes, or hearing specific lines spoken.

The in-store environment conspires against all of that. We are not static, we are moving. Our attention is attracted in several directions at once. We are in a social setting, with strangers present, not in our homes by ourselves or with just our families.

In-store video messaging must, therefore, basically be different in its conception and execution in order to adapt best to this more difficult environment.

- **Visual continuity is less important than visual content.** What I mean by that is that individual scenes should be the focus, and less so the "framework" within which they are presented. The great likelihood is that the shopper will only glimpse a portion of the video at any one time. If the video is looped, they may experience more of it as they shop through the store, but approach production with the mindset that you may only be able to communicate via single scenes.
- The brain will retain imagery and other content that it deems worth devoting attention and memory capacity to, up to a point. So making individual scenes as self-contained, impactful, and memorable as possible is more important than it might be in creating footage for a typical TV spot.
- **Portraying people is a priority.** Elsewhere you've read how the brain is fundamentally drawn to the human face. We seek community and interaction. We need to recognize other members of our species. In a hectic, crowded retail environment, where demands are continuously being made on our subconscious, the familiar/reassuring image of human faces anchors us.
- **Semantics suffer.** Unless you communicate in single words or extremely brief/concise phrases, the use of semantics in store videos is likely to be a waste. The chances that a shopper will see them in the first place are greatly diminished from what would normally be the case in the home. Neurologically speaking, unless we can connect semantics with some other information (visual and/or aural), in and of themselves those

semantics will probably not succeed in earning the allocation of valuable cognitive resources by the brain.

- **Music and more matters.** While visual stimuli are accorded priority status by the brain, audio information is hardly overlooked. In fact, in the stimulus-rich-environment of a store, the ability to capture the brain's attention with music or sound effects becomes more of a priority than it would be in the home setting. This is one category where borrowing already established musical phrases or "branded" sound effects from commercials can pay synergistic benefits.

THE MEASURED MILES: IN-STORE NEUROLOGICAL TESTING

Consider the figure 46,800. It turns out that's a very interesting and important number when it comes to supermarket shopping.

Actually, it's two numbers, slightly different, that I've combined to make my point. And here's what it is:

- The median average supermarket size is **46,755 square feet**.
- The average number of items in a supermarket is **46,852**.

That is a lot of goods in a lot of space. The prospect of having to ask consumers what they're thinking, what they're looking at, what's attracting their attention, what's engaging their emotions, and what they're remembering all while they're pushing along through 46,755 square feet, surrounded by 46,852 individual items . . . well, you see where I'm going.

You couldn't answer accurately. *I* couldn't answer accurately. *Nobody* could answer accurately. Nevertheless, this is the cathedral of commerce. This is where all the new product concepts, the packaging designs, the marketing campaigns, the displays, and the slotting fees have to pay off—in sales.

So it's critical to find out *what* consumers are reacting to, and *how* they're reacting.

Because $547.1 billion dollars are riding on it (that's the latest annual total of supermarket sales).

Neurological testing is the solution. The brain will tell us the answers to all those questions—in real time, with pinpoint accuracy. There are two ways to measure the brain's responses to the actual shopping experience.

• In-store EEG testing

One of the great advantages of EEG-based neurological testing is the fact that the equipment is easily adapted for **portability/mobility.** We can capture the same brainwave activity in the linguini section as we do in the laboratory.

A test subject can stroll the aisles and shop just as they normally would. All the while, EEG sensors acquire brainwave activity at 2,000 times a second, across multiple regions of the brain, and that data is recorded on a portable hard drive for processing and analysis.

Simultaneously, eye-tracking equipment is capturing the shopper's precise focal location, enabling the brainwave data being gathered to be matched with exactly what they were looking at, at any given millisecond.

But what if, for any number of reasons, there is a need to measure shoppers' neurological responses outside the actual store environment? Perhaps it's a need for repeated passes down a number of aisles. Perhaps it's because a client wishes to alter certain aspects of the shopping experience, to determine consumers' different reactions, and to attempt to do so with real shoppers in a real store setting would be prohibitively time-consuming/expensive.

In those circumstances, there is a fascinating alternative:

• Video Realistic Technology

Digital technology has advanced to the point where the in-store shopping experience can be replicated, with startling realism, without a test subject ever having to step foot inside an actual store.

Video Realistic methodology allows subjects to push a virtual shopping cart down virtual aisles, all the while scanning virtual products on virtual shelves. But the technology doesn't stop there.

Shoppers can pause and pick up products, examine them on all sides, and replace them on the shelf. The high-definition video codec enables a subject to read the fine print on a label, experience the rich colors of the packaging, or see the smile on the face of the infant on the bottle of apple juice.

It is **a fully immersive shopping experience, without the store.** The brain responds in the same fundamental ways that it would in an actual retail setting. From a neurological perspective, the stimuli are much the same: the aisle looks real, the shelves are stocked, and the package looks like a real package. Everything is in the correct scale. Even other shoppers are in place.

The tactile sense is not the same—the subject doesn't feel the weight of the package, for example—but for most market research purposes, that exception isn't a mission-critical one.

The flexibility of Video Realistic is one of its greatest virtues. Store environments can be changed with a few keystrokes. Packages can be moved, substituted, altered in any way desired. Displays can be changed, signage can be shifted—this attribute and others makes Video Realistic a very viable alternative, and increasing numbers of marketers are discovering its value.

THE RESOLUTION: DELIGHT THE MIND WITH SOFT AND SOOTHING DESIGNS

For our cookie/cake mix client considering a new placement of products, we tested several different end cap designs, ranging from traditional, square end caps to newer, rounded-end caps. We paid particular attention to the Emotional Engagement scores that each generated. We found that the rounded end caps incorporating natural elements and imagery reflecting a "home-looking" design worked best. What the client had hoped to do was to create a layout creating the impression of two particular products together in a pleasant, homey kitchen, without spending a fortune on materials and square footage, and it worked. Not only did sales go up for the featured product on the end cap, sales went up for their entire category.

3D MATRIX

Fresh out of our laboratories is a technology we call 3D Matrix. In the post-Avatar world, 3D will become more and more the norm for the consumer experience, and therefore increasingly so for the market research field. Glasses and touch gloves enable our test subjects to experience starting levels of perceived reality.

FUTURE SHOPPING

What can neurological testing tell us about the future of retail, and in-store marketing? There are lines that we can draw out over the horizon, starting with what we know about the brain and how it functions—what it likes and doesn't like.

We know **the brain delights in novelty**. As humans, we are predisposed to seek out the new. So retail environments could benefit from fresh designs, new applications of lighting, sound, and textures, innovative ways of presenting merchandise. For example, we know that **the brain dislikes straight lines**—so a creative retailer might decide to design a store setting that emphasizes curves rather than hard angles.

We know that **the brain prefers natural textures over artificial textures**. Technology is likely to bring us advances in synthetic materials that almost perfectly mimic their real, organic sources of inspiration.

We know that **the brain assigns priority to our sense of sight**. So expect to see much more use of video and other moving images in the retail setting.

My prediction is that as marketers and retailers become more knowledgeable about neurological testing and realize its potential, they will also come to appreciate and apply the power of neuromarketing methods like Neurological Iconic Signatures.

The future of shopping will hold even more delights for consumers, and more potential rewards for marketers, as retailers gain a deeper understanding of the brain, how it interacts with the store environment, and how to leverage that knowledge to create a more effective shopping experience.

Takeaways:

1. The brain avoids sharp corners. Let's face it, how many 90-degree angles do you see in nature?
2. The brain approaches the store the same way it approached the Serengeti: in hunting, gathering mode. It's a serious task.
3. Humans engage with the shopping experience in seven dimensions: information, environment, entertainment, education, simplicity, self-worth/social worth, and community. These are all critical for a superior shopping experience.

CHAPTER 16

THE BUYING BRAIN AND ADVERTISING

At the end of this chapter, you'll know and be able to use the following:

- Specific neurological best practices to enhance the effectiveness of advertising messages
- Four key neuroscientific principles that form the basis for the most effective advertising
- The importance of priming

ADVERTISING EFFECTIVENESS FRAMEWORK

Measuring the brain's responses to advertising is valuable to agencies and clients in several ways. The 10 elements of the Advertising Effectiveness Framework enable analyses that are *unique and beyond* what conventional audience research methodologies can deliver. These elements are:

1. **Second-by-Second A-E-M Response:** The core NeuroMetrics of Attention, Emotion, and Memory are gathered for every second of a commercial. This helps **diagnose effective or ineffective segments** of the spot and aids in understanding which elements are lacking. These deep diagnostics into which of the core elements of the ad are contributing or lacking—the attentional component, the emotional component, or the memorability—are very useful in improving the content and implementing best practices. These diagnostics are not available through any other testing methodology.

   Assessing the effectiveness of the ad in the first five seconds helps us determine whether the ad runs the risk of viewer flight or tune-out.

193

Similarly, the way the spot ends is important, because brand logos and product messaging are placed near or at the end. Endings that are weak neurologically lessen the memorability of those brand logos, taglines, and value propositions.

Second-by-second response measurements enable precise identification of the high points and lulls of emotional engagement. We have found that ads that have lulls (low points of neurological effectiveness) in excess of four seconds suffer risk of viewer flight. Careful analysis of thousands of effective and ineffective ads has revealed that there are natural rhythms of neurological effectiveness in successful ads. Comparing typical profiles of effective ads to any ad identifies areas for, and potential degrees of, improvement. Note that these techniques do not favor any one kind of creative approach or another, but merely point out that there are natural rhythms for effective ads that a good agency or brand team can leverage. Aggregating the second-by-second scores into measures of Attention, Emotional Engagement, Memory Retention, and Overall Effectiveness helps us compare one version of an ad to another along multiple dimensions.

2. **Deep Subconscious Response:** We gather the unarticulated Deep Subconscious Response to the core creative brief, the brand image, price points, and other attributes and components of an ad. This neurological measurement gets at the implicit emotional and memory priming the ad evokes. The paradigms for this testing use implicit testing methods to gather neurological signatures in time intervals of **300 milliseconds or less**.

   An ad serves a number of purposes. In addition to conveying product and brand attributes that are meant to motivate a consumer to purchase, the ad conveys targeted messaging of a more general nature. Those messages may not be registered consciously or explicitly recalled by the subject, but they may (or may not) be registered by the subconscious. It is critical to know which messages have been received by the subconscious mind of the consumer, and which have not. Using the Deep Subconscious Response method provides a marker for what has been logged and tagged in the consumer's mind. We find it useful to measure the Deep Subconscious Response to the Brand Essence prior to having test subjects watch the ad, and then perform the Brand Essence test again after this viewing to determine what has changed. This reveals which of the brand elements have resonated from the ad.

3. **Wear-In and Wear-Out:** We gather NeuroMetrics through repeated exposures to the ad and diagnose whether the neurological

effectiveness of the ad remains unchanged or increases (Wear-In), or decreases (Wear-Out). Wear-In and Wear-Out metrics help an advertiser **optimize media buys** through managing reach (recommended for higher Wear-Out ads) and frequency (recommended for higher Wear-In ads). Since media buying is usually the most expensive component of the advertising budget, this particular metric can be of significant value to advertisers.

We have found that effective ads with a sharp Wear-Out profile, meaning high levels of effectiveness that drop sharply with repeat viewings, lend themselves to being virally spread through the Internet rather than through reach-based gross rating points (GRPs) on television.

4. **Neurological Compression:** Our proprietary neurological compression software automatically picks out the most neurologically salient seconds of an ad, and performs smoothing around these sequences to produce a compressed and neurologically optimized version of the ad. Our algorithms produce an **8- to 10-second version** of a 30-second spot. This optimized rendering enables advertisers to adapt expensive commercial productions for efficient and effective use in alternative video platforms, such as the Internet and mobile communications, where shorter lengths are required for viewership. Our observation, gained from many instances of creating neurologically compressed ads, is that effective commercials still tell a cogent and complete story when they are reduced from their original lengths.

   We have also created Purchase Intent-based compression, where the moments of maximal Purchase Intent are used to define the compression. We have found that ads compressed using the Purchase Intent Neuro-Metric tend to be well suited for display on TV screens in store aisles and at points of purchase. Similarly, we have found that the compression of ads using novelty creates treatments that are most effective on mobile phones and the Internet. These key neurological metrics provide significantly different lenses that enable us to create nuanced compressed versions of ads that are suited for different market purposes.

5. **Parietal (Taste/Touch/Smell) Brain Stimulation:** We directly monitor stimulation of the brain areas responsible for taste/touch/smell as the ad evolves, and when actual product consumption is featured. We have found that in effective ads, the ad does not just tell a story, but the imagery and story actually stimulate the areas of the brain corresponding to the core features of the product being enjoyed. This index of direct brain stimulation is valuable, especially for food and beverage makers. We have found it to be a powerful way to navigate between the need

to tell a compelling story and the need to showcase the features of the product that stimulate a direct brain response.

6. **Reach Propensity, Immediate Consumption, and Mirror Neuron System Activation:** While the neurological mechanisms behind the Mirror Neuron system are very complex and represent the current frontiers of neuroscience, this system has immediate applications in the world of marketing and advertising. (See Chapter 9 for a description of Mirror Neurons.) If the ad shows the product **in the act of being handled or consumed**, we look to Mirror Neuron activation to see whether the consumer's brain activates a mirror response to what it sees on the screen.

We have found interesting correlations between this Mirror Neuron activity and the desire for immediate consumption of the product, or the propensity to reach for the product. This metric reveals the extent to which an ad invites and stimulates the viewer to handle or consume the product immediately. A problem that vexes manufacturers and advertisers is that sometimes consumers buy a product, put it away, and never use or consume it. Determining the extent to which a consumer is motivated to practice consumption of the product while watching the ad could become an important metric for evaluating the effectiveness of the ad.

7. **Neurological Iconic Signature (NIS) Embedding:** Neurological Iconic Signatures are the unique moments in the product consumption experience that generate the highest levels of brain engagement. NIS responses are identified through Total Consumer Experience (TCE) testing, and can then be applied to verify how well the "face and voice" of the product are embedded through the length of a commercial. We identify overt embedding of the NIS, as well as the implicit embedding of the NIS through the entirety of the ad. We have found that ads that embed the NIS score higher across most dimensions, and **generate significantly higher Purchase Intent**. There are many nuanced and subtle methods of embedding the visual and audio elements of the NIS. We measure the effectiveness of each to calculate the overall weight of NIS activations in the ad. As mentioned, we have found that ads containing implicit and explicit activations of the NIS score higher on overall Effectiveness, and generate significantly greater Purchase Intent than ads that do not embed the NIS.

8. **Audio Coherence and Music/Voice Effectiveness:** Because we measure activity across the entire brain, we are able to measure the separate and combined effectiveness of music and narrative in an ad.

Music provides emotional context to advertising, and the brain uses context to interpret and understand the meaning and message of an ad. Music and voice are powerful factors in advertising Effectiveness, yet are poorly measured by conventional techniques. Our full brain processing algorithms tackle this task efficiently, and we generate critical metrics that indicate the level of emotion generated by music and voice in a spot. This capability is also very useful in identifying the optimal music and voice fit among competing choices at any stage along the ad production process, including preproduction and animatics. In addition, by analyzing the overall Effectiveness of the ad in conjunction with different music treatments, we can diagnose and identify whether any problematic sequence in the ad can be fixed by music alone, rather than requiring more expensive and time-consuming fine-tuning and modification.

9. **Character/Spokesperson Effectiveness:** Through intelligent blending of eye-tracking and brainwave data, we are able to isolate the effectiveness of a character or a spokesperson in an individual ad or for full campaigns. Through application of both the Deep Subconscious Response technique and our character coding metrics, we are able to isolate successful characters as well as ineffective characters, and **diagnose the underlying dynamics** of each. This is useful for determining whether a character in an ad—for example, a person, an animal, or a cartoon character—has enough deep neurological impact to justify creating an entire portfolio of ads featuring this character. We have found that when a character contributes strongly to ad effectiveness, exposing the character in additional ads can create a portfolio win, such as that achieved for the Aflac duck or the Verizon "Can you hear me now?" guy.

10. **Out-of-Home (OOH) and In-Store Advertising NeuroMetrics:** We are able to isolate components of an ad that are particularly suitable for display and viewing in-store, as well as on billboards and other OOH venues. These are moments in the ad that generate the greatest Purchase Intent and Novelty. The display of static or dynamic versions of the ad using the Purchase Intent metric have been found to result in **significant increases in sales**. Isolating moments of an ad that generate significant Purchase Intent can produce immediate economic value by helping to differentiate your product from the clutter of competitors on the shelf.

The best neuromarketing is based on the best neuroscience. So it won't surprise you to learn that the most effective advertising is also based solidly on the best neuroscientific principles, as outlined in the Advertising Effectiveness Framework.

Of course, what I just said may come as a complete surprise to many of you. Science? Applied to the creative heart of advertising? I can just hear the dismay arising spontaneously at advertising agencies—and perhaps from some clients as well. But the fact is, as you have read or will read throughout this book, the brain does have specific preferences. It has things it likes and doesn't like; there are things it looks for and things it dismisses. These are sometimes quite distinct—we know, because we encounter and measure them daily.

We've identified these factors for brands, products, packaging, and retail environments. And we've found them for advertising.

Now that I've got blood pressure levels elevated in every creative department worth the title, let me clarify. We don't dictate the creative process. In fact, we have the highest respect for it, because in many ways it represents what is finest about the human brain. Creativity is one of the hallmarks of our advancement as a species.

We are fans of great advertising, and admirers of an **art that actually assists commerce.** We see the authentic effects that great ads can have on consumers, because we measure and report on those effects day in and day out. Neuromarketing is not the enemy of creative enterprises. In fact, it is quite the opposite. It stands to become a central pillar upon which breakthrough advertising is built.

As we explain to advertising practitioners, done correctly, neurological testing delivers knowledge and insights that can help guide the development of the most effective messages. Adapting that knowledge, and applying those insights, is the responsibility, and the genius, of the most gifted creative people. In our view, science serves art and commerce in this regard. As consumers, we can all benefit from better advertising, if we define *better* as more relevant, likable, interesting, informative, entertaining, memorable, and, therefore, motivating.

So now that I've hopefully defused the mistaken notion that science and creativity are mutually exclusive fields, I'll introduce you to motion, novelty, error, and ambiguity. And you will discover even more of the mind's deeply hidden secrets.

MOTION, NOVELTY, ERROR, AMBIGUITY

As far as formulas go, that's a fairly perplexing one, isn't it? From any perspective, it doesn't seem to have any pattern and the words lack any obvious interconnection. And yet these four words **form the basic platform** upon which the most effective advertising and other messaging is predicated. How can I state that with such certainty? Because the brain says so.

Research in neuroscience laboratories worldwide has resulted in greater understanding not only of how the brain functions, but also the characteristics of the stimuli it notices and values. Four of the most important are motion, novelty, error, and ambiguity.

Motion

Our brains are built to seek out, recognize, process, and evaluate motion as a top priority.

Viewers' subconscious minds will immediately focus on elements that are in motion in commercials. Static imagery draws far less attention.

From our earliest days in sub-Saharan Africa, we've attuned ourselves to our surroundings. The ability to perceive motion translated directly to survival—*see the prey before it sees you*. Notice movement before it turns fatal. Identify quickly and accurately when activity is benign and when it is threatening.

We developed acute visual systems and coupled those with highly sensitive neurological systems for deciphering and responding to what we see. Now that we no longer have to expose ourselves to mortal dangers just to go and find something to eat (that is, unless you're forced to take the freeway at rush hour for takeout), our brains retain those remarkable capabilities.

We are programmed to pay the highest attention to visual stimuli. That is the simple explanation for why TV advertising almost immediately became the most powerful form of commercial communication. *We're geared to watch.*

So, communicate the most critical information in TV advertising through visual means; don't rely on the sound track alone.

This also explains why mobile video advertising is emerging so rapidly as a global marketing force. We love our smart phones, in part because they reward us with what we are fundamentally built to want, appreciate, and value—activity in visual form that sparks responses in our subconscious.

Narcissus fell in love with his shimmering but static self-image reflected in that pool. Just imagine how enamored he would be if he could watch nonstop videos of himself on his iPhone!

Now I want to get down and practical with this concept. How can you use motion to maximum advantage in advertising?

The Clock Face   I never understood just how elemental that phrase really is until I became immersed in neuroscience and neuromarketing. Now I find it positively profound.

> We're neurologically **designed to prefer clockwise motion**. So, if you're concocting a storyboard or an animatic—especially if you're planning on testing consumers' reactions to them—design your material so that the motion flows in a clockwise direction (if you're a cinematographer or commercial director, think in circles, too!).

Does that mean that you have to have your commercial populated by people or objects moving around the screen according to a strict 12-3-6-9 paradigm? No, it simply means that when you're setting out to map the action in a TV spot, remember to avoid counterclockwise activity. Instead, keep the flow in a clockwise direction. It doesn't have to be a fully circular motion (although that would be optimum, neurologically speaking).

A brief aside here: The other part of *the clock face* phrase that is so elemental is the "face" reference. Elsewhere you'll read about how we humans are completely and utterly drawn to the human face. Again, this is because we're basically neurologically wired that way.

Now I'm really going to get specific.

There is a guideline we offer advertisers, agencies, and entertainment companies about where to feature motion on a screen. This guideline applies to featuring motion on any screen, from TVs to computers to mobile phones, movie screens, iPads, video game platforms, and more. Our studies across multiple categories and platforms confirm the effectiveness of following this guideline.

 You already know that motion that resolves clockwise is neurologically superior. Now you also know that motion in the periphery is also neurologically favorable.

Figure 16.1
Motion at the periphery of the screen attracts the brain's attention.

Source: NeuroFocus, Inc.

I'll take this one step further:

Motion from the periphery of the screen in toward the center is superior to motion from the center outward toward the periphery. The brain has certain specific preferences for the way in which stimuli are delivered. Matching those can mean that your material is given more attention and earns higher Emotional Engagement, better chances for Memory Retention, and higher levels of Purchase Intent at the point of sale.

Novelty

Depending on where you may have started reading this book, you have perhaps already encountered this fundamental discovery:

The brain craves that which is new.

So what? So, by emphasizing what is novel, you automatically appeal to the brain's priorities, and in doing so you help ensure that your messaging is accorded priority.

You encounter this concept again here because it is such a central tenet of modern neuroscience. In fact, it may help explain why modern advertising has naturally gravitated toward emphasizing newness:

We humans are built to seek what is novel in our surroundings.

The reason for that is twofold: First, being able to identify a change in the immediate environment has served us well in terms of sheer survival. Second, as we evolved, developing a **drive to discover new things** led to improvements in everything from finding new food sources to creating new technologies, such as metal weapons to hunt with, steam cylinders to revolutionize manufacturing and transportation, and advanced forms and methods of communication, among many others.

When we find something new that is pleasing, our brains want to highlight and retain that data for future reference. So our brains actually build internal *reward circuits*, new neurological networks that develop in response to information from our senses that represents new experiences. How does this translate into actionable guidance for creating advertising that is more effective?

Almost any way that you can telegraph to the brain that something is new will grab its attention. Attention is the first step toward the ultimate goal of raising awareness, stimulating initial product or service trial, motivating repeat purchase or viewing intent, building brand loyalty, and many of advertising's other core objectives.

The Pop-Out Phenomenon   Figure 16.2 is a good example of what we call the "pop-out phenomenon." The image pretty well explains what that is—your eye, and, therefore, your brain, is immediately drawn to that unusual imagery.

Pop-outs are one application of the **novelty principle**. They're a particularly effective one. That's why you'll see them used—in bold—throughout this book.

Look for visual and audio ways to incorporate pop-outs into your advertising with the use of color, unique sounds, contrast, and large versus smaller images. Creative people can find amazing ways to leverage this neurological building block. (We've actually compiled a collection of them for our clients.) Pop-outs

Figure 16.2
The brain loves pop-outs

Source: Photo courtesy of adsoftheworld.com

can win the brain's attention, which, as I just stated, is the essential ingredient in the neuromarketing mix.

Here are some of our neurological best practices for using pop-outs:

 Pop-outs can appear anywhere in the visual field.

 Keep the number to one or two. Any more and you risk having the brain become fatigued and discarding them all.

 Image pop-outs are better in the left visual field.

 Semantic and quantitative pop-outs are better in the right visual field.

Error

Why would I advocate something like deliberately incorporating error into your advertising? Because from the brain's point of view, it's attractive, engaging, and often irresistible. Aren't those the attributes that effective advertising strives mightily to achieve?

Figure 16.3 is a good example of what I mean by "error."

When you just saw that image in Figure 16.3, your brain slammed the brakes on. There's an obvious, immediate, striking disconnect between what the brain recognizes as a "bird" and what it also recognizes as a "dog." But the brain knows that there's no such thing as a "dogbird"—or at least it has never encountered that creature before.

So it is intrigued. There's something new here! Suddenly it has to allocate additional cognitive resources to that image in its continuing mission to make sense of the world around it.

Now, if we were to ask a focus group or survey participant to comment on the image in Figure 16.3, we might hear words like *weird* or *funny*, or some other adjective reflecting our conscious mind's struggle to articulate our subconscious reaction.

But the subconscious just finds it fascinating, with no value judgments one way or the other.

Figure 16.3
Novelty is always compelling to any brain.

Source: Photo courtesy of adsoftheworld.com

So finding **ways to incorporate "error"** into advertising can help your messaging stand out amid the clutter. The moral of this lesson is: When the brain is involved, sometimes a "wrong" does make a "right."

Ambiguity

Our culture has attached a certain negative connotation to the concept of ambiguity. We think of it (consciously, that is) as something wishy-washy, imprecise, and mildly undesirable. But the brain doesn't.

In fact, the **brain finds ambiguity downright compelling** in some key respects. And the proof is in Figure 16.4.

The portrait of Mona Lisa has been the subject of more attention over the centuries than any other painting. We're positively drawn to it. We hypothesize endlessly about "Who is she? What is she thinking? Is she smiling or not?"

Why? What is it about this portrait that commands our attention so completely, across cultures and centuries? Once again, neuroscience offers the answer: **because we can't readily figure it out.**

Figure 16.4
What is Mona Lisa thinking? The ambiguity grabs us, every time.

Source: Photo courtesy of WordPress.com

Mona Lisa's expression is perhaps the classic definition of ambiguity. It defies easy explanation and resists simple categorization. We're hard-pressed to feel as though we have her all scoped out—because even after all these years, we don't.

The brain loves puzzles.

So what? So, in cluttered messaging environments, using elements that have inherent appeal to the subconscious can help cut through the clutter and attract the brain's attention.

The brain is a massive parallel processor of signals. It is designed solely and explicitly for that purpose. It is further designed to process, analyze, and sort out what those signals mean, for our very basic survival all the way up to the most abstract theories we may contemplate.

The brain is built to search for answers. Standing in front of the portrait of Mona Lisa, our brain attempts to calculate the message being conveyed. It strives to sort through the stimuli and find a familiar pattern, a recognizable path.

Failing to uncover that, the prefrontal cortex directs its servant neurological centers spread throughout the brain to redouble their efforts. If something *still* doesn't turn up, the brain will actually form new connections to register and accommodate this new information.

One way or the other, the brain will find a way to wrap itself around this phenomenon—and prevail.

Within all this searching lies yet another key benefit: As our brains recalculate and process, we're spending more time with the stimulus overall. As focused as we are on Mona Lisa's smile (or mysterious lack thereof), we're also aware of her surroundings, her clothing, the other elements in that painting. If you apply the principle of ambiguity to some (not all) advertising, you engage the brain to that same basic extra degree. And by doing so, you increase the chances that the overall messaging you're conveying will be better and more fully absorbed by the subconscious.

For more contemporary proof of the efficacy of ambiguity, I direct your attention to just about any runway in the fashion capitals of the world. Pay special attention to the expressions on the models as they traipse across the elevated platform. They are deliberately, uniformly ambiguous—neither smiling nor frowning.

Result? Fascination. Look at the faces of the observers seated and paying rapt attention. Is it the latest creation from the House of Dior that has them riveted? Or are their brains fixated on the models themselves, particularly their faces?

Go one step further—if you watch one of these shows on TV, take conscious notice of where you yourself are looking. I think you'll be surprised to discover how much time you're spending looking at the model's faces. (This is a brief reminder that our brains are designed to pay special attention to human faces.)

Another example in an allied field is cosmetics marketing. Some smart advertisers feature models with ambiguous expressions in their print advertising. Skim through a beauty book and you may find a few of these ads—though not many, because most advertisers in this category are still featuring smiling women. If they learn about the brain's real preference, that may change and they will benefit.

We know that neurologically it is the ambiguity of the models' expressions that helps attract and then hold our attention. Of course, we're going to look at the haute couture or the cosmetics; they're the stars of the show. But we are drawn to pay attention in part because our brains are presented with a little mystery along the (run)way.

And now you know that the brain just loves a good mystery—but **be careful not to make it work too hard.**

I encourage you to explore how you might factor that knowledge into your next brilliant ad campaign.

EYEDROPS, AWARENESS, AND AUDIENCES

What can neurological testing tell us about the effectiveness of advertising? A great deal.

Here's a real-world example: A major international pharmaceutical company wanted to evaluate how effective a TV commercial was for its brand of allergy-relief eyedrops.

The Problem: Tough Category

This is the kind of category where it can be difficult to get good, reliable answers through conventional market research techniques. Asking consumers what they thought or how they felt or what they remembered about using a product like eyedrops is a challenge itself. Attempting to distill those reactions to a TV spot for the product adds height to the bar. Respondents will make a good-faith effort—but as explained in these pages, accurate articulation is hindered by the brain's basic structure and functions.

The Complication: New Message

This particular ad introduced a new product that was once-a-day eyedrops, compared to the previous version of the product that required two applications per day. From long experience, the company knew that asking people if they got the message about the new feature did not always yield a reliable response. **Just by asking the question, the response is compromised**, depending on which choice you list first, even if you put the choices at equal level on the screen like this:

Once a day   Twice a day

Still, one has to come first. That confounds memory recall and thus your research.

The Solution: A Second-by-Second Deep Dive

A typical TV spot is only 30 seconds long, but can cost millions to produce and air. So those 30 seconds have to do some heavy lifting. Key questions the client wanted answered were:

- What is the overall Effectiveness of the TV spot?
- Is there a different response based on gender?
- Does the spot promote Purchase Intent?
- Is the "once-a-day" message received? Are other messages received?
- Which parts are particularly memorable and interesting?
- How quickly does the spot wear out?

We tested an even 50/50 split of female and male subjects, who each saw the ad three times. (Keep in mind the critically important point made in Chapter 10 about sample size. Because neurological testing measures at the deep subconscious level, at the early stage of the cognitive timeline, fully scientifically valid results are achieved using **sample sizes that are 1/10th the size** required by surveys.)

We measured how strong the concepts and attributes of "once-a-day," "fast-acting," and "relief" resonated, deep in the subconscious.

Because full-brain EEG-based neurological testing combined with eye-tracking and GSR measurements generate such an enormous volume of research data—**a typical ad study like this one produces approximately 5 billion data points, and we apply some 40 billion floating data points of computational processing power to analyze them**—the results are extraordinarily rich in detail.

We were able to present the client with precise information on the exact levels of Attention, Emotional Engagement, and Memory Retention that the spot stimulated, as well as an overall Effectiveness score. We broke those NeuroMetrics out further into male and female demographics. Eye-tracking pinpointed, at a pixel level, where visual focus was located at any specific second—data we also broke out into male/female metrics.

Neurological compression technology isolated and highlighted the individual frames of the commercial that scored the highest in terms of test subjects' subconscious responses (once again, split into genders for even more knowledge of what was most effective). These results enable a TV spot to be edited down into shorter lengths for application in alternative formats, such as the Internet and mobile advertising platforms, where shorter videos are the norm, while retaining the most neurologically effective scenes and elements. They also enable an advertiser to adapt individual frames for use in print and outdoor advertising and other mediums requiring still images.

Testing demonstrated that the Wear-Out factor for the spot was clearly superior to the norm (our proprietary research into advertising effectiveness shows that the typical commercial registers measurable habituation after three to five viewings).

Beyond the results, we provided the client with a set of six specific recommendations on how to improve the neurological effectiveness of the spot even further, how to alter the copy to achieve even higher scores with both men and women, a strategy for maximizing media buys in terms of reach versus frequency levels, and more.

When millions are at stake, and in this example a critical new product formulation is being introduced in a very competitive category, EEG-based full-brain neurological testing can deliver extremely detailed knowledge and insights about how well advertising will perform, and specific, actionable ways to improve that performance.

NEUROLOGICAL NEIGHBORHOODS

One of the issues that have been kicked around in advertising and marketing circles for more than a few years is the subject of priming. The debate has centered around whether it's an actual phenomenon, and if so, how it actually works.

For those of you not in the advertising or television business, *priming* is defined as the degree to which viewers' perception of and response to advertising within a certain program is affected by the nature and content of the program itself. Conversely, and to a lesser extent, it can be defined as the extent to which the *advertising* affects viewers' outlook on and responses to the *program* material it sponsors.

In laypersons' terms: For viewers, does a program impact ad effectiveness? Do ads impact programs? If so, how much and under what circumstances?

The question has lingered in the industry because of the difficulty inherent in parsing out the variable effects of the ad/program. You can certainly measure viewership levels quantitatively, and that tells you how many viewers were tuned in at any given moment. But **were they "tuned in" in the other sense of the phrase?** Were they moved in any measurable way (up or down) in terms of Attention, Emotional Engagement, Memory Retention, Purchase

Intent, perception of Novelty, and Awareness—the key NeuroMetrics—by the interaction of the advertising and programming?

The majority of clients who bring us advertising or television programming to test ask us this question. That's how central an issue it continues to be.

And this is what we tell them:

> Priming not only exists, but it is even more important than anyone thought.

Raising the importance of priming as a key factor in the media planning and buying process can result in commercials gaining more Attention, Emotional Engagement, and Memory Retention—and spurring Purchase Intent, Novelty, and Awareness as a result. Improved return on investment (ROI) for advertising budgets can be the outcome.

To shed some light on this subject, I'll offer another real-world example. It's one that, in light of the increasing popularity of so-called reality programming, has more relevance than ever.

Neurological Nitty-Gritty

The A&E Television Network brought us a very interesting study to conduct. One of its top-rated shows is *Intervention*. It's a program that has attracted both critical praise and viewer interest and loyalty, in no small part due to its gritty realism and powerful emotional content.

The series features families, friends, and coworkers intervening with individuals who are suffering from a variety of conditions, from alcoholism to drug addiction and other serious afflictions. These souls have reached, or are rapidly approaching, the nadir of their lives. It's no exaggeration to say that, barring a turnaround, some of those lives are at real risk.

But for advertisers, the question that often arises with programming this intense is: How will viewers perceive my brand/product/service/message in this environment? Will I gain or lose Awareness, Impact, or Effectiveness? Will consumers be more, or less, **motivated to try or rebuy** my offering? Will my brand benefit, or not, by being present?

More than broadcast advertising dollars hang in the balance. Priming can also influence brand image, corporate reputation, and other critical company assets. So understanding priming and how it really works plays a central role in deciding which ads to air with which programs. We designed a testing methodology that would tease out the answers where they're actually formed: deep within the subconscious.

Carefully screened subjects were shown two programs. One was an episode of *Intervention*, and the other was a successful prime-time dramatic program from another network featuring powerful and highly personal story lines. Both shows demonstrated strong levels of viewer engagement and loyalty.

We inserted a set of six commercials, featuring a cross section of advertisers, in commercial pods (groupings of various commercials) within each program. Categories included automotive, food, insurance, personal care, retail, and telecommunications. Each set of spots was exactly the same, and their placement in commercial pods was also the same.

The findings were clear and compelling. Neurological testing revealed that, far from negatively impacting viewers' perceptions, ad placement in the emotionally powerful program environment of *Intervention* **actually enhanced viewers' engagement with the advertising**.

A small sampling of the results:

- Three of the six commercials scored significantly higher for overall Effectiveness in *Intervention* than in the competitive drama. The other three scored essentially the same in both shows.
- In our key NeuroMetric of Emotional Engagement, *Intervention* scored highest in each of the six advertising categories.

The research went on to document that viewers remained highly engaged with *Intervention* throughout the duration of the program. That level of emotional involvement resulted in ad placement later in the show suffering no drop-off in overall Effectiveness.

The top-line takeaway from this research was that the priming effect on commercials was quantified and unequivocal: **Advertising benefited from appearing in this emotionally strong programming environment.**

OUT OF SYNC, OUT OF SALES?

How else can neurological testing help advertising become more effective? One thing learned from neuroscience that can help a number of current advertisers (and definitely future ones) is what we know about a neurological syndrome known as Audio/Visual Synchrony.

A major car manufacturer runs an annual end-of-the-model-year clearance TV campaign featuring an animated main character. This fellow is featured prominently in each of the several spots in this ongoing campaign, and he's got a catchy tagline that closes each commercial. He's friendly, attractive in a sort of average man way, and allows the auto marketer to combine animation with live action shots of the product.

The only problem is that **he bothers the brain**.

Why? Because his mouth movements are chronically out of sync with the voice track. Our brains are structured to match *what* we see someone saying with *how* we see them saying it—the way their lips and tongue move in synchrony with the sounds we hear. When you introduce a break in that connection—when the brain encounters a disconnect between those two interrelated stimuli, what we hear and what we see—it causes what neuroscientists describe as a "mismatch negativity." That is not a good thing for advertising, I assure you, when you have all of 30 seconds to sell.

Our brains are forced to work overtime, simultaneously capturing and analyzing what our auditory and visual cortexes are receiving, and comparing that data with what our subconscious mind *expects* those stimuli to be. When they match up, as they do in normal conversation, our brains perceive that all is working as it should in the world.

But when they don't align, the brain is presented with mismatch negativity. The upshot is that we devote precious cognitive resources to attempting to interpret what is going on, and we can be distracted from the main message.

Next time you watch TV, look more carefully at the animated commercials for a popular online insurance company, an online hotel reservations booking site, and others. See if you also spot badly lip-synced live-action ads; they're out there pretty regularly (and the disconnect doesn't have to be pronounced to produce that infamous mismatch negativity). When you do see them, you'll now know what's going on in your own brain as you watch. That maestro of cortical coordination, your prefrontal cortex, is putting extra effort into trying to sort it all out. The advertiser who just spent several hundred thousand dollars to air that message is unaware of the reduced effectiveness built right into it. But your brain recognizes it right off the bat.

This is an excellent opportunity to tell you a little about another very important neurological syndrome called Sensory Integration (SI). It's linked directly to the Audio/Visual Synchrony effect I just described.

Neuroscience research has discovered that, contrary to previous beliefs, the auditory cortex and the visual cortex in the brain interact early in the perceptual process—and take special note of this—**one sense can prime the other.** What do I mean by "early"? It can take less than 200 milliseconds for these two separate senses to integrate in the subconscious. A properly synchronized multisensory experience is not just additive; it has a multiplicative effect.

Research shows that the more precise the synchrony is between auditory and visual stimuli, the faster that integration between them can occur. The reward of such fast, accurate Sensory Integration for marketers is called the "multiplier effect." Here's how Dr. Robert T. Knight, one of the world's preeminent neuroscientists and NeuroFocus's Chief Science Advisor, describes the value of SI:

"If the auditory component in a commercial is X and the visual component is X, when you don't have synchrony between the two the best result you can get is basically 2X. When you do have synchrony, though, you get a multiplier effect—you achieve 3X or more. This is what we describe as the power of Sensory Integration, and we see both effects in many of the brain measurements we've done over the years."

Another leading neuroscientist (and NeuroFocus on-staff expert), Dr. Michael Smith, adds another critical point to this subject:

"The crossover effect of Sensory Integration can actually enhance your perceptual experience, because it can prompt your brain to anticipate what you're about to hear based on what you're seeing, and vice versa. We synthesize these two streams of stimuli to render the world consistent with our experiences and expectations. So when Audio/Visual Synchrony is 'off,' and the brain has to work harder to reconcile the conflict, the less Sensory Integration occurs and what does occur happens later in the perceptual process."

Dr. Smith makes another related point that is particularly critical for marketers looking to leverage neuromarketing knowledge and methodologies for their products and services:

"Both the auditory and visual cortexes are located in the lateral and posterior regions of the brain. Unless you measure those areas with electrodes positioned to capture brainwave activity generated in them, you will be missing this vital data. This is why **neuroscience laboratories rely on full-brain coverage for their research**. The brain is a vastly complex and interconnected series of neural networks. Unless you capture their activity with sensors arrayed across the surface of the whole brain, you are almost completely missing the massive flows of brainwave activity that occur between critical regions of the brain; and you are incapable of detecting the synergistic effects of multisensory integration."

The lesson here for marketers is that only full-brain measurement will deliver accurate, reliable, and actionable results. For those who tell you otherwise, there is only one course of action to take: Ask for their neuroscientific credentials and check them carefully—because no neuroscientist worth his or her Ph.D. would endorse anything less than this full-brain coverage standard.

I'll cite a recent real-world example of how neurological testing can tease out information that would escape capture using conventional methodologies.

We have a client in Asia who wanted to test two of its commercials for its dishwashing liquid against the competition. The interesting thing about both the client spots was that they were virtually identical; the only difference was that in one ad there was a scene that had a caption saying, "These images are simulated." This scene would appear and then disappear in two or three seconds. It was really difficult to test this through traditional research methods, since this difference would not be easily discernible, and often memory-based methodologies are not well suited for use in evaluating such minor differences.

We completed the study and found that both ads were equal in their overall Effectiveness scores. However, when we looked in detail at Purchase Intent scores, the ad without any caption scored significantly higher than the ad with the caption, indicating that if the client went ahead with this ad (with no caption) it was more likely to persuade consumers to buy. We also looked at second-by-second "noodle chart" results showing where the Effectiveness started to drop. Interestingly, the Effectiveness of both the ads was identical until we came to the particular scene where the caption was mentioned. The Effectiveness dropped immediately after the caption was shown. The client went ahead with the ad that we recommended and within eight weeks saw a marked increase in market share.

This was a great marketplace demonstration of the power of neurological testing to isolate and identify the effects of specific advertising elements, even one this relatively small, and proved once again how our NeuroMetrics are closely tied to, and can produce, specific recommendations that can positively impact market performance.

What are the other ways that neurological testing can benefit advertising? One way is through creative development:

- Basic concepts can be tested to determine, with precision, how the sub-conscious responds to them. The savings in cost and time that result from this streamlined approach can be significant. Multiple creative solutions need not be pursued past the initial stage in the hope of deciphering which solution may be more effective; the brain will indicate the answer, with clarity, at the earliest conceptual stage. The assurance that the concept will appeal to consumers at this most fundamental and essential of levels enables the creative team to design and execute messaging with confidence that their strategic platform is proven to be neurologically sound.

- Copy testing similarly produces clear and precise results. Rather than having to rely on test subjects' articulated responses to proposed copy, neurological testing reveals exactly how subjects react at the subconscious level, in real time. The brainwave activity data recorded provides detailed knowledge and metrics.
- Storyboards, animatics, ripomatics, and rough cuts can be tested to determine neurological responses. The results can offer clear indications of which specific elements are most effective, leading to more efficient creative development and production processes.
- Finished ads can be tested to ascertain their overall Effectiveness against campaign objectives, as well as which elements are neurologically best suited for adaptation to alternative media. Neurological compression can be applied to isolate key video frames and scenes, enabling the original creative material to be used efficiently and effectively in platforms requiring shorter-length formats.
- Priming studies can be conducted to measure the effects of programming on advertising effectiveness, and vice versa.

For new product launches and brand extensions, neurological testing can be used as a stand-alone measurement of advertising effectiveness, and also be applied in conjunction with brainwave activity measurements connected with product design, packaging, and in-store environments. This multiple testing methodology can give marketers the most comprehensive view of how these separate components work together, and where there are specific opportunities to improve their individual and collective effectiveness.

Neurological testing can also deliver critical knowledge and insights into how multimedia campaigns perform, including interactive campaigns. It can also gauge how effective creative concepts and specific elements are when deployed in different mediums.

Neurological testing can also be used to measure the effectiveness of otherwise difficult-to-determine components, such as spokespeople, music, graphics, special effects, animation versus live action, and other creative or production considerations.

For major advertisers and their agencies, the application of neurological testing over time can produce a database of the most effective individual ads and their specific components. This library can be a very valuable resource, providing examples of previous successes and the specific neurological best practices employed to achieve them, when new campaigns for existing brands or for new products or brand extensions are in development. The cost and time savings gained as a result can be substantial.

PRINT ADVERTISING—LEARNINGS USING THE FRAMEWORK

Logos and symbols:
- Place logos and symbols primarily in the central visual field.
- Option: Place logos or other symbols with a slight bias to the left visual field.
- Avoid more than two logos or symbols overall.

Print advertising/websites:
- Place images on the left and semantics on the right.
- Use human imagery to engage viewers.
- Create layouts that use a circular/clockwise visual exploration pattern.
- Use just two or three major visual elements for maximum neurological impact.
- Use interesting, unique fonts to increase Attention and Novelty factors.
- Use ambiguous imagery and puzzles that resolve in four seconds maximum.

Screen partitioning:
- If you split imagery into multiple units (say, separate faces), use no more than three.
- Insert a space between each partition.
- Use vertical, not horizontal, placement and separation.

Elsewhere in the brand, product, packaging, and in-store chapters you'll find more best practices that in some instances also apply to advertising.

As you now know, one of the central themes of this book is a simple, straightforward, but exceptionally important concept: The brain is built to buy.

In fact, **the brain *wants* to buy**. Rather than the conventional wisdom that has informed some marketing and advertising thinking in the past, I encourage you to embrace that neurological knowledge and allow it to influence how you create advertising.

You still need to sell. But know that you don't have an adversary inside your consumers' heads—you have an amazing entity that is primed to receive and respond to your messaging.

I hope this book will help you create messaging that the brain finds the most appealing, interesting, attention–getting, involving, synchronized, ambiguous, emotionally engaging, momentarily puzzling, persuasive, and memorable. As consumers, we will all benefit if you do.

Takeaways:
- You now have a grasp of how neurological testing can provide **previously unobtainable research data** across all advertising mediums, and in extreme detail about individual components of specific ads.
- You've read how other companies have used brainwave activity measurements to improve the effectiveness of their advertising.
- You have a set of actionable best practices to apply to make your advertising the most neurologically effective it can be.

CHAPTER 17

THE BUYING BRAIN, SCREENS, AND SOCIAL MEDIA

At the end of this chapter, you'll know and be able to use the following:

- The critical differences in terms of consumers' subconscious responses between viewing content and messaging on traditional TV, the Internet, and mobile platforms
- Why faces are so important across these three mediums
- How to create the most effective video materials for each of the mediums
- How to create the neurologically most powerful content for social networks

One of the most fascinating dichotomies of neuromarketing is this: we're dealing with an organ that hasn't changed for 100,000 years; and yet we're measuring its responses to new technology appearing in the marketplace in the time frame of months, if not weeks.

A prime example is the three screens phenomenon. The word "phenomenon" gets tossed around all too readily, but in this case, it truly fits. The scale of growth in any one of these three media—traditional television, the Internet, and mobile devices—is simply stunning. The modern world has never experienced anything like it. In fact, as this book goes to press, the "three screens phenomenon" has morphed into something like the 15-screen phenomenon, and growing.

For those who regard TV as a mature medium, the figures say otherwise. While I've stayed away from citing streams of statistics in this book, this is a category where the numbers tell the story better than words.

Total adult daily viewing time devoted to watching all screens: approximately **8.5 hours.** (That actually grows to **9.5** hours for viewers age 45–54.) TV viewing amounts to **98 percent** of viewers' time devoted to watching video material on screens.

So the notion that "traditional" television is losing ground to alternative screen-based media is misleading. The whole pie is growing. As I like to say, the brain is a glutton. It can, and will, handle a bigger pie with ease.

Of course, the **"three screens" terminology is already inadequate** to describe our daily exposure to screen-borne messages. When you add: videos you encounter in the retail environment; back-of-the-seat entertainment in SUVs, taxicabs, airplanes, and so on; video feeds in medical office and pharmacy waiting rooms and even at gas station pumps; plus a host of other so-called "out of home" venues from bars to sports stadiums, the exposure level is striking.

But does the brain process all this moving image material the same way? The answer is no. Functionally, the brain *receives* video stimuli in an identical fashion, no matter the source. However, as with other aspects of neuromarketing, this finding is only part of the picture. There are marketing implications to be drawn from what we've learned about how the subconscious *responds* to video in various formats, from the JumboTron at the sports coliseum to the smallest cell phone screen in the palm of your hand. See Figure 17.1.

Figure 17.1
The world of three screens is already over.

Source: Photo courtesy of Dreamstime.com

There are differences and those differences will become increasingly critical for marketers as the communications spectrum continues to splinter and expand, especially as mobile communications accelerate their share of our video viewing time. Marketers must differentiate their approach to using each motion-based medium to achieve optimal neurological impact and effectiveness.

Neuroscience already has tools designed specifically to address this need. Right now, for example, we apply a unique technology known as **Neurological Compression** to render one form of video communications functional and effective for other, alternative formats.

The compression codec identifies, isolates, and edits together the most neurologically powerful scenes from material such as a TV commercial. A typical application would create a 10–12-second version of a 30-second spot. This enables companies to take existing (usually expensive to produce) footage and run it in shortened lengths on the Internet or mobile devices, where such short video clips are the norm (and where longer-length clips are neurologically much less effective). The cost and time savings realized from this effective use of current materials are considerable. But the best payoff is being certain that the shorter messages have the greatest possible neurological impact. See Figure 17.2.

THE CONVERGENCE CONUNDRUM

Trends, especially technology-based ones, tend to take on a life of their own. One of the more persistent ones—stimulated by the trinity of technological advances, manufacturer marketing, and consumer behavior—is the migration of Internet-based material to the living room TV set. So much has been forecast for this movement that, even though it has not yet happened on a large scale, it has long had the air of inevitability about it.

As interconnectivity becomes easier the boundaries between screens is beginning to drop away. Once connected, you can surf the Internet from your sofa as easily as on your 50-plus-inch high definition liquid crystal display (LCD) screen as you can on your wireless laptop, netbook, your smart phone, and your iPad. It's already occurring as Internet access-equipped new TVs are penetrating showrooms and homes.

But there's a hidden risk in that for marketers. And speaking from the perspective of the brain, it's a big one.

If marketers believe that they can create one video production, run it across all video screens, and achieve the same messaging impact regardless of format they will be making a major mistake.

Figure 17.2
Mobile phone screens engage the brain differently
than other screens.

Source: Photo by NeuroFocus, Inc.

Our research has shown that the brain responds to the presentation of certain kinds of content quite differently on one screen size versus another.

FACES ARE FUNDAMENTAL

You will read elsewhere in these pages how the brain is designed to pay attention to faces. Our ability to discern emotion and intent is founded largely on our brain's highly developed facial recognition capabilities.

Why are faces so central to marketing campaigns on each of the three screens? For one very simple reason:

> We need to be able to read someone's face to extract data about their emotions and intent.
>
> So what? So, I need to be able to see you clearly and directly to divine the unspoken messages you are conveying to me, and that my brain is acutely attuned to receive, analyze, and respond to. I also need to be able to look at your eyes (humans are the only animals with "the whites of the eyes," or scleras), gauge the shape of your mouth, and scan your whole visage for any signs of your mood or your plans that I can glean.

I can do that just fine on my large-diameter high-definition flat screen in the relative peace and quiet of my living room. I can also manage that reasonably well—though not as finely—on my desktop or laptop computer. I may miss some fine detail, but I can still get the gist of what you're all about.

But on my mobile device, I really can't see your face in any detail at all. I can't determine with reliable accuracy what your eyes have to tell me. You're too small for my brain to decipher the full message your face is conveying.

"So," you may be saying to yourself, "what's your point?" "That faces don't 'play' well on cell phones? Okay, understood. So what?"

So what is important to you, as a marketer or consumer, is that you want to send, or receive, marketing messages that capture your attention, engage your emotions, and merit retention in your memory.

Faces convey emotions. If I can't see your face properly, I won't pay attention to it. If I don't pay attention, my emotions are not going to be engaged. If my emotions remain unengaged, I am not likely to remember you—or what message you are trying to send me.

What all this means for marketers is what our research has revealed:

- For the brain's purposes, faces play best on larger screens. Therefore, emotion-based messaging is best suited for large format video displays. Target messages that rely at their core on evoking **emotional responses** to these larger-format devices.
- Target more **fact-based** messaging to smaller screens. This is not to say that fact-based commercials won't play well on big screens—but they are well suited for smaller devices where consumers can retrieve and absorb data quickly and easily.

Put another way, there's a downside to trying to convey emotionally laden content effectively on handheld screens, while there's an upside to portraying them on large screens. Conversely, while there may not be a downside per se to trying to communicate fact-based messages on big screens, they match up more closely with how consumers actually use handheld/mobile devices—meaning short viewing times spent acquiring (or transmitting) brief bursts of data.

This basic alignment takes on more importance and urgency when you see viewing trend figures.

A recent study commissioned by the Council for Research Excellence and conducted by Ball State University revealed some compelling data (full disclosure here: the Council is sponsored by the Nielsen Company, which is a strategic investor in NeuroFocus).

- Young adults age 18–24 consume **nine** forms of screen-based media for 10 minutes or more per day
- In contrast, older adults 65-plus consume only **five** forms of screen-based media for that same duration daily

When you couple that information with:

- The fact that a study by the Federal Centers for Disease Control shows that 40% of 18–29 year olds now rely exclusively on their mobile phones rather than land lines
- That comScore recently reported that within the space of one year, the number of people in the United States who accessed news and information on the mobile Web rose by 200 percent; and that 35 percent of those individuals did so daily, the scale of this phenomenon comes into sharp focus

We are becoming a society increasingly centered around mobile devices.

The ultimate point is that we will be living amidst an even larger sea of different screens at various sites, and the smartest marketers will learn to create messaging content that mirrors what consumers respond to best on each of them.

That's what our brains want, need, and will come to expect.

ACTION, BANNERS, AND WOMEN

I'll share one more detail drawn from our in-depth studies into the three-screen world. Keep in mind that the traditional three-screen categories are TV, Internet (meaning desktop/laptop viewing), and mobile (cell phones and other small portable screen-based devices).

Overall Effectiveness: Ads with high dynamism, fast-paced action, banner-like messaging treatments, and a focus on women perform better in the **Internet** setting.

Attention: Attention was highest for most of the ads in the **mobile** platform. Voluntary attention is increased on the mobile platform because the smaller screen size requires heightened focus to extract the message.

Emotional Engagement: The larger screen size of the **TV platform** helps the human elements and the fine details shown in commercials to have the highest emotional engagement. But, **fast-paced images** flashing through are more engaging in the **Internet** platform. The **mobile platform** has lower emotion due to its smaller screen size, which does not help in clearly depicting human faces and other key emotional elements in commercials.

Memory Retention: The **mobile** and **Internet** environments give a significant boost in memory retention for most of the ads tested. This is a benefit derived from the intense need to focus voluntarily on the smaller screen.

Purchase Intent: Both the **Television** and **mobile** platform screens— where the focus is on the video without any distracting elements—manage to motivate viewers very well.

Novelty: Novelty performance is highest in the **mobile** platform, making it very suitable for new product introduction ads.

SOCIAL MEDIA

Social Operating System

Are four hundred million Facebook members creating new metrics for marketing to mass audiences? A study that NeuroFocus did on a major Winter Olympics sponsorship strongly indicates they and other social media subscribers are. The results prove that what we've defined as the global "Social

Operating System" is remaking marketing, and through brainwave measurements and analysis we are quantifying the effects on consumers' subconscious responses across multiple platforms.

The focus to date has been on hardware (three screens) and media distribution channels, but that perspective misses the larger phenomenon that is altering marketing on a worldwide front. Companies would be wise to stop dwelling on these silos and shift their attention to this new 'Social Operating System.' **The medium is no longer the message; instead, it's context that influences how consumers conceive of your brand.**

In the first study of its kind, NeuroFocus applied its full-brain measurement technology to discover how consumers responded to "Trip For Life," a TV commercial featured in "Go World," VISA's multimedia campaign centered around the 2010 Winter Olympics. We measured viewers' subconscious responses to that advertisement by placing it on the special website and Facebook pages created to be VISA's Internet marketing platforms for the Vancouver event, as well as testing the commercial as shown on television during the Games. (The study was conducted solely for NeuroFocus' own research; neither VISA nor any of its vendors or other entities commissioned the report.)

The brainwave-based research revealed the power of social media as a marketing communications platform. Topline findings are:

- Highest overall Effectiveness for the ad, especially with women: Facebook
- Purchase Intent generated by the ad: highest on both Facebook and TV
- Messaging carried by the ad strongest on: Internet platform, with Facebook stronger than website
- Highest attention-getter: Internet
- VISA brand perception lifted most strongly: TV

This study marks the first time that a major global consumer marketing campaign was neurologically measured for its effectiveness across the most important communications platforms of our age. The findings reflect how pervasive and powerful social media are today. But they can't be defined by delivery systems any longer—Facebook is now available on your high-definition big-screen TV as well as your iPhone, your laptop, your desktop, and your iPad. There are powerful strategic implications of this global 'Social Operating System' for companies looking to optimize their marketing communications investments. Up until now, they haven't known with scientific certainty the role that social media especially plays in that marketing mix. We used full-brain, EEG-based testing to get at the answer to that critical question, because it is the most accurate and reliable means of measurement—which is why clients rely on it for decision-making.

As more people and more companies enlist on social media networks and incorporate them into their daily lives and marketing programs, neuromarketing principles will undoubtedly play a more prominent role in this fast-growing phenomenon. In fact, the social networking category is ideally suited for the application of what we already know about how the brain works, from a neuromarketing perspective.

Faces Come First

Without our conscious minds being aware of it, one of the key reasons we are so drawn to the Facebooks, MySpaces, and Twitters of our world is the fact that they feature faces. Neurologically, we are irresistibly drawn to the human visage. For marketers, the message is clear: employ faces as a core element of your presence on these websites.

Fit through the Filters

One of the core neurological principles that we see at work at the forefront of social media networking, and mobile communications at large, is **"filtering."** This is the process that the prefrontal cortex initiates and coordinates on a real-time basis, continuously on the behalf of the other regions of the brain. When you try to enumerate all the stimuli coming our way, every second of every day, from every direction, through every sense, in every setting, you get a small idea of what a large undertaking our subconscious manages in this regard.

It is a selection process. **A juggling act.** A traffic-control tour de force that makes O'Hare or Heathrow airport at peak travel time look like a simple game of tic-tac-toe.

The brain filters incoming stimuli and decides what is essential and what is not; what must be accorded priority status and what can be safely ignored or discarded. When the stakes are upped, as they increasingly are now in our multichannel, multidevice, multitasking daily life, the brain kicks into higher gear. If the brain allowed an uncontrolled flood of data to overwhelm us, we would be neurologically gridlocked. Life and death situations would share the same space as what to have for lunch. In essence, we would be paralyzed.

In your living room, as the flat screen flickers and you Twitter on the sofa, switching to the nearby laptop or desktop to summon something else of interest, your subconscious is simultaneously monitoring everything that you're doing and everything that is bombarding your senses. It is screening megabytes of data in milliseconds, making split-second decisions about what rates your attention and what does not.

The steep challenge for marketers in this multiscreen, multimessage world is how to fit through the filters that the subconscious applies. Following are some neurological best practices to apply when marketing through social media networks.

Attract Attention ASAP

The brain will only afford your message **a very brief "window"** of time to gain its notice. Exceed the limit, and your material is either overlooked or erased. Therefore, it's imperative that messaging be extremely well crafted to grab the attention of the subconscious. The devices you can use to do that include:

- Employing "action" words. The brain will afford these greater significance than milder/passive language.
- Please with puzzles. Quick, simple-to-solve puzzles attract the brain. Visually-based puzzles are preferable to semantic-based.
- Pose questions. This self-involving, community-themed approach can work well for primarily female audiences.
- Call for quick replies with male audiences. Direct "appeals to action" trigger the subconscious to respond.

Simplify

The easier you make it for the brain to **receive and absorb your message,** the better. When it comes to marketing messages, more is not necessarily better in the social media world.

Sustain

Different websites have different formats, which some marketers mistakenly believe call for fundamentally different messaging. While it's not desirable to try to cram your Facebook material into a Tweet, the goal should be to maintain as much core similarity/uniformity across the various social media platforms where your company/brand has a presence. Focus on key language (see above for "Action" words), key visuals (faces), and other central elements.

The brain seeks familiarity. It searches for connections that it can recognize in the ocean of information that washes over it on a constant basis. By giving it such identifiable landmarks, you enable the brain to register this connectivity, and you enhance the chances that the subconscious will award your message the ultimate prize: attention and transfer to memory.

Tempt with Triggers

Colors, sounds, unusual/stand-out words, symbols, and other unique characteristics that you can insert into your messaging can work to draw the brain's attention. To the point above, when you use these devices as consistently as circumstances allow across different social media platforms, you "please" the brain by proactively meeting its desire/need to search for and find familiar touchpoints.

Leverage Three-Screen Learnings

The brain requires context for emotionally-based messaging to work at maximum effectiveness. This is a prime reason why the relatively large and longer-form of the traditional TV format works well for such messaging. By definition, social media platforms tend to be viewed on smaller screens, and aren't consistent with longer-form messaging. The trick is to find ways that evoke certain primal emotional responses quickly, with the minimal amounts of stimulus that social media platforms tend to allow compared to conventional mediums.

Fine-tune the use of action words even further, focusing on those that may evoke more basic reactions than others. "Win," "earn," "learn," and "gain" are examples that can stimulate the subconscious to pay attention.

Takeaways:
- Use traditional TV for more emotion-based messaging.
- Mobile and Internet platforms are well-suited for fact-based messaging.
- Faces are fundamental—but they're not nearly as effective on small screens.
- Mobile platforms are particularly suitable for new product launches.
- Please with puzzles and pose questions in social media outlets.

CHAPTER 18

VISION OF THE FUTURE

There is no more fascinating subject than the human brain. And what fascinates the human brain is what this book is all about.

Through these pages, I hope you've gained a new appreciation of your own and your clients' and consumers' brains—what attracts, engages, and delights them, and what compels them to try and buy.

Consumers in this global economy are confronted with millions of marketing messages and countless purchase opportunities every day. They will collectively spend trillions of dollars this year to vote on the success or failure of your brand, product, package, message, or retail environment. Trust me: They **want** to listen to you, **if** they are addressed with purpose, relevance, and clarity.

So, rather than depending on creative guessing or research techniques that do not reach below the surface of casual verbal observations, I hope you'll use the principles in this book, based on the latest neuroscience findings, to hone in precisely on the real needs and wants of your consumers.

I believe that providing products and messages that leverage the emerging sciences of the brain will usher in a new era of partnership between marketers and consumers. That new day begins with messaging that's aligned with consumers' desires, with content that's compelling, and with products, packages, and environments that know the brain inside and out and that acknowledge, respect, and reflect how our brains are built and how they work—all designed with people's true but unarticulated desires and needs in mind.

The strategies outlined in this book succeed because they focus on what the brain **loves** and what it needs to make good choices and decisions—all presented in the most "brain-friendly" ways possible. We invite you to build upon these principles and examples to launch a **new era of creativity** in your own marketing and product development activities, with fresh, new insights drawn straight from neuromarketing's proven best practices.

RECAP

As I promised in the very first chapter, in this book we've learned how the buying brain functions; what's attractive to it; how it decides what it likes and doesn't like; and, ultimately, how it makes that all-important transition from being a "shopping brain" to becoming a "buying brain."

As we saw when we journeyed back to a day in the life of our ancestors, our brains haven't changed very much in 100,000 years, but the world around them has. That new combination—**the primal brain in the modern world**—creates huge challenges and opportunities; it has not existed in human history before.

PERFECT STORM

In fact, the vast majority of what we know about the brain today has only been learned in the last few years. And, amazingly, what we know today is just the **tip of the iceberg.** We are at the crest of a huge wave of incipient knowledge. What we're learning about the brain and our new ways of learning about it are growing beyond what we can imagine.

Sometimes, very rarely, as history moves us along, a confluence of events occurs, and new vistas appear. These are the horizons we see at the end of "perfect storms," crackling with clarity and tingling with the electricity of new ideas and methods for implementing them. For example, when astronomy and the ability to navigate by the stars coincided with our capability to build ships that could sustain life on the open sea for months at a time, the world changed from flat to round. When steam and electricity were harnessed and made available to the populace, our agrarian society formed cities and the Industrial Age was born. When Watson and Crick discovered the double helix in 1953, they set in motion a flood of new discoveries about the human genome that has revolutionized medicine and continues to this day. Concurrently, when 79 million Baby Boomers came of age together, they reinvented childhood, adolescence, and every other life stage they entered. Along the way, they stopped a war and changed the world.

Today, the ability to monitor **the full brain in real time,** combined with the computational capability to make sense of the results, applied to the needs for more effective and accountable marketing expertise, have launched us into our own perfect storm of consumer insights. As we look now into the bright blue sky that follows, here is a little taste of what we can expect—both in the world at large and in our (growing) corner of it.

THE $1 TRILLION BARGAIN

In the future, neuroscience insights will impact everything. Alarm clocks will wake us in concert with our REM sleep cycles. Exercise machines will coach and motivate us as we stride toward fitness. On the way to work, the car will monitor our moods, and provide us with music, information, or phone conversations depending on how we feel.

Entertainers will use neuroscience to create material that suits every taste. Chefs will discover new and delightful ways to surprise our palates. Musicians will fine-tune melodies based on brain responses. Educators will create textbooks and interactive materials that surprise and delight the learning brain. Videogame designers will learn how to make games that adapt to the way *individual* brains play. Brain fitness will become as serious as physical fitness, and feeding the brain will be seen as just as important as providing good nutrition for the body.

Those manufacturers, advertisers, and retailers who take the time to know us at our deepest subconscious level will survive. Those who brandish buggy whips (or treat us like nameless statistics in a survey) will fall, swiftly, to the wayside.

Rather than resisting the inevitable and innovative, research teams will blend **cutting-edge neuroscience** into their product offerings. Traditional statistical methods like "conjoint analysis" will join hands with neuromarketing. Market mix models will blend seamlessly with neuromarketing parameters and indices. Surveys will become much more reliable indicators of preferences and trends, blending verbal information with neural insights.

In fact, many of these inroads are already in the works. As you read these words, universities are beginning to introduce neuromarketing into their MBA programs and create a new generation of brain-based marketers. Ad agencies are hiring neuromarketers to augment their creative teams. Psychology departments are experiencing a boom in cognitive neuroscience enrollment.

NeuroLabs are spreading around the world, becoming larger and studying more components of the corporate world. Neuromarketing has gone global, viral, and tribal—and its benefits extend to every corner of the globe.

Luckily for every brain who shares this gorgeous planet, the cumulative effect of the neuroscientific revolution extends far beyond who buys what product and why. It's not hubris, but rational optimism, that leads me to believe that the advances we see today will make all of our lives a little bit better in the future, and some of our lives radically better than they can be today. For example, over the next few years expect neuroscience to provide much better therapies for the severely disabled, including:

- Ways for "locked in" patients to communicate their thoughts and feelings by simply looking at a computer keyboard;
- Robotics that respond to minute brain signals from paralyzed patients, who will be able to navigate their worlds successfully for the first time;
- Artificial retinas that work with signals from the optic nerves to restore sight to the blind;
- Ways to read nerve signals in patients with spinal cord injuries to help them control prosthetics to relearn how to walk, sit, stand, and *be* in the world; and
- New understanding and effective therapies for many disorders, including Alzheimer's, Parkinson's, Attention Deficit Hyperactivity Disorder (ADHD), Autism, Cerebral Palsy, Depression, Anxiety, Fibromyalgia, Neuropathic pain, Bipolar Disorder, Manias, Schizophrenia, and Sleep Disorders.

We can also look forward to:

- Mobile personal digital assistant (PDA) body scans to allow us to monitor our health and react to changes with remarkable, life-saving speed.
- Paradigm-shifting ways to educate our children—and our adults. Teaching methods that engage and delight the brain, that capture and use our twenty-first century knowledge of what works to create emotion, attention, and memory retention in the eager, learning brain.
- Architectural designs that encourage creative thinking and have a positive impact on the inhabitants' cognitive, emotional, and physical health.

I end with a quote from Bharata from 200 B.C. In the *Natya Shastra*, he says:

Where the hands go, the eyes have gone.
Where the eyes have gone, the mind has flown.
Where the mind has flown, there has gone emotion.
Where there is emotion, there goes life.

I think Bharata figured neuromarketing out long before I arrived on the scene.

NOTES AND SOURCES

T hese notes provide guidance to the reader looking for source references and additional reading opportunities on the topics covered in *The Buying Brain*. As I have written this book for readers who are not professional scientists, references to scientific source materials are kept to a minimum.

Chapter 1

The vast difference in information processing capacity between the conscious and subconscious parts of our brains is documented in Timothy D. Wilson, *Strangers to Ourselves: Discovering the Adaptive Unconscious* (Cambridge MA: Belknap Press of Harvard University Press, 2002), 24.

Chapter 2

The basics of EEG data collection, including minimal standards for electrode counts and artifact collection, are covered in any neuroscience graduate program. An excellent source is Paul L. Nunez and Ramesh Srinivasan, *Electrical Fields in the Brain: The Neurophysics of EEG* (Oxford: Oxford University Press, 2006). See also David Regan, *Human Brain Electrophysiology: Evoked Potentials and Evoked Magnetic Fields in Science and Medicine* (New York: Elsevier, 1989).

"When asked how to recount how it reacted to something ... the brain actually alters the original data it recorded." For an excellent example of this phenomenon from the world of advertising, see Kathryn Braun et al., "Make My Memory: How Advertising Can Change Our Memories of the Past," *Psychology and Marketing* 19, no. 1 (January 2002):1–23.

On sample sizes for EEG studies, the key is to calculate how many data points are required to achieve a statistically significant differentiation between expected effects. This is covered in most statistics texts. The classic reference is Jacob Cohen, *Statistical Power Analysis for the Behavioral Sciences* (New York: Academic Press, 2nd Edition, 1988).

On the shortcomings of fMRI as a way to measure consumer responses, see the Mind Hacks blog post, "The fMRI Smackdown Cometh," June 26, 2008, and links at http://www.mindhacks.com/blog/2008/06/the_fmri_smackdown_c.html.

Strengths and limitations of biometric measures are covered in a huge literature. A good introduction is John L. Andreassi, *Psychophysiology: Human Behavior and Physiological Response*, 5th ed. (Mahwah, NJ: Lawrence Erlbaum, 2007).

Chapter 3

"Our brain is the most metabolically expensive organ to operate . . ." See Este Armstrong, "Relative Brain Size and Metabolism in Mammals," *Science* 220, no. 4603 (June 17, 1983), 1302–1304.

For evolution, altruism, kin selection, see Richard Dawkins, *The Selfish Gene*. (Oxford: Oxford University Press. 1976).

Lee Alan Dugatkin, *The Altruism Equation*. (Princeton: Princeton University Press, 2006).

On deception, see "Deception http://www.sunypress.edu/p-158-deception.aspx" December 1985.

William A. Searcy and S. Nowicki. *The Evolution of Communication: Reliability and Deception in Signaling Systems* (Princeton: Princeton University Press, 2005).

For a discussion of the human "bottleneck" in evolution, see Richard Dawkins, *The Ancestor's Tale: A Pilgrimage to the Dawn of Life*. (Boston: Houghton-Mifflin, 2004), 416.

Chapter 4

For brain anatomy, see Malcolm Carpenter and Jerome Sutin, *Human Neuroanatomy*, 7th ed. (London: Williams & Wilkins, 1976).

Chapter 5

For a lush and beautiful overview of our five senses, see Diane Ackerman, *A Natural History of the Senses* (New York: Vintage, 1991).

For an overview of how the body "maps" sensory experiences, see Sandra Blakeslee and Matthew Blakeslee, *The Body Has a Mind of Its Own* (New York: Random House, 2007).

For the effects of physical appearance, see Ray Bull and Nichola Rumsey, *The Social Psychology of Facial Appearance*. (New York: Springer-Verlag, 1988);

Kate Lorenz, "Do Pretty People Earn More?" CNN.com, July 11, 2006; and Helene Cavior, Steven Hayes, and Norman Cavior, "Physical Attractiveness of Female Offenders," *Criminal Justice and Behavior* 1 (1974): 321–331.

The neurobiology of food cravings is explored in C.E. Fairburn and P.J. Cooper, *Identical Twins and Food Cravings* (Toronto: University of Toronto Press, 1982).

To learn more about dogs and their amazing ability to smell, see Hywell Williams and Andres Pembroke, "Sniffer Dogs in the Melanoma Clinic," *The Lancet* (April 1, 1989).

Chapter 6

For the latest statistics on Alzheimer's, see "Alzheimer's Disease," *New York Times*, Thursday, February 4, 2010.

For a discussion on the positive aspects of the aging brain, see Roberto Cabeze et al., "Aging Gracefully: Compensatory Brain Activity in High-Performing Older Adults," *NeuroImage* 17 (2002): 1394–1402.

Gaolang Gong et al., "Age- and Gender-Related Differences in the Cortical Anatomical Network," *The Journal of Neuroscience* 29, no. 50 (2009): 15684–15693.

Dixon Gunning et al. "Age-Related Differences in Brain Activation during Emotional Face Processing," *Neurobiology of Aging* 24 (2003): 285–295.

Elizabeth Kensinger and Daniel Schacter, "Young and Old Brains Differ in Encoding Positive Information." http://mitpress.org/cgi/content/20/7/1161.

—. *Neural Processes Supporting Younger and Older Adults' Emotional Memories.* (Boston: MIT Press, 2008).

M. Mather et al., "Amygdala Responses to Emotionally Valenced Differences in Brain Activation during Emotional Face Processing." *Psychology Science* 15 (2004): 259–263.

Sara Reisand-Long, "Older Brain Really May Be a Wiser Brain." *New York Times*, May 20, 2008.

Patricia A. Reuter, and Cindy Lustig, "Brain Aging: Reorganizing Discoveries about the Aging Mind." *Current Opinion in Neurobiology* 15 (2005): 245–251.

Barbara Staunch, "How to Train the Aging Brain," *New York Times*, December 29, 2009.

Williams et al., "The Mellow Years? Neural Basis of Improving Emotional Stability over Age," *The Journal of Neuroscience* 26, no. 24 (June 14, 2006): 6422–6430.

Chapter 7

For a definitive overview of the female brain, see Louann Brizendine, *The Female Brain* (New York: Broadway Times, 2006).

For details on the female brain in the modern workplace, see Helen Fisher, *The First Sex: The Natural Talents of Women and How They Are Changing the World* (New York: Ballantine Books, 1999).

To see how maternity enhances the female brain, see Katherine Ellison, *The Mommy Brain: How Motherhood Makes Us Smarter.* (New York: Basic Books, 2005).

For a more thorough discussion of self-esteem in girls, see Robert Josephs, et al., "Gender and Self-Esteem," *Journal of Perspectives of Social Psychology* 63, no. 3 (1993): 391–402.

For the economic clout of women, see Michael Silverstein and Kate Sayre, "The Female Economy," *Harvard Business Review* (September, 2009), 46–53; Marissa Miley and Ann Mack, "The Rise of the Real Mom," *Advertising Age*, White Paper (November 16, 2009).

For a discussion on speaking styles of both genders, see Deborah Tannen, *You Just Don't Understand: Women and Men in Conversations.* (New York: William Morrow, 1990).

For an insider's view of a woman's brain, see Jill Bolte Taylor, *My Stroke of Insight.* (New York: Penguin Books, 2006).

Chapter 8

For a great overview of recent research findings on the maternal brain, read: Katherine Ellison, *The Mommy Brain: How Motherhood Makes Us Smarter.* (New York: Basic Books, 2005).

For a sociological perspective on modern motherhood, see Sarah Hrdy, *Mother Nature: Maternal Instincts and How They Shape the Human Brain.* (New York: Ballantine Books, 1999).

Groundbreaking research into the changes that occur with motherhood are presented in Craig H. Kinsley and Kelly Lambert, "The Maternal Brain," *Scientific American* 294, no. 11 (January 2006): 72–79.

The details on sleep loss are from James B. Maas, *Power Sleep: The Revolutionary Program that Prepares Your Mind for Peak Performance.* (New York: Harper Perennial, 1998).

Michael Merzenich and I had a long conversation about the plasticity of the maternal brain.

For brain changes in the maternal brain, see Michael Numan and Thomas Insel, *The Neurobiology of Parental Behavior*. (New York: Springer, 2003).

To learn more about the creation of new neurons in the "Mommy Brain," see T. Shingo et al., "Pregnancy-Stimulated Neurogenesis in the Adult Female Forebrain Mediated by Prolactin," *Science* 299 (January 3, 2003): 5003.

For more about the changes maternity presents to the brain, see C. Xerri et al., "Alterations of the Cortical Representation of the Rat Ventrum Induced by Nursing Behavior," *Journal of Neuroscience* 14, no. 3 (March 1994).

Chapter 9

The two definitive sources for groundbreaking material on Mirror Neurons are:

Marco Iacoboni, *Mirroring People: The New Science of How We Connect with Others*. (New York: Farrar, Straus & Giroux, 2008).

Giacomo Rizzolatti and Laura Craighero "The Mirror Neuron System," *Annual Review of Neuroscience* 27 (June 2004): 169–192.

Chapter 10

Metrics and measures described in this chapter have been developed by NeuroFocus based on a wealth of academic research that has been adapted and tested to meet the unique needs of our commercial and consumer research clients.

Examples of the foundational research we have leveraged can be found in the following seminal studies and literature reviews.

On attention: Jin Fan, Michael I. Posner et al., "The Relation of Brain Oscillations to Attentional Networks," *The Journal of Neuroscience* 27, no. 23 (June 6, 2007), 6197– 6206.

On emotional engagement: James A. Coan and John J.B. Allen, "Frontal EEG Asymmetry as a Moderator and Mediator of Emotion," *Biological Psychology* 67 (2004): 7–49.

On memory: Wolfgang Klimesch, "EEG Alpha and Theta Oscillations Reflect Cognitive and Memory Performance: A Review and Analysis," *Brain Research Reviews* 29 (1999): 169–195.

On persuasion: John Cacioppo and Richard Petty, "The Elaboration Likelihood Model: The Role of Affect and Affect-Laden Information Processing in Persuasion," in Patricia Cafferata and Alice Tybout, Editors, *Cognitive and Affective Responses to Advertising*. (Lexington, MA: Lexington Books, 1989).

On novelty: Robert T. Knight, "Contribution of Human Hippocampal Region to Novelty Detection," *Nature* 383, no. 19 (September 1996): 256259.

On awareness, understanding, and comprehension: Sabine Weiss and Horst Mueller, "The Contribution of EEG Coherence to the Investigation of Language," *Brain and Language* 85 (2003): 325–343.

Chapter 11

The Consumer Journey is a proprietary framework developed by NeuroFocus to integrate neuroscience metrics with the full spectrum of consumer responses to brands, product selection, advertising, in-store shopping, product usage, and post-purchase behavior.

Chapter 12

The Brand Essence Framework is a proprietary tool developed by NeuroFocus to delineate the major dimensions or elements of brands in the marketplace.

A large and fascinating literature exists on the topic of brands and the brain. Some classic studies that explore this relationship include Tim Ambler et al., "Brands on the Brain: Neuro-Images of Advertising," *Business Strategy Review* 11, no. 3 (2000): 17–30); Samuel McClure et al., "Neural Correlates of Behavioral Preference for Culturally Familiar Drinks," *Neuron* 44 (October 14, 2004): 379–387; Chris Janiszewski, "Preattentive Mere Exposure Effects," *Journal of Consumer Research* 20, no. 3 (December 1993); ABI/INFORM Global, p. 376); Michael Schaefer and Michael Rotte, "Favorite Brands as Cultural Objects Modulate Reward Circuit," *Brain Imaging* 18, no. 2 (January 22, 2007); and Hilke Plassmann et al., "What Can Advertisers Learn from Neuroscience?" *International Journal of Advertising* 26, no. 2) (2007): 151–175.

Chapter 13

The Total Consumer Experience methodology is a proprietary tool developed by NeuroFocus to compare and combine sensory product experiences using direct neurological measures rather than, or in addition to, articulated responses. Here are some examples of foundational research using brain imaging to measure sensory experiences:

For taste, J. O'Doherty et al., "Representation of Pleasant and Aversive Taste in the Human Brain," *The Journal of Neurophysiology* 85, no. 3 (March 2001): 1315–1321.

For olfaction (smell), Tyler S. Lorig, "The Application of Electroencephalographic Techniques to the Study of Human Olfaction: A Review and Tutorial," *International Journal of Psychophysiology* 36 (2000): 91–104.

For audition (sound, music), Eckart Altenmüller, "Hits to the Left, Flops to the Right: Different Emotions during Listening to Music Are Reflected in Cortical Lateralisation Patterns," *Neuropsychologia* 40 (2002): 2242–2256; also Margaret M. Bradley and Peter J. Lang, "Affective Reactions to Acoustic Stimuli," *Psychophysiology* 37 (2000): 204–215.

The New Product Effectiveness Framework is a proprietary tool developed by NeuroFocus to assess neurological responses to new product concepts expressed in words. The methodology is based on a rich literature on cognitive and emotional response to words in written and spoken form. Some of the foundational research in this area is summarized in Marta Kutas and Kara D. Federmeier, "Electrophysiology Reveals Semantic Memory Use in Language Comprehension," *Trends in Cognitive Sciences* 4 no. 12 (December 2000). Many techniques have been adapted from studies of language disabilities; see, for example, Dennis L. Molfese et al., "The Use of Brain Electrophysiology Techniques to Study Language," *Learning Disability Quarterly* 24 (Summer 2001).

A key neuroscience tool for assessing new products and novel concepts is a cognitive response called the "expectancy violation" reaction. This is an automatic process by which the brain "resets" its expectations when it encounters an item in a flow of experience that does not "fit" with the rest of the flow. An example of this phenomenon and how it can be used to measure pricing sensitivities is William J. Gehring and Adrian R. Willoughby, "The Medial Frontal Cortex and the Rapid Processing of Monetary Gains and Losses," *Science* 295, no. 22 (March 2002).

Chapter 14

The Packaging Effectiveness Framework is a proprietary tool developed by NeuroFocus to measure the impact and effectiveness of different packaging treatments. The notion of "pop-out" is central to packaging assessment. Pop-out is referred to as "bottom-up attention" in the neuroscience literature and has been the subject of thousands of studies. The path-breaking work in this area was carried out by Anne Treisman and colleagues in the 1980s and 1990s. An accessible introduction can be found in Michael S. Ambinder and Daniel J. Simons, "Attention Capture: The Interplay of Expectations, Attention, and Awareness," Chapter 12 in Laurent Itti et al., editors, *Neurobiology of Attention*. (Burlington, MA: Academic Press, 2005).

Chapter 15

"The brain dislikes straight lines and sharp edges ..." See Moshe Bar and Maital Neta, "Humans Prefer Curved Visual Objects," *Psychological Science* 17, no. 8 (2006): 645–648.

The Shopper Experience Framework is a proprietary tool developed by NeuroFocus to test neurological responses to shopping and point of sale environments. Observations throughout this chapter about subconscious responses to different dimensions of the shopping experience are drawn from NeuroFocus client studies undertaken in both real and virtual shopping environments.

Chapter 16

The Advertising Effectiveness Framework is a proprietary tool developed by NeuroFocus to assess brain responses to advertising messages. Observations throughout the chapter on the impacts of motion, novelty, error, and ambiguity on advertising effectiveness are derived from hundreds of advertising analyses performed for NeuroFocus clients. For readers interested in the neuroscience and cognitive psychology underlying these findings, here are some good starting points.

For the attentional attraction of motion, see Charles L. Folk and Roger W. Remington, "The Structure of Attentional Control: Contingent Attentional Capture by Apparent Motion, Abrupt Onset, and Color," *Journal of Experimental Psychology: Human Perception and Performance* 20, no. 2: (April 1994: 317–329). See also Steven L. Franconeri and Daniel J. Simons, "Moving and Looming Stimuli Capture Attention," *Perception & Psychophysics* 65, no. 7 (2003): 999–1010.

For novelty, see Mark M. Kishiyama and Andrew P. Yonelinas, "Novelty Effects on Recollection and Familiarity in Recognition Memory," *Memory & Cognition* 31, no. 7 (2003): 1045–1051.

For a general review of sources of attention, see Daniel J. Simons, "Attentional Capture and Inattentional Blindness," *Trends in Cognitive Science* 4, no. 4 (April 2000).

Chapter 17

Results reported in this chapter are derived from a confidential research project performed by NeuroFocus for a European advertising company wanting to know what ad elements to emphasize in designing ads for different media and screen sizes.

Chapter 18

The Natya Shastra is an ancient Indian treatise on the performing arts, attributed to the Sage Bharata Muni, that describes in great detail principles for the presentation of fine arts, including theater, dance, and music. Bharata was also an early student of the brain. He outlined a set of eight rasas, or emotional states, to categorize different moods of Indian dance, music, and theater—love, laughter, fury, compassion, disgust, horror, heroism, and wonder.

INDEX